THE
WELL BEING—
GOOD HEALTH
HANDBOOK

A publication of
Leisure Press.
597 Fifth Avenue; New York, N.Y. 10017

Library of Congress Catalog Card Number: 83-80739

ISBN: 0-88011-194-1

Book design: Brian Groppe
Cover design: Julie Garrison
Cover photograph: David Madison

THE WELL BEING– GOOD HEALTH HANDBOOK

by David K. Miller

LEISURE PRESS

NEW YORK

Dedication

To my wife Roselyn and our daughter Kathryn
For their love and patience

Contents

Preface

There are no quick gimmicks that can produce good health. Well-being and good health come about only when your lifestyle is conducive to them. *The Well Being—Good Health Handbook* shows you how you can improve your quality of life. You can acquire the skill and confidence to set realistic health goals and design a health program that meets your own particular needs. Following the recommended guidelines and procedures, you choose the methods you will follow to

1) develop a positive view of life
2) develop circulorespiratory fitness, muscular strength, muscular endurance, and flexibility
3) enjoy a nutritious diet while learning to manage your weight
4) learn to cope with stress and depression.

No matter how many other health programs you've tried and dropped, *The Well Being—Good Health Handbook* can help you change your lifestyle to suit your needs. The good life can be yours!

Introduction

*If I had known I was going to
live this long, I would have
taken better care of myself.*
  Gene Autry, Age 72

A 1978 nationwide survey by Louis Harris and Associates indicated that most Americans have unhealthy habits and live unhealthy lives. The survey revealed that 92% of the American public believes that if we would live healthier lives, eat more nutritious food, smoke less, maintain proper weight, and exercise regularly, it would do more to improve our health than anything doctors or medicine could do for us. Nevertheless:

- Only 37% engage in regular exercise and 62% are overweight.
- 37% of all adults still smoke.
- 20% do not believe they get enough sleep.
- One-third of all adults report that they or a member of their family have experienced emotional problems, nervous conditions, stress or anxiety which has affected the physical health of the people concerned.

Why do we practice such poor health habits?

A study of the elderly's attitude toward health and physical activity found that many of them believed they were active enough, that their weight was normal, and that their physical fitness was above average. Yet, investigators were able to demonstrate how wrong these beliefs were. How do such faulty beliefs arise?

Another study found that once he is over 50, the sedentary male executive tends to remain sedentary, unless he has a strong personal motivation to be active. The same study concluded that the younger more physically active executive will probably only maintain a fitness program if it is handy and reasonably priced. What is the strong personal motivation that the older executives need? And with all the accepted benefits of exercise, why will the younger executives participate in an exercise program only if it is handy?

Prior to age 30, the human body can take a large amount of neglect and abuse without any apparent harm; but after this age the results of abuse will begin to appear, and most of us will die of diseases directly related to over-consumption, luxury, and neglect of health. Why are we not willing to assume the responsibilities of taking care of our bodies? Why do we fail to appreciate our health until we no longer have it?

As a nation we have fostered the belief that at retirement we should "slow down," rest, and perform as little physical exertion as possible. As a result of this dreadful misconception, many older people have limited expectations and undergo rapid physical deterioration. Why do we have such a negative attitude toward a lifetime of physical activity?

In addition to being overweight and physically unfit, many of us think very little of ourselves, experience depression, and have difficulty tolerating stress. Why do we have such poor self-images? And why don't we learn to manage stress?

The answer to all these questions involves two concepts: information and motivation. We have not been informed of the value of health and how to obtain it, and we have not been motivated to seek health. If we are to experience healthful living, we must have the right information, accompanied by the right kind of motivation.

Just to strive for a minimal level of healthful living should not be our goal. We should seek health+. To experience health+ we must have:
● a positive view of life
● circulorespiratory fitness
● a nutritious diet
● an acceptable weight (or % body fat)
● adequate flexibility
● adequate muscular strength and endurance
● the ability to manage stress
An optimum health+ program will seek to develop and maintain all of these things.

To carry out a succesful health+ program you must (1) know what to expect from the program, (2) know how to design and conduct your own particular program, and (3) have the inner motivation to succeed with your program. Too many individuals fail to meet these requirements prior to undertaking a health+ program. Without any sense of direction, they embark on a fanatical effort to improve their health. Blind with enthusiasm, they expect instant weight loss, instant physical fitness, and an instant cure for their mental problems. No appeal can be made to their reason. They expect too much too fast, and they cannot be persuaded to compromise their expectations.

Such people are not really true believers in the programs they are following; they are only zealous converts. Their dissatisfaction with themselves has created a desire for change; but, lacking the initiative to design a program for themselves or failing to find security and self-assurance in their own individual resources, they cling to whatever health improvement program they happen upon. They follow it not because of its worthiness, but because they are looking for a shortcut to their needs. And rather than trust their own judgment, they are ready to follow unthinkingly the example of others.

In blindly following the example of others, they rarely make a true commitment to a program. The commitment is absent because they fail to realize their own particular needs and abilities; they fail to understand the basic concepts of a health+ program; and they fail to have the necessary inner motivation to succeed. Their only concern is whether the program will do for them what they believe it has done for someone else. When it fails to live up to their expectations, they abandon it, bewildered by their failure.

It is possible for you to succeed with your own health+ program. The purpose of this book is to show you how. Hopefully, you will recognize the need for health+ and be motivated to design and follow a program which best meets your needs and abilities. You will have to ask yourself some searching questions, and try out a variety of new experiences. You will be asked to make a sincere commitment to health+. If you make this commitment, if you have the patience to give yourself ample time to progress, and if you believe in yourself, you can experience an improved quality of life. You can achieve health+.

1

Motivation

First say to yourself what you would be; and then do what you have to do.
Epictetus
Discourses

Have you ever attempted some type of a health improvement program? Did you begin with high hopes of reaping the benefits of your efforts, but then experience failure and dissatisfaction? Do you know people who follow a particular diet successfully and reduce their weight, while when you attempt to follow the same diet, you are unable to reach your desired goal? Does a specific technique for stress management work for others but not for you? Are others faithful to an exercise program that you discontinued after a short period of time?

Failure in endeavors of these kinds is quite common—and so are the reasons for failure. If you attempt a health+ program without really knowing what to expect from it and without knowing how to design and conduct a program well suited to your own particular needs, your chances for success are small. Moreover, knowledge and ability alone are not enough. You must also feel a personal need to change your lifestyle. A good health+ program can only succeed if you possess the desire to alter your behavior and lifesyle. You must see the need to assume responsibility for your health, and to account for your present and future health.

Being in command of your own health means that you will undertake a health+ program only because you choose to do so, and not because someone else exhorts you to do so. Your commitment to the program will be internal rather than external. You will undertake a health+ program because you see an opportunity to renew and revitalize your sense of well being through change, and adjustments in your lifestyle. You will not seek external rewards or recognition, but you will emphasize the fulfillment of your needs. You will want to put forth the necessary efforts to meet your needs. The success of your program will be determined by you

It is essential that you avoid the belief that you should "be like so-and-so."
No two people are alike. You are unique.

alone, and your reward will be knowing that your reached your goals.

It is essential that you avoid the belief that you should "be like so-and-so." No two people are alike. You are unique. If you undertake a health+ program because others follow it, you may come to resent your efforts after a very short time, and you will very likely give up before you reap any benefits.

Everyone does not have the same health+ needs, nor does everyone respond to exercise, diet, or stress in the same way. You must choose to follow a particular health+ program only because you believe it is the best program for you. If you choose to modify your diet, do so because you sincerely believe the changes are best for you. The same can be said for the management of depression, stress tolerance, circulorespiratory fitness, or any other component of health+. The design of your program should have nothing to do with the programs of others; it should be based solely on your own health+ needs and desires, and your own way of responding to experience. Have the attitude, "It's not what's happening in their program that counts; most important is what I choose to do, and how it will affect me."

Hopefully, by the time you finish this book you will realize what your own needs are, what changes you must make in your lifestyle in order to achieve health+.

It is also my hope that, once you are aware of your need for change, you will be aroused to action, and will possess a real inner motivation to sustain that action and succeed with your program, knowing that only effort can lead to success. If you have the inner motivation which moves you to action, an inner force which says, "I want to, I can, I will," the chances for success with your program are unlimited.

Once you feel the internalized desire for change, work to keep the desire alive. Cultivate a burning desire which looks to success. Avoid fear of failure. Motivation from fear is not the kind of inner motivation you want. Forget any failures you have experienced with past health+ programs; in fact, forget all failures of any kind that you have experienced. Expect to succeed. Dwell on success. Imagine how you will feel experiencing total mental and physical relaxation. Imagine how you will look after shedding unwanted body fat. Remember, the success of your program is dependent upon your burning drive, on your inner motivation.

Perhaps you are the type of person who recognizes the need for a health+ program, but just can't get very excited about modifying your life-style, especially if exercise or sacrifice is involved. If so, get yourself started by pursuing just those components of a health+ program that

You should undertake a health + program only because you wish to do so.

you are willing to attempt, perhaps those requiring a minimum of exercise or sacrifice. Remember, you must undertake a health+ program only because you alone wish to do so. You may need to spend some time cultivating that wish. For example, if you are reluctant to plunge right into a vigorous exercise program, begin by spending a few minutes each day imagining yourself walking, bicycling, swimming, or performing some other similar activity. Imagine a relaxing, rhythmic, moving sensation as you mentally perform one of these activities. There are no painful sensations. Think of it as an opportunity to relax and escape from all your concerns or problems. It may be that if you continue this practice often enough and long enough, the desire to attempt an exercise program will develop. If the slightest desire does occur, dwell on it. Think about it more and more. Read about the advantages and disadvantages of different excercise programs. You will move in the direction on which you dwell. In this way, you can develop the inner force that will move you to action; you have only to try.

2

Goals

"Cheshire—Puss," she began, rather
timidly. . . "Would you tell me, please,
which way I ought to go from here?"
"That depends a good deal on where you
want to get to," said the cat.
"I don't much care where. . .", said
Alice.
"Then it doesn't matter which way
you go," said the cat.

Lewis Carroll
Alice in Wonderland

Goal setting is a part of our culture. Most Americans are achievement oriented. Having achieved one goal, we search for the next one. We perform best when we have goals. Goals direct our actions toward some long-range outcome. We believe that goals directly affect our behavior so we take interest in setting them. Many of us are unable to find happiness without goals to conquer and achieve. We sincerely believe that life is more worthwhile when we are striving toward our declared goals. Our feelings about personal success are dependent upon the extent to which we reach our goals.

The ability to establish goals, to determine ways of achieving them, and to know when they have been achieved is basic to your health+ program. You must state your goals, plan how to fulfill them, and believe that there is no substitute for this planning. Your ability to maintain your initial inner motivation depends upon your success at meeting your stated goals. Without goals you may tend to neglect your program, or permit it to be influenced by unrelated random events. And without goals to direct and mobilize your efforts and to evaluate your efforts day-by-day, you will probably wander aimlessly. Goal setting will influence your efforts, direction, performance level, and persistence. In addition, health+ goals may give more meaning to your life; the fulfillment of these goals can provide you a satisfaction that you have never experienced before.

Examine the goals you have for all aspects of your life. Are you able to state them? Do you really know what you want out of life and what you want to accomplish with your life? Make a list of the goals you now have. Be honest. This self-evaluation can help you determine whether your goals are reasonable and within your control. Are the goals you listed your own goals; or have you been influenced too much by what other people think and expect of you? Perhaps you have been influenced by the goals you have heard other people set for themselves. The importance of achieving your own goals, as opposed to responding to the goals of others, cannot be overemphasized. Your goals must have personal meaning, and only you can really determine what your goals should be. If you attempt to measure up to some other person's goals, you may feel miserable and second rate. You may even conclude that something is wrong with you. In addition, you will work much harder to fulfill your own accepted goals than you will work for the goals that others have described. You may fulfill their goals, but you will not be satisfied. You will not be happy striving to fulfill someone else's goals. Your goals must reflect your own values.

Now look at the total number of your goals. Do you have too many? Maybe you have not fulfilled many of your goals because they are too numerous. If you believe this to be so, determine an order of priority for your goals. Do you still believe all of them are of value?

Count the number of materialistic goals you have. Have you included any health+ goals and placed them at a high priority? Setting and prioritizing your goals is vital to the success of any health+ program. If you truly believe that materialistic goals are more important than your health, you will have difficulty maintaining a health+ program. Your priorities will allow you to make such excuses as, "I don't have time today," or "It will not matter if I fail to fulfill my health goals this day." Health goals must have a high priority in your life if you really wish to fulfill them. You must realize that if you do not attain your health goals, if you do not have the health to really enjoy life, your materialistic goals will rapidly cease to have any value. Without vigor, without zest, without the spark that health+ can provide for you, other aspects of your life will be less important.

As I said above, maintaining that inner motivation which is necessary for you to succeed with your program is directly related to your success or failure at meeting your declared goals. You will evaluate your achievements in terms of how well you reach your aspirations. In order to persist in your program, you must experience success in some form. Therefore you should plan your goals only after carefully weighing all options, risks, and potential for success. Inadequate planning of what you really want from your program can lead to failure. Worse, the frustration that comes with failure can cause you to lose your desire to persist in the program.

Before you declare any health-fitness goals, you should be aware of the following guidelines:
- Establish a background of information on which to base your goals. Without this background you may very well plan unrealistic goals that are virtually impossible to reach.

Consider for example, the area of weight loss. Many individuals attempting to lose weight lack a basic understanding of the importance of a sound diet, caloric balance, and the role of physical activity in weight reduction programs. Nor do they understand that it is impossible to lose body fat as fast as is claimed by the promoters of some diets. Because of this lack of understanding, these individuals set unrealistic goals and fail to experience a permanent reduction in body fat. In addition, as a result of their poorly thought out programs, they often experience physical and/or emotional problems that are worse than the problems created by the excessive weight. Another example is in the area of exercise. Without a background in the appropriate prescription of exercise, many individuals attempt to perform physical feats for which their bodies are not properly prepared. Their efforts only result in soreness or injuries, and an unwillingness to ever again take up exercise. If you attempt to formulate a component of your health+ program without the proper background knowledge, you may do yourself more harm than good. Furthermore, poorly conceived goals can lead to attempts to short cut your program, which in turn will lead to failure. Do not formulate your health+ goals until you have the necessary background. Wait until you have completed this book before attempting to state your goals.
- Set your goals low. While it is very possible for goals to be unrealistically high, it is impossible for any goal to be too small.

Avoid the belief that any goal is too small to fulfill. Not only can the attainment of any goal, large or small, be the spark which provides the inner motivation to continue your program; it can also help lead to the development of a positive self-image.

As you only can control the present, begin with the present in the formulation of your goals. Don't be too concerned about long-term goals and certainly don't plan for drastic, immediate changes in your lifestyle. It is very important that you have initial success with your health+ goals, so begin with small or moderate goals that can be reached within a short period of time. You may wish to limit your goals to a day-by-day basis as you undertake your program. Don't be too ambitious and don't make your list of goals so long that you can't possibly fulfill all of them. At the end of the day, or whatever short period of time you have allotted for the achievement of your goals, you may wish to rearrange your list of priorities. Keep a record of the goals you reach; strike from the list the goals you fulfill. The purpose of beginning with small goals, and proceeding in this step-by-step manner is to develop the confidence you need to succeed with your program, enabling you eventually to seek higher and more difficult goals.

Following is an example of how one might go about setting small, short range goals in a weight loss program:

Frustrated by his repeated failure to lose 40 pounds on a diet, Mr. Williams decides to take a new approach, proceeding one small step at a time. First, he acquires some necessary background information, averaging his daily caloric intake over a 7 to 14 day period. He then sets the goal of decreasing his caloric intake for day 1 by 300 calories. Having reached this goal, he sets a new goal of maintainig this decreased caloric intake for a period of 5 more days. He feels that once he has attained this second goal, he will have the confidence to decrease his daily caloric intake even further for day 7; and his confidence will help him stick to his diet modification program in the long term, setting one short-range goal after another.

Goals to develop all components of health+ should be planned with the same insight and patience. Attempts to develop muscular strength and endurance too fast will result in soreness and/or injury. Attempts to develop circulorespiratory fitness too fast will not only cause unwanted fatigue, but also can result in injury. Don't set goals which lead you to attempt to perform at a level or intensity which will create more problems than benefits. Remember, the achievement of one goal will open doors to other goals. Also, short-range goals provide a means for self-evaluation. Constant awareness and rating of your success will provide good motivation for you.

A word of caution should be given at this point. It is very probable that as you fulfill some of your goals, you will expect to see improvement in some area of health+. Don't expect immediate noticeable improvement. For example, if you embark on a sensible weight loss program, but choose to weigh yourself every day, you will probably get discouraged; it is unlikely that you'll be able to observe daily changes in your weight. Instead, you should accept and focus on the fact that a realistic reduction

Begin with small goals and proceed in a step-by-step manner in order to develop the confidence you need to succeed with your program, enabling you eventually to seek higher and more difficult goals.

in caloric intake, combined with a moderate exercise program, will lead to a gradual reduction in body fat. Similar disappointment can result if you want to progress too fast in the development of circulorespiratory fitness. Failure to see a marked decrease in the time it takes to complete a specified distance of walking, running, bicycling, swimming, etc., can lead to frustration and dissatisfaction. You should expect to see improvement in your health if you make a commitment to a health+ program, but only after a reasonable period of time. And you will be more faithful to the program if you progress slowly.

● In planning your health+ goals, be very specific. The more specific and detailed your goals, the more clearly you will be able to visualize them.

You will work harder for a goal that you can visualize and recognize when you reach it, than you will work for a generalized goal. Working to reach a specific goal is more productive than simply attempting to "do the best you can."

You should visualize in words and pictures how you will fulfill each goal. Furthermore, you should visualize them in the first person. Many individuals are unsuccessful with a health+ program because they do not practice within what they want without. Try to imagine the mental, physical, and emotional satisfaction that you will experience upon successfully reaching each of your goals.

In addition to detailed, mental visualization of succeeding in your goals, imagine how to avoid failure. Think about possible situations which might stop you from attaining your goals and how you will not allow this to happen. Mentally practice functioning productively in diverse settings. Anticipating and planning how to cope with possible obstacles will help you avoid being caught off guard, yielding to various pressures and failing to fulfill your goals.

If you follow and remain faithful to a specific plan to reach your goals, you can develop staying power and a positive attitude about your program. You can develop confidence in yourself and your program.

The success story of Bruce Jenner illustrtes the value of setting specific goals in the first person. Prior to the 1976 Olympic trials, Jenner wrote down what he believed he had to do in all 10 events of the decathalon in order to qualify for the Montreal Olympics and at the same time to break the world record for the decathalon. He recorded the needed scores to the tenth of a second and quarter of an inch. Jenner hit every one of those marks and broke the world record. For the Olympics he believed he had to better his scores in six events in order to win the gold medal. He came close, as his scores were higher in five events. He missed improving in another event by only one-half of an inch. Jenner believes that specifying his goals and working toward them in this way is what enabled him to finish first in the Olympic decathalon. Stating your health+ goals in the first person will increase your efforts and potential for success.

- Set only one goal at a time for each area of your health+ program and don't provide yourself with an alternative.

  It is not good practice to tell yourself that you want to reach one goal but you'll try for something else if you fail. You may not get beyond the "if"; you are already writing failure into your goal. If you find that your goal is too high to reach, lower it, but be firm about where you are aiming. Don't hedge.

- When working toward your goals, do it with enthusiasm, a positive attitude, and a pleasant outlook.

  Believe in the value and worthiness of your health+ program. You must work toward your goals with intensity, vigor, and sincerity. If your goal is to avoid certain high caloric foods, avoid them with positive enthusiasm. If your goal is to perform certain exercises, perform them with enthusiasm and a pleasant state of mind. Once you have lighted a fire of enthusiasm within yourself, only you can put it out. Add more enthusiasm to the fire, keep it burning. Any fire will die without fuel. Be a self-starter; don't depend upon anything or anyone other than yourself to keep your program going. Make your health+ goals an important part of your life. You can succeed.

3

A Positive View of Life

I can love others because I love myself.

Someone once said that the happiest moods are those when there is really no particular reason for which to be happy. The happy mood is just the result of feeling good, enjoying the present, and having a positive view of life. Think about the following questions. Are you usually in a good mood? Do you rarely have occasions in which you appear to be angry with the world? When these times do occur, do they last only for a short period? Are you able to bounce back from disappointments, disagreements with others, or major setbacks, with renewed enthusiasm and a sense of direction? If you honestly were able to answer "yes" to all of these, you are very fortunate. May you continue to enjoy life. But, if you found yourself having to say "no" perhaps you need to examine your self-image and your ability to avoid depression.

Self-Image

For our purposes self-image is defined as what you think about yourself, the mental picture you have of yourself. It is what you believe your inner and outer self to be. If you like yourself, you have a positive self-image. If you dislike yourself, you have a negative self-image. Self-esteem is sometimes defined in the same way.

The self-image is a human attribute that must be developed. It does not exist at birth; it is not given to you, and the development of it is a continuous process throughout life. It is determined by what you expect of yourself, what you believe others expect of you, and the ratio of successful experiences to failing experiences.

Your self-image and your habits are directly related, and 95% of your behavior, feelings and responses are habitual. You will feel, act, and perform in accordance with what you believe about yourself. Your self-image is the key to your personality.

Your self image is influenced by many things, including your confidence and abilities, body image, needs, values, and resources, as well as your feelings of acceptance or rejection by others, and the degree of fulfillment you find in your life and work. Unfortunaltely, many people have inaccurate pictures of themselves. They unknowingly embrace some symbolic role based on their own ideas. Are you one of these people? The following pages should help you break free of this problem, working toward a positive, accurate self-image—an important component of health+.

Positive Self-Image (I like and love myself.)

Record the names of several people you admire. They may be historical figures, living or dead, friends, relatives, co-workers—anyone you think highly of. Now write down the qualities you like in these people. Now what do you consider to be your good qualities? Be honest with yourself and make a complete list. Do you have any of the qualities you listed for the people you admire?

Do you believe that you have a positive self-image? If so, the following statements should apply to you: You view change and adjustment as opportunities for further development of your well being. Any problem encountered in personal adjustment are viewed as challenges to your inner strength and not as a threat to your well being. You don't focus on any inadequacies you might have, but you concentrate on what you can do. You realize it is not what you are that holds you back, it is what you think you are not. You center your attention on any given task; you don't think about reasons why everything will fail.

Perhaps this approach to life can be illustrated with the following story:

"An old Indian chief once called together all the young men of the village and said, "Tomorrow I am sending you to climb the mountain that rises high across the valley. You are to bring me a leaf from the plant you find at the highest point to which you climb."

Before the rising of the sun the young men started out, each with high hopes and eager to succeed. It was not very long until the first young man returned, holding a piece of cactus, and explaining that he had twisted his ankle. The old chief said, "But my boy, you did not even cross the desert." Soon, a second young man returned, holding a spray of cedar. He had climbed as far as the first slide rock. By mid-afternoon, a third brave returned with a piece of brickthorn. The chief smiled and said, "You were halfway up the mountain." By late afternoom another brave returned with a sprig of pine. The chief accepted it and said, "You were three quarters of the way to the top.' Eventually all the braves except one returned without reaching the top of the mountain.

The sun had gone down before the last man returned. He stood straight and tall, but his outstretched hand was empty. "Oh chief," he said, "where I climbed to, there were no trees, no plants, only snow and rocks. But oh chief, I saw the shining sea."

If you have a positive self-image, you view change and adjustment as opportunities for further development of your well being.

The old chief clasped the young man's hand and with great feeling in his voice said, "I know it. You didn't need to tell me. It shines in your eyes; it rings in your voice. You have felt the uplift. You have tasted the glory of the mountain."

If you have a positive self-image, you are like that young brave. You focus on the mountain top instead of on the obstacles you may encounter along the way. You remember the satisfaction of succeeding. You see yourself as being able to do. You take responsibility for your own life and do not give in to doubt and fear. You are not afraid of making the wrong choice on your way to where you are going and what you are seeking. You are behind the wheel of your own life; you are responsible for your present and your future.

In addition to these qualities, your positive self-image makes you aware of your capabilities, limitations, and potential. You accept and like yourself. You are capable of planning realistic goals in all aspects of your life. You have your own consistent system of values, but you are able to appreciate the values of others. You accept the blame and credit for your decisions; with confidence and self-control, you function in diverse settings. Not only are you a self-starter, you have staying power to complete difficult tasks. Because you like yourself, you usually act with modesty and do not feel it necessary to draw attention to yourself.

In all probability, the strongest outgrowth of your positive self-image is that you do better than most people in reaching your innate potential, achieving self-actualization. You attempt to become everything that you are capable of becoming. You concentrate on building up your resources for better meeting your needs and the needs of others. You live for yourself in order to give yourself to others. However, you recognize that self-actualization is not an objective in itself, but a product of reaching other life's goals; you are not self-conscious in your achievements. Self-actualization is not a condition to be reached; it is a continuous process. It is by focusing on your specific goals, activities, interests, and interpersonal affiliations that you come to realize your potential. As a self-actualized person you feel accepted, admired, loved, recognized, understood and respected for what you are.

Negative Self-Image (If I don't like myself, how can I expect others to like me?)

Now list what you consider to be your bad qualities. If you have a negative self-image, it will be obvious. You will not only see yourself as less adequate and less acceptable, you will see your peers as less acceptable. In addition, you will show an inefficient and less effective approach to problems you encounter, and less freedom of emotional expression. You lose touch with your strengths, concentrate on your weaknesses, and maintain a rigid, safe outward appearance. Because you have doubts about yourself and a low estimate of your ability to cope with problems and change, you always have excuses available. It is not uncommon to hear you say, "I don't have the time," or "I'm too busy," when asked to do something that involves a risk to the image you maintain.

You often underestimate your abilities and overestimate the difficulties facing you, and your feelings of inadequacy and nervousness result in underachievement in your endeavors. The negative feelings that you have about yourself probably cause you to be less persistent in trying to reach goals because you believe you have little chance of success.

If you find that many of thse descriptions apply to you, you need to better your self-image. Your health+ program should include goals that lead to a positive self-image.

Achievement and Self-Image

There is positive correlation between the successful performance of physical skills and the improvement of a child's self-image. In addition, children with a positive self-image, conditioned and fortified by performances they believe to be successful, appear far more likely to expect success in their social and academic endeavors than do children with a negative self-image. On the other hand, the "failure syndrome" (unsuccessful performance of physical skills) experienced on playground will be generalized to the classroom.

Studies with college students indicate that achieving students rate themselves higher in ability than do underachieving students. The achieving students also show smaller discrepancies between their perceived and actual levels of college ability. Achieving students know themselves better than do underachieving students.

Successful experiences strengthen your self-image. They give you an enhanced sense of self-worth, effectiveness and opportunity. Successful individuals have a positive self-image.

Development of a Positive Self-Image

The development of your self-image is a continuous process throughout your life. You are capable of improving a weak self-image. The most important factor in developing a positive self-image is that you must exhibit a desire to change your image. You must be willing to risk your image, to choose freely between alternatives in any given experience or encounter. You must be willing to "experience," you can't change your image through intellect alone. The belief that you have more capabilities than you ever use is also essential. And you must communicate with and listen to yourself; you must attempt to motivate yourself into positive action.

Denis Waitley in *The Psychology of Winning* offers the following guidelines for the development of a positive action.

- Keep your self-talk in the affirmative. Your manner of responding to any devaluation or lack of success is very important. Don't be too critical of yourself for any failure that you may encounter. Even though you should attempt to succeed in all your endeavors, you must recognize that 100% success is unlikely. Learn from your unsuccessful experiences, then forget them and concentrate on the positive.
- Accept responsibility for your incorrect decisions, but also accept praise. When others compliment you, say, "Thank you." Believe that you have earned their praise and recognition. Don't pass off their comments with responses like, "I was lucky," or "It was nothing."
- Dress and look your best. Clothes don't necessarily create a positive self-image, but if you believe you look well dressed, it will give you additional confidence.
- Enjoy volunteering your name when meeting new people. Pronounce it in a confident way. You may have to force yourself to do this, but after a few successful tries, you will find it progressively easier.
- Develop the habit of sitting up front at meetings instead of looking for a seat in the back. Sitting at the front will make it easier to participate in the meeting. Publicly affirming your beliefs will help your self-image.
- Walking slowly with slumped shoulders conveys the impression of someone with a poor self-image, so walk erect and at a moderately fast pace. After a period of time you will feel comfortable walking in this manner.
- Set your own life's goals. Only you should decide what commitments to make with your life. Plan your goals in a positive way and eliminate phrases like, "I have to," or "I can't."
- Seek to understand, accept, and enjoy yourself. If it is possible to change or modify the things that you don't like about yourself, make the commitment to do so. However, accept what cannot be changed and have a positive attitude about it.
- Keep your self-development an on-going process. Seek to discover your very best possible self, to become all you are capable of becoming. Self-evaluation and self-reinforcement can help to improve your self-image.

Self-evaluation and self-reinforcement can help to improve your self-image.

- Remember your worth as a person. Recognize the things you do well and give yourself respect. Your values, aspirations, and uniqueness are important.

Physical activity and Self-Image

There is ample evidence to support the use of physical activity to improve self-image. Participation in vigorous acitivity produces physically fit people, and physically fit people are more likely to have a positive self-image. Individuals who have made the commitment to a lifetime of regular physical activity have greater self-confidence, emotional stability, and feelings of self-worth.

Collinwood and Willett found that a program of jogging, calisthenics, and swimming not only increased obese teenagers' physical fitness, it also improved significantly their self-acceptance and their attitudes toward their bodies. Similar results were seen among college students learning to swim. Participation in outward bound programs often creates a significant change in young people's attitudes. They see themselves as more active, stronger, more positive, and less alienated. They begin to see others as individuals in their own right, and they see themselves as having a more mature goal orientation. They have a more positive attitude toward participation and believe they have a greater potential to reach positive goals.

Participation in physical activity can improve the image that you have of your own body. Physically fit individuals, because they have initiative and a sense of power, like their bodies better. Satisfaction with your body-image can improve your self-image.

It appears that challenging goals, which a physical activity program can offer, and the perception of your own physical fitness, are both important aspects of your self-image. Remember, the self-image is changed by doing, not just by thinking. Physical activity may do more to improve your self-image than any other single thing.

Words of Caution

If you undertake a program of physical acitivity with the goal of improving your self-image, plan realistic goals. If you perform below your self-image level, you will adjust. If you attempt to perform above your level, however, tension will develop within you. Remember, you alone determine the success of your program; stay within yourself. Guidelines for planning a physical activity program are discussed in the chapter on Exercise Prescription.

Depression

Depression is the most common psychiatric disorder found in large-scale population surveys. The American Medical Association claims that the prevalence of depression is rising and probably 17% of the U.S. population currently suffers from it. It is sometimes called the common cold of mental illness because it is so widespread. It underlies many of the physical complaints physicians are asked to treat, and it hospitalizes hundreds of thousands every year. It also is responsible for the high suicide rate among teenagers.

Depression is usually related to some sort of loss or disappointment. What depresses you is viewed as having already had an irreparable impact on the present and the future; this gives you a feeling of helplessness. When depressed you become a captive of your mood. You seem unable to do what you want or control the way you feel.

Such factors as your job, homemaking responsibilities, financial obligations, parental responsibilities, and the stress of marriage or being single can contribute to depression. Other factors associated with depression include not knowing what is expected of you in the performance of a role or task, and the failure to fulfill your personal expectations. The more of these factors experienced at once, the greater the chances for depression.

Depressed individuals often exhibit one or more of the following traits: poor appetite, a lonely feeling, a tendency to withdraw, little interest in other people or things, low sexual interest, trouble getting to sleep or staying asleep, low energy, preoccupation with unhappiness, thoughts about suicide.

The tendency to overwork has also been associated with depression. Some individuals lack the ability to regulate their work-rest-recreation balance and have guilt feelings when they are not working. With their compulsive need to work, they deny the existence of fatigue and push themselves beyond their limits. To cope with their lack of concentration and fatigue, they force themselves to stay long hours at their duties. To compensate for their diminished efficiency, they lenghten their workday. By taking these misguided measures they make things worse rather than better, usually eliminating exercise or recreation time, and further diminishing their capacity to recover.

Things to do for Depression

Individuals suffering from severe depression should be urged to seek medical help. Drugs, electroshock therapy, sleep deprivation, and counseling have all been used to treat extreme cases. However, there are also things you can do to help yourself for many types of depression.

- Face up to reality. Analyze yourself to become aware of things that trouble you. Don't expect everything to be pleasant all the time. Unpleasant tasks are often a part of life and must be faced, especially when seeking goals. The belief that there should be no unpleasantness in your life will only lead to disappointment.
- Don't strive for unattainable perfection. Anger at yourself is often the root of depression. Expecting to always perform flawlessly can cause unnecessary stress and tension.
- Anytime you have an unpleasant task to perform, do as much advance preparation as possible. Plan how to cope with the unexpected.
- When attempting new tasks or to reach new goals, begin at a level in which you will experience success. Initial success in your endeavors will help your self-image, and depressed individuals experience elation as a result of assuming a more positive self-image. Recalling past successes may be good therapy. However, it is important to take on new projects, to try to experience new successes, rather than rely on recalling past successes.
- Visualize the rewards of fulfilling your goals. Talk to yourself about the rewards. Often it is possible to talk yourself into a positive attitude and mood.
- Seek a pleasant environment as often as possible. There is a definite relationship between engaging in pleasant activities and a positive mood.
- Evaluate your attitude towards your work. You must keep in mind that people differ in their energy levels, their recuperative powers, and their enjoyment of work. Seek to balance these factors against the realistic demands of your job and the goals they require. It just might be that a vacation or rest will do wonders for your depression.
- Manage your time. If you manage it well, you can avoid feelings of being rushed or pressured. Avoid wasting time that can be of use to you. Always allow some time of the day for yourself, however. There should be time for you to "get away from it all."
- During your times of being alone—relaxation, meditation, exercise, etc.,—think pleasant thoughts. Try to empty your mind of unpleasant things; don't allow them to intrude on the part of the day that you have set aside for yourself.

If you follow these practices, they may help you to become the master of your moods, instead of allowing depression to be your master.

Physical Activity and Depression
As early as the 1940's certain veterans's hospitals used running as a means of treating depressed patients. Today more and more medical authorities are prescribing physical activity programs as therapy for

depression. They are impressed by the benefits that many depressed individuals obtain from extended, systematic periods of regular physical exercises such as walking, jogging, swimming, bicycling, tennis, and racquetball.

There are numerous studies to support this treatment for depression. Dr. W.P. Morgan demonstrated that, as the physical working capacity was increased, the depth of depression decreased in male psychiatric patients. Another study found that depressed adult males experienced a significant reduction in depression following six weeks of chronic exercise. In addition, in experiments at the National Institute of Mental Health, depressed persons placed on a regular exercise program experienced mood elevation. Patients at the University of Wisconsin were able to decrease depression symptoms through a running program, and a study with 100 college professors found a reduction in the occurrence of depression with participation in programs such as jogging, swimming, cycling, and weightlifting. Female college students who improved their circulorespiratory endurance through a jogging program became less depressed, more confident, more efficient at work and experienced more restful sleep. It also has been demonstrated that physical activity can be effective in repelling the depressed pessimistic moods occasionly experienced by healthy people.

Even though physical activity is recognized as an acceptable therapy for depression, research has failed to show how it relieves depression. Most authorities believe there are biochemical changes in the brain and other nerve tissues of the body when physical activity takes place. It is possible that these biochemical changes help move the individual out of depression and toward a more normal functional state. Studies are being conducted to determine whether such biochemical adaptation takes place.

Dr. Robert Brown, University of Virginia, has studied changes in blood and urine specimens to find a relationship between physical activity and depression. According to Brown, depressed individuals experience an anti-depressant factor at about two hours after they complete their exercise. He was unable to determine whether this anti-depressant factor was due to salt loss, change in nervous transmission, an increase in body temperature, or to some other reason.

Dr. Brown is not waiting for all the answers before prescribing exercise for his depressed patients, however. He does not prescribe anti-depressant pills as freely as he once did, and he now jogs with his patients, both to be with them and for his own health benefits.

Dr. Thaddeus Kostrubala, psychiatrist and author of *The Joy of Running*, is another medical doctor who is not sure as to the how, but is convinced of the value of physical activity for the treatment of depression. He believes that there is a distinct physiological or neurochemical basis to the effect physical exercise has on the mind. According to Kostrubala, running stimulates the unconscious and is a powerful catalyst to the individual pshche. When some of Dr. Kostrubala's depressed patients took up running but maintained their usual dosage of anti-depressant drugs, they developed more side and after effects from the same drug dosage. It was as if they had increased their drug dosage.

Dr. Marjorie H. Klein, University of Wisconsin, also believes that exercise such as running may well be an antagonist to depression. Since the way we feel in our minds can make us feel bad physically, she suggests it may work the other way too. Dr. Edward Greenwood of the Meninger Foundation states that the body and the mind don't operate on different levels independently of each other. If one breaks down, the other necessarily suffers. Any change in the physiological state is accompanied by a change in the mental state; any change in the mental state is accompanied by a change in the physiological state. If he is right then strengthening the body clearly will help the mind.

Some medical authorities believe that physical activity provides depressed individuals the satisfaction of mastering a task they perceive as being difficult. Through exercise they can meet a goal and accomplish something. Thus, they recognize their ability to change themselves for the better. The depression is also relieved through their improved physical health, appearance, and body image.

The role physical activity plays in the treatment of depression really may be very simple. Walking, running, bicycling, or other similar activities may serve to stimulate daydreaming and unconscious mind release. The mind is allowed to "spin" and relax, blue moods leave, and anxiety and anger melt away during the solitude provided. The freedom and renewed capacity to think creatively during this time greatly relieves individuals who are depressed.

In fact, the environment in which such activities take place may be an important part of the healing process. The smell, touch, and feel of the outdoors provide distractions which prevent you from concentrating on your problems. You become more aware of the self and the environment than at any other time.

How Much Exercise?

The anti-depressant effect of exercise may depend on the type, intensity, duration, and frequency of the physical activity. Dr. Robert Brown demonstrated anti-depressant effects with activity that was not very vigorous, such as softball. Similarly, walking three miles within 45 minutes several times a week relieved depression. In comparing the influence of tennis and jogging on depression, he found both to be effective. However, jogging five days a week for 10 weeks caused a greater reduction in depression than playing tennis or jogging for three days a week. In addition, when allowed to select their exercise program, most depressed subjects selected the most vigorous activity. Brown's belief was that there is more therapeutic value in vigorous physical activities. Dr. Kostrubala's patients experienced the best therapeutic results when they ran for one hour at 75% of their capacity, three times a week.

Apparently, better results are obtained when the activity pursued develops the components of physical fitness (circulorespiratory endurance and muscular strength and endurance). Walking, jogging, tennis, racquetball, squash, handball, swimming, cycling, and weightlifting have all been effective in relieving depression. Even individuals who score normal on the depression scale improve their scores as they become physically fit. Brown claims he has never treated a physically fit person for depression.

If you decide to help relieve your depression through exercise, what type of exercise should you choose and how hard, long, and often should you perform? It is probable that the best results are obtained when the physical acivity involves rhythmic movement of large muscle masses and is performed at least four to five times a week at a moderately high intensity. (See the chapter on Exercise Prescription.)

Whether you exercise alone or with someone is up to you. Activity can be effective therapy for you. The depression-free time that occurs during your physical activity, even if short-lived, may renew your outlook on life.

Words of Caution

Exercise is not a panacea. Some individuals will not respond to exercise therapy either because they fail to follow proper guidelines, or because they fail to understand both the benefits and limitations of an organized physical activity program. Others will not respond because they are so seriously depressed that they need professional help to determine the source of their problem.

4

Circulorespiratory Fitness

"You gotta have heart."

Circulorespiratory fitness is determined by the ability of the heart, lungs, and blood vessels to deliver oxygen to the body cells and to remove carbon dioxide and other by-products of chemical processes (metabolism) from them. If this function is hindered, as it is in cardiovascular diseases, serious health problems can occur.

Coronary Heart Disease

Cardiovascular diseases (high blood pressure, atherosclerosis, heart attack, stroke, congestive heart failure, rheumatic heart disease, and congenital defects) account for about one-half of all deaths in the industrialized countries. In the U.S., 40 million people are afflicted with cardiovascular disease, leading to about one million deaths a year, or 52% of deaths from all causes. The mortality rates for men are several times higher than those for women, but American women have a higher death rate from cardiovascular diseases than the women of any other country.

Coronary heart disease (CHD) is the most prominent form of cardiovascular disease. Even though the number of deaths due to CHD has declined in recent years, it remains the leading cause of death in the U.S. About one million heart attacks occur each year, resulting in more than 600,000 deaths.

A brief description of the heart's blood vessels will help you to understand this disease better. The heart is composed of muscle tissue, called the myocardium. It requires a continuous blood supply, as do all body cells. This supply does not come directly from the blood being pumped through the heart, however. It is transported through a special set of arteries, the coronary arteries, which surround the heart.

These and all other arteries should have a smooth interior to function effectively. The arteries in small children are relatively smooth, but over the years, the arteries become less efficient. As fatty deposits collect along the inside of the blood vessels, the walls thicken. The blood is forced through a roughened, narrowed channel. This condition, known as atherosclerosis, may occur anywhere in the body, including the kidneys, legs, and brain. When it occurs in the coronary arteries, the rate of blood flow and the amount of blood going to the cells of the heart may be reduced. If the blood flow is reduced to the point that the cells of the heart fail to receive enough oxygen to function, a coronary heart attack occurs. In some cases the immediate cause of the attack is a blood clot (thrombus) which blocks an artery already narrowed by atherosclerosis. This type of heart attack is known as a coronary thrombosis.

Atherosclerosis may also cause a condition known as angina pectoris. Characterized by pain in the chest, this condition is caused by the inability of the coronary arteries to supply the heart with adequate oxygen. The pain, which may be mild or severe, is usually not present when one is at rest but occurs during physical or emotional exertion. It extends from the chest to the shoulders, jaw, and arms and usually subsides with the cessation of the exertion.

Death from atherosclerosis usually occurs in later life (although nearly one-fourth of all heart attack deaths occur under age 65), but signs of its development apear much earlier. In fact, the early stages of atherosclerosis have been observed in children. Some medical experts believe that the type of diet and lack of physical activity contribute to the development of atherosclerosis in children.

Evidence of early and gradual accumulation of fatty deposits in the arteries is found in the often-quoted study of 300 U.S. soldiers killed in the Korean Conflict. The soldiers averaged only 22 years of age, but more than 70% of them showed signs of coronary artery disease. The disease varied from a slight thickening of the artery linings to complete blockage of one or more main artery branches. Many of these young men had impaired coronary circulation long before any symptoms would have appeared. Autopsies performed on Korean soldiers killed in this war revealed no evidence of similar coronary damage. The study was repeated during the Vietnamese Conflict and similar results were observed. Studies in other countries (such as autopsies of accident victims) demonstrated again that early atherosclerosis is more common among young American men than it is among young men elsewhere in the world.

It is obvious that CHD is not limited to the older population. The buildup of fatty substances in the arteries begins at an early age. It is a progressive condition, developing over a long period of time. It is not something that appears suddenly one morning in middle age.

Some medical experts believe that the type of diet and lack of physical activity contribute to the development of atherosclerosis in children.

Risk Factors

The most widely accepted theory regarding the development of CHD involves multiple factors. It appears that the more risk factors you possess, the greater your chances for CHD become. Risk factors which have been found to be associated with this disease are:

- heredity
- gender
- carbohydrate intolerance (diabetes)
- emotional stress
- obesity (overfatness)
- cigarette smoking
- high levels of blood fats
- hypertension (high blood pressure)
- electrocardiographic abnormalities
- lack of physical activity (sedentary living)

Heredity

If you have a blood relative who had coronary heart disease prior to the age of 50, the odds are increased that you may have heart problems, other factors being equal. Some medical researchers use the age of 60 as a cutoff point, and others list only blood relatives who died of heart disease as a risk factor. The odds are even greater if more than one blood relative has had heart disease. If your family history also includes diabetes and/or hypertension, you may be even more susceptible.

Even though heredity has been associated with an increased risk of heart disease it is often difficult to separate hereditary influences from environmental influences. Certain environmental factors in family living patterns may contribute as much to the development of heart disease as do the genetic factors. Poor diet management, cigarette smoking, and physical inactivity may be a significant part of the family living pattern.

Several studies indicate the importance of living habits. The incidence of CHD among new immigrants to the U.S. is many times greater than that found in their country of origin. Within one or two generations it approaches the magnitude of CHD found in the general population of the U.S. A study of Irish brothers found that the brothers who lived in the U.S. ate more, weighed more, walked less, and had a higher death rate from CHD than did the brothers who remained in Ireland.

Such studies support the belief that CHD is due to multiple factors rather than heredity alone. However, if your family history does indicate an early development of CHD, it may be especially wise for you to undertake a risk-management program. Other family members, including children, should be included in the program.

Gender
Prior to the age of 40, men are 20 to 30 times more likely than women to suffer CHD. From 40 to 49 years of age men are only five times more likely than women to develop heart disease. After menopause women become more susceptible to this disease, although they still do not reach the same risk level as men.

Exactly why women are less prone to CHD is not yet fully understood, but investigation has pointed to several possible explanations. One suggestion is that the female sex hormone estrogen acts as a protector of the heart and blood vessels. After menopause, when estrogen productions drops, incidence of CHD increases among women.

Another possible explanation may have to do with the arrangement of cholesterol found in the female's blood. Women are found to have a higher percentage of high density lipoprotein (HDL) in their blood cholesterol than men. Recent research indicates that the concentration of HDL in the blood bears some relation to the incidence of coronary heart disease. (See Blood Fats.)

Other factors may also be involved in the female's resistance to CHD. Women tend to smoke less than men. It may also be that differences in the social and professional status of men and women in the U.S., and differences between men and women where weight and diet are concerned, play some role. However, the number of women suffering from heart disease is rising. Some speculate that this increase may be due to the entry of more women into certain kinds of stressful professions. It has also been noted that not only are more women smoking, they are smoking a greater number of cigarettes per day.

Whatever the reason, the more masculine the male, the more prone he is to CHD. For reasons that are not yet clear, the more hair on a man's chest, the less hair on his head, and the thicker or more athletic-looking his body, the greater his risk of heart disease.

Carbohydrate Intolerance (Diabetes)
When the pancreas either doesn't produce enough insulin or the body is unable to use insulin efficiently, the condition of diabetes occurs. Insulin is needed to transport glucose (sugar) through the cell membranes in most tissues; therefore, if insulin is in short supply, the metabolism of glucose is disturbed. Glucose is the cells' preferred energy source. If the blood sugar is not transported to the cell, you will experience chronic fatigue; your cells will have to utilize protein and fat as energy sources. Higher levels of sugar in the urine and/or abnormally high amounts in the blood (hyperglycemia) may be indications of diabetes. Complete dependence on protein and fats for energy sources causes severe

acidosis. This condition can ultimately result in diabetic coma and death.

About eight percent of the population of the U.S. has some clinically detectable degree of diabetes and this number is increasing each year. With the use of insulin many diabetics may live a fairly normal life; however, complications can arise even in treated diabetes. The most common complications are CHD, stroke, gangrene, and blindness.

Heredity is an important factor in diabetes, but research suggests that the disease can be postponed or accelerated, depending on personal habits and lifestyle. Obesity and heavy sugar consumption are recognized as contributing factors to the disease. The American Diabetes Association states that the odds of developing diabetes are 20 times as high in the obese. In addition, studies of "adult-onset" diabetics (over 40 years of age) show that more than 80% of them are overweight.

There are ways to bring down or control your blood sugar levels.
- Maintain your acceptable body weight or % body fat. These topics are discussed in the Weight Management chapter.
- Maintain a low intake of sugar in your diet. Sugar is discussed in the chapter on nourishment.
- Maintain a regular physical exercise program. Exercise utilizes glucose quickly, reducing the demand on the pancreas to produce insulin. It also helps to control your weight and improves blood circulation. These three practices have replaced medication and lowered the risk of developing CHD for many diabetics. However, if you are a diabetic, do not cease your medication without the approval of your doctor. If you are not a diabetic, these practices can lessen your risk of developing diabetes.

Emotional Stress

Emotional stress has very profound, and possibly very detrimental effects on your body. Your cardiovascular system is particularly sensitive to such stress. The heart rate and the amount of blood pumped with each contraction (stroke volume) increase under stress. The blood vessels in the skin, kidneys, and most internal organs constrict, decreasing the amount of blood flowing to these areas. Systolic blood pressure and the volume of blood circulating per minute increase. There is an increase in the amount of fatty acids in the blood, and the resistance to flow (viscosity) and the coagulability of the blood increase. All of these reactions to stress place a strain on the heart. Stress and ways to manage it are discussed in the chapter on stress.

Obesity (Overfatness)

The more extra fat you possess, the greater the load on your heart, and the greater your risk of heart disease. High blood pressure is twice as frequent, and hardening of the arteries (arteriosclerosis) is three times more frequent in the obese. When your blood has to be forced through vessels that are crowded with fat deposits, there's increased strain on your heart. Obesity is discussed further in the chapter on weight management.

Cigarette Smoking

The use of tobacco has been known in Western society since the discovery of America by Christopher Columbus in 1492. Former President Harry S. Truman once stated, "Columbus brought syphilis to the Indians and they gave him tobacco. It is doubtful which is worse." However, at that time the American Indians considered smoking a sacred ritual. They seldom smoked and certainly were not addicted to the smoking. Smoking in the United States did not become a major health hazard until the invention of the cigarette during the early part of the twentieth century.

Until the 1950's smoking was not considered very harmful. However, as evidence against smoking began to mount, warnings against the possible dangers of smoking were issued from the Office of the Surgeon General of the United States. In the 1964 report, *Smoking and Health*, and in later reports, the surgeon general's team evaluated three major types of evidence linking tobacco smoking to disease.

1. Evidence from animal studies: The tissues of animals were damaged when they were given nicotine and other chemicals found in tobacco smoke.
2. Evidence from clinical and autopsy studies: Tissue damage occurred most often in smokers.
3. Evidence from population studies: The smoking habits of individuals with a particular disease were studied, and groups of smokers and nonsmokers were observed over a period of years to record the presence of certain diseases. All studies indicated a link between smoking and disease.

The Office of the Surgeon General concluded that the total amount of tobacco smoke inhaled is the key factor in the connection between smoking and the occurrence of disease. Smoking many cigarettes per day, inhaling deeply, smoking cigarettes down to small butts, and beginning to smoke at an early age increase the risk of disease. Many diseases have been linked with tobacco smoke. The more prominent ones are diseases of the respiratory system, lung cancer, other forms of cancer, and CHD. Peptic ulcers are also associated with smoking. Studies show that smokers have a higher rate of absenteeism from work, take more sick days, and have more hospital stays than nonsmokers.

The danger of smoking is most commonly associated with lung cancer. Specialists believe that perhaps 90% of all lung disease is tobacco related. However, if you smoke more than one pack of cigarettes a day, you are more likely to die of a heart attack than of cancer. You are three times more likely to die of a heart attack than the nonsmoker when you smoke more than two packs per day. According to some estimates, the light smoker has a 50% increase for CHD and the heavy smoker has a 500% increase.

Before the number of women smokers increased significantly, sudden death from CHD claimed only 1 woman for every 12 men. The ratio is now more than 3 women for every 12 men. The average age of death from sudden heart attack for women who are heavy smokers is now 48 years. For women who don't smoke it is 67.9 years of age.

The physiological effects of cigarette smoke are caused primarily by three different toxic components: carbon monoxide, nicotine, and tar. Carbon monoxide readily combines with red blood cells, decreasing their capacity to transport oxygen. The heart must then pump more blood to transport the same amount of oxygen to the cells of the body. Since there are minute amounts of carbon monoxide in the air, even nonsmokers have a slight decrease in their oxygen-carrying capacity. But, depending on the number of cigarettes smoked, the smoker shows a loss of 10% or more in this capacity. This lower concentration of oxygen also slows the breaking down of cholesterol by the cells. Thus, cigarette smoking may promote the accumulation of cholesterol in the cells and facilitate atherosclerosis.

In addition, the smoker's make-up of cholesterol appears to be affected. There is a strong inverse relation between the number of cigarettes smoked and the proportion of high denity lipoprotein (HDL) in the blood. The heavy smoker has lower HDL. (See Blood Lipids.)

The nicotine found in just one cigarette significantly elevates heart rate and blood pressure. Nicotine increases the secretion of adrenaline which makes the resting heart rate go up by 15 to 25 beats per minute and systolic blood pressure rise 10 to 20 mm Hg. Diastolic blood pressure rises 5 to 15 mm Hg.

Nicotine also affects the body in other ways. It causes constriction of the small arteries supplying the skin, accounting for the cold hands of many smokers. Their skin temperature drops due to the decrease in blood flow. The blood clotting process is hastened by smoking, increasing the possibility of clot formation in the heart and brain blood vessels.

Emphysema is another condition associated with smoking; it rarely occurs in nonsmokers. This disease causes the heart to work harder, to pump more blood through less resilient lungs in order to pick up needed oxygen.

It also has been demonstrated that cigarette smoke can be harmful to a nonsmoker with heart disease. Without doubt, cigarette smoke is harmful to your body.

Do You Want to Quit the Habit?

It is much easier never to begin smoking than it is to quit the habit. Buy you can reduce your chances of CHD and cancer by quitting. There are two avenues for you to follow. You may attend a clinic for group therapy, or you may choose to stop smoking by yourself. Smoking clinics provide an environment which helps the smoker, but once the program ends the environment is no longer present. And without the environment the behavioral reinforcers that maintain abstinence may no longer be present. When the reinforcers disappear, the new behavior often goes with them. For this reason, the number of individuals who are able to kick the smoking habit after attending a smoking clinic is small.

It is possible for you to stop smoking, but you must have an inner motivation, a positive attitude, and the desire to change your behavior. You must recognize what needs to be done and be willing to do it, cheerfully and with enthusiasm; you must find personal satisfaction in it. You must believe that you can reach your goal.

You should first concentrate on the benefits of not smoking. Do not dwell on the unpleasant aspects of being deprived of your tobacco, but think about your health+ goals. Then you should examine your dependency on tobacco. Ask yourself why, when, and where you smoke. Your answers to these questions will help you select the best approach to stopping smoking.

There are different approaches to help you change your behavior. The self-monitoring program has proven successful for many. For each cigarette you smoke over a certain number, penalize yourself in some way. Consider not allowing yourself to attend or participate in some pleasurable event, or force yourself to put away a specified amount of money as a fine. The goal is to decrease the number of cigarettes smoked each day, or in a period of days.

For some individuals smoking is reinforced by being associated with pleasant environments such as parties and drinking. You may need to be especially aware of your smoking in such environments. The contract method may work for you. Sign a contract with a friend, spouse, or someone close to you, stating that they may penalize you in some way if they see you smoking. You probably will continue to smoke, but only when you are alone. The pleasure of smoking may be so reduced that you will want to stop.

An exercise program can help you curtail your smoking. There are several reasons for this. Smoking a cigarette temporarily elevates blood pressure, heart rate, and free fatty acids. The smoker feels relaxed after smoking. Rhythmic exercise has the same effect. In addition, the heaviest smokers are often the individuals least involved in physical activity. Upon exercising many of these individuals begin to take pride in their body and health. Exercise also helps prevent the weight gain associated with the cessation of smoking.

You may want to keep track of each cigarette you light up. The number will probably surprise you. At the same time keep a record of how much money you're spending on cigarettes. Then keep account of how much you save when you cut back. Reward yourself with the savings.

There are other procedures used to stop smoking, and it is important to follow the one which works best for you. If you really are unable to stop smoking, do the following:

- smoke fewer cigarettes
- inhale less
- don't smoke your cigarettes all the way down (the first half gives you 40% of the tar and nicotine; the second half 60%)
- select a cigarette with less tar and nicotine. Although the low-tar, low nicotine cigarettes may reduce your risk of lung cancer, don't expect them to reduce your risk of CHD. Decreasing the tar and nicotine does not reduce the amount of carbon monoxide produced by smoking.

Blood Fats (Lipids)

Fatty materials (lipids) are found in body tissues and blood plasma. Two of these substances, cholesterol and triglycerides, our bodies need and make. When too much of one or more of these fats is present in the blood (hyperlipidemia), it is considered a CHD risk factor. Hyperlipidemia can only be diagnosed through blood analysis.

Cholesterol

A fatty alcohol, cholesterol is a vital part of our cell walls and is used by the body in producing bile salts, sex hormones, and Vitamin D. It serves as a building block for our cells, is a structural component of nerve tissue, and facilitates the absorption of fatty acids from the small intestine. It is produced by almost all cells of the body, especially the liver, but it is also ingested in high quantities in the American diet. Such foods as animal fats, egg yolks, cheese, butter, cream, and shellfish are high in cholesterol.

The amount of cholesterol in the blood is expressed as milligrams of cholesterol per 100 milliliters of blood (mg%). There is a wide variation in plasma cholesterol levels in the U.S., but the current average is about 250 mg%. It is believed that high levels of cholesterol contribute to the development of atherosclerosis and that our national average is too high.

The following statistics support this belief:

- Among white American males from age 30 to 59, the incidence of heart attacks is about twice as high for those with cholesterol levels in the 250 to 299 mg% range as it is for those with cholesterol levels in the 175 to 249 mg% range.
- If you are a male and your cholesterol levels rise from between 225 and 250 mg% up to 300 mg% or over, the risk of your first heart attack more than doubles.
- If your cholesterol levels increase from below 194 mg% to over 250 mg%, the risk of your first heart attack triples.
- The affluent societies of North America, Central and Northern Europe, New Zealand, and Australia have high cholesterol levels and high incidences of fatty artery diseases.
- The populations of the Orient, Latin America, and the Mediterranean areas have low cholesterol levels and are relatively free from fatty artery diseases.

Based upon statistics such as these, an international panel of heart specialists and nutritional experts (sponsored by the American Health Foundation, 1979) recommended that Americans reduce their serum cholesterol levels. The panel put forth the optimal level of 160 ± 30 mg%.

The manner in which cholesterol is transported might be more important than the total amount in the blood. Cholesterol travels bound to a protein molecule (lipoprotein) in three different forms. All three forms are microscopic, but some are bigger than others. They are classified by their density. The largest and least dense are very low density lipoproteins (VLDL); the middle-sized are low density lipoproteins (LDL); and the smallest are high density lipoproteins (HDL).

The VLDL transport most of the triglycerides, so high levels of triglycerides mean high VLDL. Cholesterol is transported by LDL and HDL molecules, so high cholesterol levels can mean a high LDL, a high

HDL, or both. These three lipoproteins have different effects on your body. Although the exact reasons are not fully understood, low levels of VLDL appear to be preferable.

The significance of LDL is more fully understood. It is known that high levels of LDL particles in the blood are associated with atherosclerosis. When high LDL concentrations are inherited (a disease called familial hypercholesterolemia), it must be medically treated, or the individual typically dies in his early 20's.

As previously described, all three lipoproteins transport cholesterol. However, apparently some of the LDL particles penetrate the inner walls of the arteries and deposit their cholesterol there, leading to the development of atherosclerosis. This process is much more likely to occur if the concentrations of LDL particles in the blood are high over many years. The recommendation of the international panel of the American Health Foundation was based on the accepted opinion that high cholesterol levels should be translated to mean a high level of LDL. The committee further concluded that the ideal level of LDL cholesterol should be about 90 mg%, which works out to mean total serum cholesterol levels of 160 ± 30 mg%. At this level the LDL is still capable of delivering the cholesterol required by cells. Children should have levels of 120 to 140 mg%. If cholesterol levels are high during childhood, they are more likely to be high during adulthood.

Just as there is evidence of high LDL levels possibly leading to the development of atherosclerosis, there is also evidence of HDL, the smallest and most dense cholesterol-carrying particle, possible helping to prevent it. The HDL particles transport cholesterol away from the body tissue, including artery linings. Acting as scavengers, these particles constantly pick up the potentially damaging cholesterol and carry it to the liver for breakdown and excretion from the body.

The following research findings indicate the desirability of high HDL levels:

● Women, who have much less heart disease than men, have higher HDL levels. (Men's average HDL levels = 45 mg%; women's average HDL levels = 55 mg%.)
● Populations with high rates of heart attack tend to have low average HDL levels, and those with low rates have high average HDL levels.
● Laboratory animals traditionally having a high resistance to experimental heart attack, have high HDL levels and low LDL levels.
● HDL is reduced in several conditions associated with an increased risk of future heart disease, namely, elevated serum cholesterol (hypercholesterolemia), elevated serum triglyceride (hypertriglyceridemia), male sex, obesity, and diabetes mellitus. The Framingham

Study, which has followed the lives and heart problems of over 5000 people since October 1949, supports this claim. Comparing the frequency of heart disease at various total cholesterol/HDL ratios (TC/HDL) the researchers found that the risk of heart disease decreases as the total cholesterol decreases and the HDL increases.

TC/HDL Ratio	Risk of CHD
9.6	twice the average
5.0	average
3.4	half the average

A total cholesterol of 200 mg% or less and a HDL of 50 mg% or more would place a person in the less than average category. (Remember, there are other risk factors, however. It is important to manage all of them.)

HDL levels might be the most powerful single predictor of CHD and increasing its level could possibly prevent atherosclerosis. A reduction in the HDL concentration may do the opposite and accelerate the development of this disease. Considering the evidence, you really should seek to manage your total cholesterol levels and your HDL concentration. The following practices can help you to accomplish this goal:

- If you are overweight (overfat), lose weight. A reduction in % body fat often decreases the serum cholesterol levels significantly. Decreasing your total cholesterol will decrease the TC/HDL ratio.

- Reduce your intake of cholesterol and saturated fats. They may cause an elevation in cholesterol levels. (See the chapter on nourishment for discussion of dietary sources of cholesterol and saturated fats.) A reduction in total serum cholesterol and an increase in HDL concentration has been achieved by individuals who limit their dietary cholesterol to less than 300 mg. daily. This restriction also includes a limit of total fat and saturated fat intake.

- Increase your intake of foods high in polyunsaturated fats. For reasons not fully understood, polyunsaturated fats cause a reduction in elevated serum cholesterol levels for many individuals. Vegetable oils such as corn or safflower oil are excellent sources of polyunsaturated fats.

- Maintain an exercise program. Not all studies report a decrease in total cholesterol through exercise, but it is generally agreed that there is a strong positive correlation between the degree of physical activity and HDL and TC/HDL. Active women have a higher HDL concentration than inactive women, and active men have an HDL concentration similar to women. In a study of men between the ages 35 and 66 years, Hartung and associates found that joggers and marathon runners had significantly higher HDL than inactive men. The

researchers concluded that jogging and running, rather than diet, elevate HDL to levels associated with significant reduction of coronary risk. Hartung reported the following average HDL levels for three groups of subjects:
marathon runners—65 mg%
joggers—58 mg%
inactive men—43 mg%

- Stop smoking. More investigation is needed, but there are studies which indicates smokers have a lower HDL concentration and HDL/TC ratio than nonsmokers.

The effect of alcohol on the HDL concentration has been studied as well. There is evidence that consuming one or two cocktails per day may increase the HDL concentration and lessen the buildup of cholesterol on blood vessel walls. Before you begin a campaign for drinking, however, I recommend waiting until more evidence is available. Alcohol will elevate the triglyceride level; moreoever, there are too many known side effects of drinking to make alcohol a recommended choice in preventing CHD.

Triglycerides

These particles are synthesized in the liver from fatty acids and carbohydrates. They serve to transport fats throughout the body and are necessary for chemical activity of the body. Different values have been advised for safe levels of triglyceride, but the upper limit is generally recognized to be 150 mg%.

Individuals with both high cholesterol and high triglyceride levels have an even greater risk of CHD. It is possible that the two concentrations act jointly to create a "sludging" effect, slowing the flow of blood down and allowing the cholesterol to adhere more readily to artery walls. VLDL particles transport the triglycerides, and an increase in VLDL concentration is correlated with an increase in triglycerides. Undue caloric intake, excessive alcohol consumption and high carbohydrate diets are associated with high triglyceride levels.

You can reduce and manage your triglyceride levels in several ways:
- If you are overweight (overfat), lose weight. Most individuals experience a decrease in triglyceride concentration with weight loss.
- Reduce your consumption of saturated fats. Animal fats, luncheon meats, and poultry skin are especially high in triglycerides. Drink skim milk and eat low-fat dairy products and lean meats.
- Reduce your intake of alcohol, starches, and refined sugars.
- Maintain an exercise program. Exercise decreases the serum triglyceride concentration, but the effect is only temporary. The

triglyceride concentration can return to pre-exercise levels within 48 hours. This suggests the necessity for a regular exercise program if a triglyceride lowering effect is to be maintained.

Hypertension

Blood pressure is the force exerted on the walls of the arteries as the heart pumps blood throughout the body. It is the result of the interaction of the heart rate, contraction force of the heart (stroke volume), elasticity of the arteries, and the resistance of the small arteries to blood flow. It is highest (systolic pressure) when the left ventricle of the heart contracts to force blood into the arteries and lowest (diastolic pressure) when the left ventricle relaxes. It is expressed in millimeters of mercury (mm Hg) as a fraction (for example, 110/70). The top number is the systolic pressure; the bottom number is the diastolic.

Even though blood pressure may increase with age (though it need not), normal blood pressure ranges are 100 to 140/60 to 90. Anything above 140/90 usually is considered abnormal. Blood pressure higher than 160/95 is diagnosed as high blood pressure (hypertension), and treatment is recommended. (Some insurance companies believe the criterion for treatment should be 140/90.) When the pressure is high for no specific reason, it is called essential hypertension. When disease or infection cause an elevation in pressure, it is called secondary hypertension. Some 24 million Americans suffer from hypertension, and it is probably the most frequent cardiovascular disorder found in the practice of medicine.

Hypertension is called the "silent killer" because it presents no symptoms. However, it is a risk factor for CHD. Generally, the higher your blood pressure, the greater your risk of CHD or stroke. Consider the following facts:

- The Framingham Study shows that for all ages entering the study there is a linear and stepwise increase in mortality as the systolic pressure increases from 110 to 190 mm Hg and the diastolic pressure increases from 70 to 110 mm Hg.
- An individual with systolic pressure of 160 mm Hg or more has a four times greater risk of CHD than if the pressure were 120 or less.

Stress, obesity, diet, hormonal imbalance, and other factors have been studied as possible causes of essential hypertension. Heredity appears to be an important factor in hypertension, but, as with diabetes, personal habits and lifestyle can accelerate the disease.

Treatment of hypertension often involves antihypertensive drugs, but it is possible to prevent and treat mild hypertension through several methods.

- Limit your salt intake. Restricting the salt intake tends to curb fluid retention, thus reducing blood volume. Limiting salt intake has decreased the blood pressure of many individuals. Salt intake is discussed further in the chapter on nourishment.
- If you are overweight (overfat), lose weight. Overweight people are more likely to have hypertension because the additional fat places greater demand on the heart.
- If you experience stress and tension, practice relaxation techniques. Relaxation is discussed in the chapter on stress.
- Cease smoking, or at least reduce the number of cigarettes you smoke. Nicotine and carbon monoxide cause the heart to work harder.
- Maintain a regular exercise program. Exercise has been effective in reducing the blood pressure of many individuals, and some have been able to reduce their blood pressure medication through exercise. However, if your blood pressure is elevated, you should undertake an exercise program only after medical clearance.

Electrocardiographic Abnormalities
A resting electrocardiogram (ECG) is valuable for detecting heart disease; however a stress ECG is of more value. A stress ECG usually consists either of riding a stationary bicycle (bicycle ergometer) or of walking and/or running during a multistage treadmill test. Your blood pressure, heart, and general response to exercise are monitored by a physician during the test. In both methods, the work load is gradually increased until either you can no longer continue, a predetermined heart rate is reached, or symptoms of CHD are observed. Heart disease symptoms are more often found in older individuals using this test.

Lack of Physical Activity (Sedentary Living)
Does a physically active lifestyle protect you from CHD? Even though the death rate from coronary artery disease in the sedentary population is five times that of the active population, some investigators are reserving judgment about this risk factor. However, more and more evidence is demonstrating the relationship between physical inactivity and CHD. In assessing the nature of this relationship, four types of studies have been done:
(1) epidemiological,
(2) risk factor,
(3) cardiovascular efficiency and
(4) post coronary treatment.
In all four types of studies, appropriate kinds and amounts of exercise

have proven beneficial. In many of these studies the researchers also have offered explanations as to why these benefits occur.

Several studies involve a massive amount of data. For example, Morris categorized two million middle-aged men from England and Wales in terms of the physical activity required to perform their last occupation. He found that the more activity required in a group's occupation, the lower the rate of CHD death in that group. In another British study, researchers examined the death certificates of 31,000 employees of the London Transport System. They compared the sedentary bus drivers with the more active bus conductors. The incidence of heart attack and death from CHD was found to be 1½ times higher in the sedentary bus drivers than in the more active conductors. Sudden death following a first heart attack was two times higher in the sedentary group.

In another study led by Morris, 16,882 British male office workers, aged 40 to 64, recorded their physical activities for a Friday and Saturday. The men who recorded "vigorous" activities (continuous, uninterrupted activity for at least 15 minutes, reaching a peak energy output of 7.5 calories per minute) showed only one third the incidence of CHD than comparable men who exercised less or not at all. The researchers concluded that vigorous exercise apparently protected against rapidly fatal heart attacks and other first clinical attacks of coronary disease through middle age.

Paffenbarger and his associates also conducted studies involving large populations. In a 16-year study of 3,263 longshoremen, it was found that men with sedentary jobs expended 925 fewer calories per workday and sustained coronary death rates one third higher than men who performed more physically demanding jobs. In addition, the inactive's group occurrence of sudden death was three times higher.

Paffenbarger performed a similar study with approximately 17,000 Harvard alumni. The alumni, ages 35 to 74, were classified by energy expenditure (stairs climbed, blocks walked, sports played), and were followed for 6 to 10 years, to record the number of heart attacks. The study found an inverse correlation between heart attack and levels of activity. This trend held for all ages and for both nonfatal and fatal attacks. Strenuous sports in particular showed a strong inverse relation to heart attacks, suggesting that the greater the physical exertion, the lower the risk of heart attack. Participation in casual sports did not affect the occurrence of heart attack. Paffenbarger found that individuals who expended less than 2,000 calories a week in their exercise experienced a 64% greater heart attack risk than did their more active classmates.

The study of Irish brothers mentioned earlier in this chapter also concluded that physical activity was an important risk factor in CHD. In the nine-year study 575 pairs of brothers born in Ireland were observed. One of each pair remained in Ireland while the other immigrated to the U.S. The brothers who remained in Ireland had lower blood pressure, lower levels of cholesterol, weighed less, had less body fat, and experienced less CHD. They consumed more animal fats and at least 400 more calories each day, however. The smoking and drinking habits of the brothers were very similar, but their physical activity habits were significantly different. The brothers in Ireland were generally active while the brothers in America were sedentary. The researchers concluded that the physical activity habits of the Irish brothers played a significant role in their lower incidence of heart disease.

The Framingham Study supports a connection between physical activity and CHD. The incidence of fatal heart attacks has been consistently lower among the more active individuals than among the sedentary ones over a ten-year period. Other studies have reached the same conclusion—when variables such as age, weight, and % of body fat are held constant, the risk from any one factor is reduced in individuals who are physically fit.

Thus, research supports the belief that physically active individuals have a lower risk for the development of CHD than do less active individuals. The research is not limited to observing the incidence of coronary heart disease, however. Numerous studies are available which describe the effects of physical activity on the heart, blood, and vessels. These effects probably reduce the occurrence or severity of CHD:

- Decrease in resting heart rate (bradycardia). This decrease provides a longer resting period between contractions of the heart. The significance of this decrease can be observed by calculating the number of times your heart will contract in a 24-hour period at a rate of 60 beats per minute versus 80 beats per minute.
- More time for blood to flow through the coronary arteries. Coronary blood flow occurs primarily during the relaxation phase of heart contraction.
- Thicker and stronger heart walls.
- Increase in the amount of blood pumped into general circulation with each contraction (stroke volume). The stroke volume may vary from two ounces of blood in a very deconditioned individual to eight ounces in a longterm, very fit individual. This is due to the increased strength of the heart.
- Increase in the amount of blood pumped per minute by the heart (heart rate X stroke volume = cardiac output). This is due to the increased stroke volume.

- Increased area for oxygen to be delivered to the heart cells due to an increased number of capillaries.
- Decreased systolic and diastolic blood pressure, if they are elevated.
- Increase in the amount of oxygen extracted from the blood by the cells of the body.
- Increase in destruction of fibrin in clotted blood, resulting in dissolution of a clot (fibrinolysis).
- Less platelet clumping, decreasing clot formation.
- Increase in the total amount of blood, number of red blood cells, and percentage of hemoglobin in the blood. These changes increase the blood's capacity to transport oxygen.
- Decrease in serum triglyceride.
- Increase in HDL concentration.
- Possible decrease in total serum cholesterol.
- Reduction in blood sugar.
- Possible formation of additional coronary blood vessels (coronary collateral circulation). This provides interconnections among coronary arteries. There is disagreement within the medical profession about the development of coronary collateral circulation in human beings, although it has been demonstrated in exercise-trained animals. The exercise-induced effects of collateral circulation have been seen in people through the reduction in angina pain and improved stress electrocardiograms. If formed, these additional vessels provide alternate routes for blood flow in the event a heart attack does occur.
- Possible increase in size of coronary artery lumina. Mann and his research team examined 600 members, including 350 over age 40 years, of the Masai tribe of East Africa. This tribe lives almost exclusively on meat and fermented milk, consuming about 300 gm of fat and 600 mg of cholesterol daily. At the same time they are exceptionally active and physically fit. The research team found only one individual with electrocardiographic evidence of a heart attack. High blood pressure was unusual, and the level of serum cholesterol rarely exceeded 150 mg%.

Mann and his associates collected the hearts and aortas of 50 Masai, most of whom had died from combat or infection. The aortas had extensive atherosclerosis with lipid infiltration and fibrous changes, but little obstruction in blood flow as found. The coronary arteries showed distinct internal thickening by atherosclerosis, yet they had enlarged with age to compensate for the degree of atherosclerosis present. Mann speculated that the physical fitness of the Masai tribe somehow protected them from the effects of atherosclerosis by causing the coronary vessels to enlarge.

Each year about 75,000 coronary bypass operations are performed in this country at a cost of $10,000 and up. If the decision is life or death, $10,000 is not considered expensive, but the management of the CHD risk factors is really a bargain. You can do something to decrease your risk of CHD. Your health+ program should include goals to do so.

Aspirin

A promising development is the use of aspirin to prevent heart attacks. It is possible that regular small doses of aspirin changes the blood-clotting mechanism to make you less likely to have a heart attack, and especially, less likely to have a second one. There is disagreement as to the actual effectiveness of this treatment, but many physicians are prescribing aspirin for this purpose. Much research needs to be done in this area. Certainly, you should not neglect the management of the CHD risk factors in hopes that a daily dose of aspirin is all you need. And you should not practice the philosophy, "if a little is good, more is better." Too much aspirin can be detrimental to your health.

Risko

The following game will help give you an estimate of your chances of suffering a heart attack.

RISKO

A WAY TO ALERT YOU TO THE RISKS OF HEART ATTACK

DON'T PLAY GAMES WITH YOUR HEART. SEE YOUR DOCTOR REGULARLY AND LET HIM HELP YOU REDUCE YOUR RISK OF HEART ATTACK

The purpose of this game is to give you an estimate of your chances of suffering heart attack.

The game is played by making squares which—from left to right—represent an increase in your RISK FACTORS. These are medical conditions and habits associated with an increased danger of heart attack. Not all risk factors are measurable enough to be included in this game.

RULES:

Study each RISK FACTOR and its row. Find the box applicable to you and circle the large number in it. For example, if you are 37, circle the number in the box labeled 31-40.

After checking out all the rows, add the circled numbers. This total—your score—is an estimate of your risk.

IF YOU SCORE:

  6-11 — Risk well below average
12-17 — Risk below average
18-24 — Risk generally average
25-31 — Risk moderate
32-40 — Risk at a dangerous level
41-62 — Danger urgent. See your doctor now.

HEREDITY:

Count parents, grand-parents, brothers, and sisters who have had heart attack and/or stroke.

TOBACCO SMOKING:

If you inhale deeply and smoke a cigarette way down, add one to your classification. Do NOT subtract because you think you do not inhale or smoke only half an inch on a cigarette.

EXERCISE:

Lower your score one point if you exercise regularly and frequently.

CHOLESTEROL OR SATURATED FAT INTAKE LEVEL:

A cholesterol blood level is best. If you can't get one from your doctor, then estimate honestly the percentage of solid fats you eat. These are usually of animal origin—lard, cream, butter, and beef and lamb fat. If you eat much of this, your cholesterol level probably will be high. The U.S. average, 40%, is too high for good health.

BLOOD PRESSURE:

If you have no recent reading but have passed an insurance or industrial examination chances are you are 140 or less.

SEX:

This line takes into account the fact that men have from 6 to 10 times more heart attacks than women of child bearing age.

AGE	10 to 20	21 to 30	31 to 40
HEREDITY	No known history of heart disease	1 relative with cardiovascular disease Over 60	2 relatives with cardiovascular disease Over 60
WEIGHT	More than 5 lbs. below standard weight	−5 to +5 lbs. standard weight	6-20 lbs. overweight
TOBACCO SMOKING	Nonsmoker	Cigar and/or pipe	10 cigarettes or more a day
EXERCISE	Intensive occupational and recreational exertion	Moderate occupational and recreational exertion	Sedentary work and intense recreational exertion
CHOLES-TEROL OR FAT % IN DIET	Cholesterol below 80 mg.% Diet contains no animal or solid fats	Cholesterol 181-205 mg.% Diet contains 10% animal or solid fats	Cholesterol 206-230 mg.% Diet contains 20% animal or solid fats
BLOOD PRESSURE	100 upper reading	120 upper reading	140 upper reading
SEX	Female under 40	Female	Female over 50

41 to 50 **4**	51 to 60 **6**	70 & over **8**
1 relative with cardiovascular disease Under 60 **4**	2 relatives with cardiovascular disease Under 60	3 relatives with cardiovascular disease Under 60
21-35 lbs. overweight **3**	36-50 lbs. overweight **5**	51-65 lbs. overweight **7**
20 cigarettes a day **4**	30 cigarettes a day **6**	40 cigarettes a day or more **10**
Sedentary occupational and moderate recreational exertion **5**	Sedentary work and light recreational exertion **6**	Complete lack of all exercise
Cholesterol 231-255 mg.% Diet contains 30% animal or solid fats	Cholesterol 256-280 mg.% Diet contains 40% animal or solid fats	Cholesterol 281-300 mg.% Diet contains 50% animal or solid fats
4 160 upper reading	**6** 180 upper reading	200 or over upper reading **8**
5 Male	**6** Stocky male	**7** Bald stocky male

TOTAL

© *Michigan Heart Association*

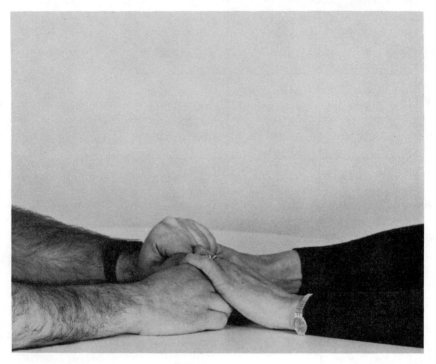

Stress is a critical factor in "RISKO."

Because of the difficulty in measuring them, these RISK FACTORS are not included in "RISKO":

Diabetes, particularly when present for many years.

Your Character or Personality, and the Stress under which you live.

Vital Capacity—determined by measuring the amount of air you can take into your lungs in proportion to the size of your lungs. The less air you can breathe, the higher your risk.

Electrocardiogram—if certain abnormalities are present in the record of the electrical currents generated by your heart you have a higher risk.

Gout—is caused by a higher than normal amount of uric acid in the blood. Patients have an increased risk.

IF YOU HAVE A NUMBER OF RISK FACTORS, FOR THE SAKE OF YOUR HEALTH ASK YOUR DOCTOR TO CHECK YOUR MEDICAL CONDITIONS AND QUIT YOUR RISK FACTOR HABITS.

NOTE: The fact that various habits or conditions may be rated similarly in this test does not mean these are of equal risk. The reaction of individual human beings to Risk Factors—as to many other things—is so varied it is impossible to draw valid conclusions for any individual.

This scale has been developed only to highlight what Risk Factors are and what can be done about them. It is not designed to be a medical diagnosis.

5

Nourishment

It matters what you eat.

Unless you are attempting to lose or gain weight, you probably do not think of yourself as being on a diet. At the same time you probably think you know all you need to know about food. You are wrong on both counts. Your diet is a habitual pattern. It involves different types of foods that affect how you feel, how much you weigh, and how you look. You certainly are on a diet, and knowing what you should eat is not as simple as it may seem.

There are many ways to be malnourished or well nourished. Good nutrition involves choosing your food wisely and being aware of what you eat. However, many Americans select their food for convenience, the artificial flavor, and the attractive packaging. Selection of food for these reasons can lead to nutritional disorders. Because of unwise selection, the diet of this nation, as in most industralized countries, is too high in fat, salt, sugar, and processed foods. It is too low in fresh fruits, vegetables, whole grains and cereals, and dried legumes, which together make up about 80% of the total calories of many nonindustralized nations.

According to a 1978 poll by Louis Harris and Associates 67% of all American adults recognize that they can be healthier if they make certain changes in their diet. They realize they should eat more fruit, fish or poultry, whole grain bread, and fresh or frozen vegatables. They also know they should be consuming less fried foods, sugar, soft drinks, salt, coffee, pretzels, potato chips, and white bread. The same poll indicated the main reasons people go on eating the foods they do even though they realize the need to change: they like what they eat, they eat many foods out of habit, and they lack the willpower to change.

Evidently, these individuals really don't believe it is worth the effort to have a sound diet. Nutritional research indicates how wrong they are. The intake of just enough calories, protein, vitamins, and minerals to provide for growth and avoid malnutrition won't necessarily be sufficient for avoiding diseases of the heart and blood vessels and other premature killers in industrialized populations. In this nation of plenty, diet is linked with six of our major killers—heart desease, cancer, stroke, diabetes, arteriosclerosis and cirrhosis of the liver. And these diseases can be prevented more easily than they can be treated.

The Nutritional Diet

The diet for health+ is based on seven food categories:
(1) carbohydrates
(2) fats
(3) protein
(4) vitamins
(5) minerals
(6) fiber
(7) water

Carbohydrates, fats, and proteins are the only substances that provide body energy (calories). The percentage of calories provided by each of these sources is important in your health+ program (See Appendix—Caloric and Nutritional Values of Foods).

Carbohydrates.

The organic compounds commonly called starches and sugars are carbohydrates. These compounds are broken down into a simple sugar, glucose, which the body uses as its primary source of energy. As with proteins and fats, it matters what type of carbohydrates you eat. Fresh fruits, vegetables, and grain products are the most desirable. These foods provide minerals and vitamins. The least desirable, sweets and sugar provide energy, but they provide very few, if any, minerals and vitamins. In addition to being the most important source of energy, carbohydrates are needed to build such important cell components as nucleic acids, connective tissues, and carbohydrate-protein compounds.

Carbohydrates should make up about 50% to 60% of your daily diet, and most of them should be in the form of starches (vegetables and grains). In the U.S., however, sugar furnishes more than 50% of our carbohydrate intake. The percentage of starches consumed has decreased by about 30% since the turn of the century.

The belief that carbohydrates are fattening, or that they are more fattening than other foods, is incorrect. Depending on the caloric content, all foods can be fattening when eaten excessively. When there is more glucose in the body than is needed, it is converted to glycogen and stored in muscle and liver cells. When needed, this glycogen is converted back to glucose. However, if the capacity of the cells for glycogen storage is reached, the excess sugar is readily converted into fat and stored in the fat tissue beneath the skin. Any food intake that is in excess

Carbohydrates should make up about 50% to 60% of your daily diet.

Fats.

More calories are found in fats, or lipids, than in carbohydrates and proteins; they have an energy content of 9.3 calories per gram. Your body requires at least some intake of fats, for several purposes:

- They provide a reserve fuel supply. They are an important source of energy for light to moderate levels of activity and in prolonged exercise there is a significant increase in the amount of fat utilized for energy. The body's fat stores may provide nearly 90% of the total energy required for exceptionally prolonged exercise. A pound of body fat stores more than twice the energy found in a pound of carbohydrate. If your energy reserves depended only on carbohydrate storage, you would be much larger. This does not imply that you should try to store more body fat; you probably now store more than you will ever need. A pound or two of fat provides enough energy to complete a marathon run (26.2 miles).
- Fats support and protect vital organs. The fat around the heart, liver, kidneys, brain, and spinal cord serves as a protective shield against injury. If the amount of fat around these organs is excessive, however, it may constitute a risk to your health.
- They help provide the fat-soluble vitamins A,D,E, and K. A diet consistently low in fat may cause you to experience a deficiency of one or more fat-soluble vitamins.
- The storage of fat provides body insulation. Fats stored beneath the skin act as an insulator to protect the body in a cold environment. Individuals with a high percentage of body fat feel the cold less than slender individuals. On the other hand excess body fat can be a disadvantage in a hot environment. The fat makes the loss of body heat more difficult, and because they dissipate body heat less readily, fat individuals sweat on warm days. The lean person, because he has less insulation, can maintain normal body temperature for a longer time before needing the cooling benefits of the sweat mechanism. The problem of heat regulation must be considered especially by fat individuals during physical activity.
- Fats are needed to maintain cell structure.
- Fats are needed to provide linoleic acid. This is a polyunsaturated fat that strengthens the capillary wall, prolongs internal blood clotting time, and possibly lowers serum cholesterol.
- Many fatty acids that are essential for life are obtained only through eating; that is, they are not manufactured by the body.

Fats are of two basic chemical types—saturated and unsaturated. The type is determined by the number of hydrogen atoms combined with carbon atoms in the fat molecules. Saturated fats have the maximum number of hydrogen atoms to which the carbon atoms can attach. They harden at room temperature and are found abundantly in beef, pork, lamb, ham, butter, cream, whole milk, and cheeses made from cream and whole milk. Saturated fats are also found in many solid and hydrogenated shortenings, coconut oil, cocoa butter, and palm oil (used in commercial cookies, pie fillings, and nondairy milk and cream substitutes).

Unsaturated and polyunsaturated fats have fewer hydrogen atoms in proportion to carbon atoms. They are liquid at room temperature, and are found primarily in vegetable foods and in liquid vegetable oils, such as those derived from corn, cottonseed, safflower, sesame seed, soybean, and sunflower seed.

It is important to know the difference between these fats because they have very different effects on your body. Most nutritionists and cardiologists believe that the consumption of saturated fats raises the level of the blood lipid cholesterol. (The American diet includes 400 to 800 mg of cholesterol daily.) Studies comparing the diets and blood lipids of various societies support this belief. One such study observed three groups of healthy, young, urban Ethiopian men differing in dietary pattern. The results showed striking increases in blood lipids when the diet assumed a more Western character. It is believed that the consumption of unsaturated fats has no effect on blood cholersterol levels and that polyunsaturated fats tend to reduce blood cholesterol levels in many individuals.

In addition, a diet high in saturated fats may be directly or indirectly related to the development of cancer of the colon, stomach, esophagus, breast, liver, and uterus. Again, studies of diets in various nations support this belief. The U.S. has a high fat intake and a high incidence of breast cancer; Japan has a low fat intake and a low incidence of breast cancer. It is possible that a high fat intake enhances the activity of cancer-producing agents, or that fats act as carriers of these agents to their sites of action.

Primitive man probably received about 10% of his calories from fat. At the turn of the century, the American diet consisted of 33% fat. Today, the average person in the U.S. consumes nearly 150 gm of fat daily. This represents 40% to 45% of the total caloric intake and amounts to 115 pounds of fat consumed per person each year. A small percentage (about 20%) of this fat is consumed in the "visible fats" of butter, lard, mayonnaise, cooking oils, and hard fat on meat. Most of the fat is consumed from the "invisible fats" of meat, eggs, milk, cheese, nuts, vegetables, and cereals. Of every 10 pounds of fat taken in, about 3.4

pounds are vegetable fat; the remaining 6.6 pounds are derived from animal sources.

Only 25% to 30% of your total caloric intake should be in the form of fat. Even this percentage may be too high if you suffer from gall bladder or cardiovascular diseases. At least one-half to two-thirds of your fat intake should be of unsaturated and polyunsaturated fats. The recommendation of many nutritional experts is to limit your cholesterol intake to 300 mg per day.

You certainly should not attempt to eliminate all fats from your diet, but you should limit your intake of the following foods:

- Organ meats—liver, heart, kidney, brains
- Fatty meats—hamburgers, steak, ham, pork, bacon, etc.
- Fatty oils and sauces—cooking oils, salad oils made with sour cream or cheese, shortening, gravy
- Fishes packed in oil
- Dairy products—eggs (no more than 3 or 4 per week), whole milk, butter, cheese
- Desserts made with whole milk and/or eggs
- Shrimp, lobster, crab and crayfish
- Nondairy products that contain coconut oil, palm kernel oil, or hydrogenated oil

Include more lean meats, poultry (without the skin), fish, skim milk, low fat dairy products, and polyunsaturated fats in your diet. And be more selective when shopping for processed foods. Check the label for the list of ingredients; they are listed in descending order by weight. If fat appears early in the list, the food is likely to be high in fat. When you do purchase fatty foods, select those with a lower fat content. For example, Parmesan cheese and mozzarella cheese made from part-skim milk have less fat than other hard cheeses; fig bars and vanilla wafers have less fat than cookies made with chocolate, cream filling, or nuts; English muffins and hard rolls have less fat than fat-rich biscuits. Also boiling, steaming and baking are preferable to frying.

Some excellent sources of polyunsaturated fats are:

- corn oil   1 tsp
- safflower oil   1 tsp
- sunflower oil   1 tsp
- walnut oil   1 tsp
- black walnuts   4 halves
- English walnuts   4 halves

At least one-half to two-thirds of your fat intake should be of unsaturated and polyunsaturated fats.

Protein.

One-half of our body (water excluded) is made up of the organic compound protein. Body cells ordinarily don't use protein for energy, doing so only if the carbohydrate and fat supplies have been depleted. Proteins are needed to build and repair tissue and are the major component of muscle, nails, hemoglobin, antibodies, and many other parts of the body. They also function as enzymes and hormones, and transmit hereditary characteristics.

There are 4.1 calories in each gm of protein. Animal meats are excellent sources of protein as are fish, poultry, milk, eggs, grains, nuts, and legumes. Your digestive system breaks down the protein from these sources into its basic components, amino acids. The body has the ability to make new protein, but all the necessary amino acids must be present for this to occur. There are at least 8 to 10 essential amino acids that cannot be synthesized by the body and must be supplied by your diet. From these 8 to 10 components the body is able to build the remaining dozen or so amino acids. Animal proteins generally contain all the essential amino acids, whereas vegetable proteins do not. It is possible to eliminate animal protein from your diet and combine or supplement vegetable proteins in such a way as to obtain the essential amino acids, but such a diet must be planned carefully. Vegetarian cookbooks usually have recipes which include all of the essential amino acids.

The body can't store protein as it does fat, so an adequate daily intake of protein is essential for your well-being. The daily requirement is 0.8 to 0.9 gm per kilogram (2.2 pounds) of body weight or 10% to 15% of your caloric intake. A few Americans may have diets deficient in protein, but most of us consume two or three times more than we need. For example, a 6-ounce steak provides the daily protein requirement for the average-size female. That same steak provides 80% of the average-size male's protein demand. The excess protein you consume is usually excreted, but if an abnormally high amount of protein is consumed over a period of time, it can be dangerous to your health. The kidneys may not be able to handle all the waste products that accumulate from the breakdown of protein. Furthermore, when you get your protein from animal sources you also take in a lot of fat and extra calories. At least 70% to 80% of the calories in beef and pork come from fat.

High protein consumption may be one factor responsible for the shorter life span of men as compared with women. Protein consumption is 40% greater in men than in women based upon total daily intake and about 20% greater when related to body weight. The metabolic cost of obtaining calories from protein exceeds that from carbohydrate and fat. And it produces no demonstratably favorable metabolic effect. This process "idles" the body engine faster. It has also been shown that the lifespan of experimental animals is increased by decreasing protein intake. Considering these studies, and reports on men and women who ate similar quantities of protein as children but not as adults, it appears that protein consumption may in some way affect the life span in human beings.

Exercise does not increase the requirement for protein. Likewise, the belief that one can increase muscle mass through a large intake of protein is incorrect. Increase in muscle mass is the result of exercise, not diet.

Following is a breakdown of the sources of protein in the American diet:

- beans, peas, nuts   5%
- cereals   19%
- dairy products   24%
- fats and oils   1%
- fruits and vegetables   7%
- meat, fish, poultry, eggs   44%

Vitamins.

Vitamins are the organic chemical compounds necessary to enable the body to utilize cabohydrates, fats, and proteins. Like enzymes, they help produce the right chemical reactions at the right time. The body can't synthesize vitamins, and when a particular vitamin is lacking in your diet, the chemical reaction it's concerned with can't take place, even if you have been eating an otherwise balanced diet. All the vitamins should be included in your diet.

The B vitamins and vitamin C are water-soluble and are not stored in the body. Since they are excreted when not used, these vitamins should be included in your diet daily. Vitamins A, D, E, and K are fat-soluble and can be stored in the liver. Deficiencies of the fat-soluble vitamins in a previously well-fed adult may not appear for years. The liver is limited in its capacity to store these vitamins, however, and overdoses of them can be dangerous. For example, large doses of vitamin A and D have been known to result in headache, nausea, hair loss, disturbance of the menstrual cycle, liver damage, and cellular abnormalities. For some individuals large intakes of vitamins B_6 and C may also be harmful.

The minimum essential amount of some vitamins required in our daily diet can be very, very small. For this reason, the Recommended Daily Allowance (RDA) for some vitamins is expressed in International Units (IU). The National Research Council of the National Academy of Sciences advises the Food and Drug Administration as to what the RDA for each vitamin should be. It represents the amount necessary to prevent deficiency symptoms.

There are probably more myths and misunderstandings about vitamins than there are about any other aspect of nutrition. Despite the abundance of foods containing vitamins A and C, many people still don't have an adequate intake of these vitamins. At the same time, others needlessly consume large quantities of vitamin supplements. This practice is shown by the fact that Americans spend over $500 million annually on vitamin preparations.

Claims have been made about the benefits of large doses of certain vitamins. The question of supplementation in moderate amounts will be discussed below, but if you do consume large amounts of some vitamins, or are considering doing so, you should be aware of the pros and cons as indicated by scientific research.

Vitamin B.

Five or six vitamins of the B-complex group interact with various enzymes that are important in energy-yielding reactions utilizing carbohydrates and fats. Because of this interaction, many physical fitness enthusiasts and athletes consume large quantities of the vitamin B group in hopes of improving their performances. Yet there is little accepted evidence to support this practice.

Thiamine is sometimes taken as an antidepressant, or to increase the body's energy. Pantothenic acid is prescribed occasionally for skin disorders and for energy. Again, there is little scientific research to support these claims.

Individuals who drink alcohol excessively do need additional vitamin B supplements. Heavy drinkers often neglect their nutritional needs, and alcohol interferes with the absorption and utilization of vitamin B.

Vitamin C.

This is a $100 million-a-year industry. Although many claims have been made about the benefits of its supplementation, scientific evidence to support most of them is lacking. But the connection between vitamin C deficiency and scurvy is accepted as fact by all. Most animals are able to produce vitamin C from sugars within their bodies, but we cannot; we must depend on obtaining it from our food.

The primary function of this vitamin is to assist in the production of collagen. This substance holds cells together, enabling them to maintain the proper physical relationship to each other. It also aids in the formation of scar tissue, necessary for the healing of injured muscles and tendons.

Perhaps the most publicized claim for an increased dosage of vitamin C is made by Dr. Linus Pauling. In 1966, Pauling used himself as an experimental subject and ingested massive doses of vitamin C. He became convinced that the vitamin prevents colds and increases the body's resistance to disease. He has since performed other experiments to support his claim. Very few studies have duplicated Dr. Pauling's findings.

Many individuals take vitamin C supplements and sincerely believe they have fewer colds. It is likely that, in addition to taking a supplement, they become "cold conscious" and monitor their behavior. That is, they probably try to prevent colds by doing certain other things, such as getting adequate rest, avoiding fatigue, maintaining a good diet, and so on. Vitamin C may play an important role in the prevention and curing of colds, but more research is needed to support Dr. Pauling's work before it will be wholeheartedly accepted by the medical profession.

Other experiments suggest vitamin C may assist in the prevention of atherosclerosis by acting as a cholesterol suppressant. Guinea pigs with a chronic margial deficiency of vitamin C have high levels of cholesterol and triglyceride and cholesterol accumulation in tissue and blood vessels. An increased vitamin C intake tends to improve these disorders.

Furthermore, individuals with high levels of cholesterol and triglyceride and a low intake of vitamin C have experienced a decrease in these levels through the long-term administration of vitamin C. In Great Britain, a significantly lower coronary death rate has been reported in regions with a higher intake of vitamin C. It also has been proposed that the increased intake of vitamin C in the U.S. has brought about a substantial decrease in the incidence of marginal vitamin C deficiency, and the correction of this deficiency may have contributed to the decline in coronary deaths.

Other possible functions of vitamin C, such as its role in the treatment of cancer, are being studied. Vitamin C may very well prove to be an extremely important vitamin for treatment of various diseases and disorders, but additional research must be performed before exhorbitant claims can be made.

Just as some research supports large doses of vitamin C supplementation, other research suggests that these doses can be harmful. There is some indication that supplementation increases the destruction of vitamin C within the body. Scurvy has been observed in individuals who have taken large amounts of vitamin C for a long duration and then returned to a diet with normal amounts. It could be that the increased rate of vitamin C destruction produced by supplementation persists after supplementation is ceased. High doses of vitamin C may also induce an allergic response which destroys the vitamin. According to another report, individuals who consume 5 gm of vitamin C per day had no differences in blood vitamin C levels from those who ate a similar diet but took no supplement. The researchers suggest that either the excess vitamin was destroyed internally or it was eliminated from the body.

In some individuals, doses as low as 500 mg have actually destroyed vitamin B_{12}, which is necessary to prevent red blood cell abnormalities and pernicious anemia. Yet another problem associated with high vitamin C supplementation is that excess vitamin C in the urine prevents accurate testing for diabetes because it gives a false reading for sugasr level. In addition, it is believed that some individuals have experienced gout, hemorrhaging of ulcers, formation of kidney stones, severe diarrhea, liver abnormalities and enhancement of copper deficiencies as a result of prolonged intake of large vitamin C doses.

Vitamin E.
This vitamin is found abundantly in fats and oils. Since the typical American diet is over 40% fat, most of us get more vitamin E than we need.

Vitamin E has been used as a treatment for skin wrinkles, sexual problems, heart disease, aging, increasing physical endurance, and many other things. The belief in its value as a protective agent against aging and for increased physical endurance is derived in part from its unique, but not fully understood, ability to protect body tissues from oxygen breakdown. Still, it is doubtful that vitamin E fulfills the claims that are made for it. In fact, very few of the benefits attributed to vitamin E have been scientifically documented, and many of the claims can be traced to poorly controlled experiments.

Vitamin E has been demonstrated to be of value in the treatment of patients recovering from heart attacks. The vitamin prolongs bloodclotting time, allowing the blood to flow more freely. Heart patients and diabetics are cautioned against taking high doses of vitamin E without proper supervision, however. Since it is a strong heart stimulant, high doses can increase the blood pressure of individuals with atherosclerosis or hypertension.

ESSENTIAL WATER–SOLUBLE VITAMINS IN THE ADULT DIET

Vitamin	Sources	Functions	Adult Requirement	Deficiency
B₁ (Thiamine)	Whole grain products, legumes, nuts, lean meats, various green & yellow vegetables	Carbohydrate and protein metabolism, nerve functions, digestion	0.5 mg per 1000 calories consumed	Beriberi, Neuritis, heart disorders, fatigue, loss of appetite
B₂ (Riboflavin)	Milk, cheese, eggs, enriched breads and cereals, nuts, legumes, meats, liver	Catalysis in cellular oxidations, tissue growth and repair, metabolism of foodstuffs	0.6 mg per 1000 calories	Cracks and sores in mouth, eye problems, anemia, fatigue, digestive disorders, headaches
B₆ (Pyridoxine)	Liver, wheat germ, lima beans, peas, sweet potatoes, peanuts, fish	Protein metabolism, cell function	1.5 mg women, 1.8 mg men	Pernicious anemia, skin disorders, nerve inflammation, neuritis
B₁₂ (Cyanocobalamin)	Meat, liver, eggs, milk, fish	Formation of blood cells, metabolism of basic foodstuffs	3 mg	Pernicious anemia, nervousness
Biotin	Present in almost all foods	Metabolism of basic foodstuffs, aids in utilization of other B vitamins	No RDA	Poor Appetite, depression, muscle pain, impairment of fat metabolism, deficiency unlikely
Choline	Egg yolk, beef, beans peas	Nerve transmission, fat metabolism, liver and gallbladder regulation	No RDA	Fatty liver, high blood pressure, hemorrahaging of kidneys, deficiency unlikely
Folic Acid	Liver, nuts, wheat germ, green vegetables	Growth and division of body cells, red blood cell formation, metabolism of proteins	400 mcg	Anemia, B₁₂ deficiency, Diarrhea

ESSENTIAL WATER–SOLUBLE VITAMINS IN THE ADULT DIET (continued)

Vitamin	Sources	Functions	Adult Requirement	Deficiency
Niacin (Nicolinic acid)	Liver, meats, fish whole grain breads, cereal, dried peas, and beans, peanuts, peanut butter	Metabolism of basic foodstuffs, health of skin, tongue, digestive system	6.6 mg per 1000 calories	Pellagra (skin disease), nervous disorders
Pantothenic Acid	Liver, beef, wheat germ, bran, wholegrain cereals and bread, peanuts, peas	Metabolism of basic foodstuffs, aids in utilization of some vitamins, synthisis of some adrenal hormones	5 to 10 mg	Vomiting, restlessness, stomach stress, increased susceptibility to inection, sensitivity to insulin
C (Ascorbic acid)	Citrus fruits and their juices, potatoes, peppers, cabbage, tomatoes, broccoli	Metabolism of amino acids, healing of wounds, strength to capillary walls, absorption of iron, formation of intercellular substance of collagenous and fibrous tissue	50 to 100 mg	Scurvy, delayed healing of wounds, bleeding gums, hemorrhages, swollen or painful joints

To understand the relative amounts needed, it may be useful to know that one level teaspoon of white sugar weighs about four grams.

ESSENTIAL FAT-SOLUBLE VITAMINS IN THE ADULT DIET

Vitamin	Sources	Functions	Adult Requirement	Deficiency Disorders
A	Liver, eggs, milk, cheese, many green and yellow vegetables	Normal growth of most cells, normal vision, growth of bones and teeth	5,000 IU	Rough, unhealthy skin, night blindness
D	Salmon, sardines, fish, butter and cream products, liver, oils, egg yolk, sunlight	Utilization and retention of calcium and phosphorus, normal bone and tooth development	400 IU	Softening of bones and teeth, inadequate absorption of calcium
E	Vegetable oils, whole grain cereals, green leafy vegetables, legumes, nuts	Prevention of unwanted oxidation of polyunsaturated fatty acids and fat-soluble compounds	12 IU women, 15 IU men	Deficiencies rare
K	Green leafy vegetables; most important source is intestinal bacterial flora, which provide adequate amount under normal circumstances	Formation of prothrombin by liver, which is needed for normal blood-clotting	No RDA	Tendency to hemorrhage, deficiency rare

Minerals.

Carbon, oxygen, hydrogen, and nitrogen make up 96% of the body's weight. The other 4% consists of minerals. Even though the total quantity of minerals is relatively small, each mineral is vital for proper function of the body's cells. Several minerals are essential for the maintenance of acid-base balances and the fluid balance between tissues and blood. They are components of enzymes, hormones, and vitamins, and they are found in muscle and connective tissues. Such minerals as sodium, chlorine, and potassium are lost during exercise, but an adequate diet replaces them.

There are six minerals required in relatively large quantities: sodium, potassium, chlorine, calcium, phosphorus, and magnesium. All of these should be present in your diet in amounts of 100 mg a day or more. The calcium and phosphorus found in teeth and bones account for 58% to 85% of all the body's minerals. The essential trace minerals are required in amounts smaller than 100 mg.

ESSENTIAL MINERALS IN IN THE ADULT DIET

Mineral	Source	Functions	Adult Requirement	Deficiency Disorders
Calcium	Milk, most dairy products, shellfish, egg yolk, green vegetables	Major component of skeleton & teeth, assists normal blood clotting, muscle action, nerve function, and heart function	800 mg	Tetany, demineralization of bones, back and leg pains
Chlorine	Table salt, bacon, bread, olives	Acid-base regulation, maintains osmotic pressure, activation of many enzymes	No RDA	Retarded growth, loss of hair and teeth, poor muscular contractibility, impaired digestion
Cobalt	Lettuce, spinach, turnip greens, cabbage, many other vegetables	Functions as part of vitamin B_{12}, maintains red blood cells, activates several enzymes in the body	No RDA	Anemia
Copper	Liver, oysters, oats, dried peas, dried beans, corn	Necessary for formation of red blood cells, part of many enzymes, works with vitamin C to form elastin	2 mg	Anemia, general weakness, skin sores, impaired respiration
Flouride	Sea foods, rye bread kidney, liver, some water supplies	Normal tooth and bone formation; may reduce tooth decay	No RDA	Tooth decay
Iodine	Seafoods, vegetables grown on iodine-rich soils, iodized salt	Formation of thyroid hormone	100 mcg women, 130 mcg men	Goiter

ESSENTIAL MINERALS IN THE ADULT DIET (Continued)

Mineral	Source	Functions	Adult Requirement	Deficiency Disorders
Iron	Liver, lean meat, shellfish, beans, lima beans, soybeans, split peas, green leafy vegetables, nuts, oatmeal	Oxygen transport (hemoglobin & myoglobin), cellular respiration, protein metabolism	18 mg women, 10 mg	Anemia, weakness, constipation
Magnesium	Nuts, whole wheat, lima beans, peas, corn, brown rice, soy flour oatmeal	Activiation of many of the body's enzymes, acts as a catalyst in utilization of carbohydrates, fats, protein, calcium, phosphorus, and possibly potassium	300 mg women, 350 mg men	Soft-tissue classifications, changes in teeth and bones
Manganese	Wheat, rye, flour, oatmeal, peas, rice, lettuce, dry beans	Enzyme activator, skeletal development, maintains sex-hormone production	No RDA	Dizziness, atoxia convulsions, paralysis hormone production
Phosphorus	Milk, cheese, eggs nuts, whole wheat, split peas, beans, poultry	Essential constituent of all cells, works with calcium to build bones and teeth, utilizes carbohydrates, fats, & proteins	800 mg	fragile bony structure, rickets, growth reatardation
Potassium	Bananas, dry apricots, raisins, peanuts, dried peas, spinach, sweet potatoes, green vegetables, molasses	Important intracellular fluid constituent, necessary for smooth skeletal and cardiac muscle contraction, affects excitability of nerve tissue	No RDA, average daily intake is 2000 to 2500 mg	Muscular weakness, nervous irritability, poor reflexes, respiratory failure, cardiac arrest

ESSENTIAL MINERALS IN THE ADULT DIET (continued)

Mineral	Source	Functions	Adult Requirement	Deficiency Disorders
Sodium	Table salt, butter, margarine, bread, celery, beet greens	Fluid and acid-base balance regulation, maintains health of nervous, muscular, blood, and lymph systems	2.5 g	muscular cramps, weakness, headache, loss of appetite, interference with heat regulating ability of body
Sulfur	Many foods	Important constituent of amino acids, hormones, vitamins and enzymes	RDA of protein provides sufficient sulfur	Deficiency unknown
Zinc	Oysters, shellfish, liver, wheat, bran	Component of insulin and male reproductive fluid, aids in digestion and healing process	15 mg	Slow healing of wounds; deficiency unlikely

Fiber is the nondigestible component of wheat (germ and bran) and the "roughage" found in carrots, celery, apples, and other fruits and vegetables.

Fiber.

Fiber is the nondigestible component of wheat (germ and bran) and the "roughage" found in carrots, celery, apples,and other fruits and vegetables. It is not found in animal cells. It is unaffected by the secretions of the small intestine and passes undigested into the large intestine. It is made up of four substances—cellulose, hemicellulose, pectin, and lignin. The proportion of each substance in the fiber varies between plants, and the total amount of fiber can be increased or decreased by the way the plant food is processed. It does not supply nutrition, but it provides the bulk needed to move other foods through the digestive tract.

The average American is believed to consume about 1 to 3 gm of fiber daily, or approximately one-third of the amount eaten prior to the mass production of processed food. According to some nutritional experts your daily fiber intake should be at least 6 to 10 gm (some recommend 10 to 15). This recommendation is based on several considerations.

- Passing through the intestine like a sponge, fiber absorbs water and other materials. It thus serves to decrease the amount of water absorbed from the intestine into the circulatory system. The water now remaining in the intestine hastens the propulsion of fecal material out of the bowel. The fiber also binds with cholesterol and bile salts (important for fat digestion), and thus, it is believed, helps to reduce the levels of fats in the blood. Cereal fiber is more effective in lowering cholesterol than fiber from fruits, vegetables, or nuts. When fiber levels are low, too much water is absorbed from the large intestine; the feces become small and firm and constipation becomes a problem. A more serious problem may be the development of outpouches called diverticula. These outpouches result from the increased pressure the colon must exert to propel slow-moving waste matter along. Pressure forces the membrane lining of the intestine out through the overlying muscle coat of the intestine. When partly digested food becomes trapped in these pouches, infection may result. This inflammatory condition, called diverticulitis, requires serious surgery for about one-half million Americans each year. Cereal fiber diets are often used to treat this disease.
- A high-roughage diet requires more time and energy to chew. Because the food content is bulkier, you are more likely to reach the point of satisfaction sooner, decreasing your caloric intake.
- Low-fiber carbohydrates are more readily converted to glucose than high-fiber carbohydrates. Glucose enters the circulatory system quickly and increases the demand of the pancreas to produce insulin. This process may predispose a person to develop diabetes.

• The evidence is not conclusive as to why, but in societies where food is less refined and more fiber is consumed, cancer of the colon is rare. The populations of South Africa consume nearly five times more fiber than the typical American; colon cancer is rare in these populations. The Japanese eat less meat and fat and more fiber than we do; colon cancer is rare among the Japanese. However, when the Japanese migrate to the U.S., and eat a typical American diet, the incidence of colon cancer increases. Successive generations of Japanese-Americans have an even higher incidence of this cancer.

Fat consumption in Denmark and Finland is similar, but cancer of the colon is four times more frequent in Denmark that in Finland. The Finns consume 80% more fiber than the Danes do, mostly in the form of rye. The state of Utah has an overall cancer mortality 22% lower that the general U.S. population does. Mormons, who compose three-fourths of the Utah population, have an extremely low incidence of colon and rectal cancer. The Mormons do eat a diet high in meat content, but in addition, they eat a high-fiber diet. This fiber is consumed in seasonal fresh fruits, vegetables, home preserved foods, and from ample intake of grain products, including home baked breads.

Several possible reasons for the decreased incidence of colon and rectal cancer associated with a high-fiber diet have been proposed. The water absorbed by the fiber helps to dilute any cancer producing agents (carcinogens) produced by intestinal bacteria during the digestive process. Propelled through the intestine more quickly, these carinogens remain in the digestive tract for a shorter period of time. The fiber also causes the feces to be more acidic and reduces the breakdown of bile acids by bacteria into potential carcinogens. Furthermore, the fermentation of fiber in the colon may assist in the removal from the intestine of ammonia, a product of protein digestion which in large amounts may be carcinogenic.

Sources of Fiber.

Not only has the quantity of fiber in our diet decreased, the quality has been altered too. Because we are able to store, can, and freeze fresh fruits and vegetables, we eat fewer starchy staples. A list of common sources of fiber is provided for you. These foods should be included in your health+ program, but your diet should not be based solely on fiber sources. Excessive fiber intake may have the effect of binding vitamins and minerals, reducing their absorption. Remember, more is not always better. Take a balanced approach to nutrition.

COMMON SOURCES OF FIBER

BREADS, FLOURS, CEREAL, GRAINS, AND GRAIN PRODUCTS

Bran Flour
Buckwheat
Cereal (many commercial cereals
   are good sources)
Corn Flour
Cornmeal Flour
Millet Flour
Oatmeal

Rice Bran Flour
Rice Flour
Rye Flour
Soy Flour
Spaghetti
Wheat Bran
Wheat Flour
Wheat Germ

FRUITS

Apples
Apricots
Avocados
Bananas
Blackberries
Blueberries
Coconuts
Cranberries
Currants
Dates
Elderberries

Figs
Gooseberries
Grapes
Guavas
Kumquats
Limes
Loganberries
Loquats
Mangos
Papayas
Peaches

Pears
Persimmons
Pineapples
Prunes
Quinces
Raisins
Raspberries
Strawberries
Tangerines
Watermelons

NUTS AND SEEDS

Almonds
Brazil Nuts
Cashews
Chestnuts
Hazel Nuts

Peanuts
Pecans
Sesame Seeds
Sunflower Seeds
Walnuts

SOUPS

Bean Soups
Cream of Asparagus
Cream of Celery
Chili Beef
Minestrone

Split Pea
Onion
Tomato
Vegetable

COMMON SOURCES OF FIBER (continued)

VEGETABLES

Alfafa
Artichokes
Asparagus
Bamboo Shoots
Beans
  Azuki
  Black-eye Peas
  Chickpeas
  Green
  Lentils
  Lima
  Mung
  Pinto
  Red Kidney
  Soybeans
  Yellow Wax
  White
Beets
Beet Greens
Broccoli
Brussels Sprouts

Cabbage
Carrots
Cauliflower
Celery
Collards
Corn
Cress, Sprigs
Cucumbers
Dandelion Greens
Dock (Sorrel)
Eggplant
Ginger Root
Jerusalem Artichokes
Kale
Kohlrabi
Leeks
Mushrooms
Mustards Greens
Okra

Onions
Oriental Radish
Parsley
Parsnips
Peas
Peppers
Pickles
Pimientos
Potatoes
Pumpkins
Rutabagas
Sauerkraut
Shallots
Spinach
Squash
Sweet Potatoes
Swiss Chard
Tomatoes
Turnips
Turnip Greens
Yams

Water.

The most important substance in your body is water. All chemical reactions in your body take place in water. Food, oxygen, and waste products enter and exit the cell with the aid of water. Water is involved with the movements of the internal organs of the abdomen, and with lubrication of the joints. It cushions the spinal cord and brain, keeps the tissues moist, and helps regulate body temperature.

Forty to 60% of your body weight is due to water. The actual amount in your body is determined by your particular body compositon. It makes up approximately 72% of muscle tissue weight, but only 20% to 25% of fat weight. The leaner your are, the more body water you have. The greater your % of body fat, the less water will be found in your body. Generally, because the male has less body fat than the female, he has more body water. Approximately 55% of the male's body weight is water, while in the female it is 50%.

You can live for many weeks without food but only for a few days without water. Usually, your natural response to thirst will maintain the body's water at a safe level. However, during hot weather and/or after vigorous exercise your thirst mechanism may not cause you to drink enough water. Even following the habit of drinking five to eight glasses of fluids per day may not provide an adequate water intake. If the average male loses two quarts of water, he will be thirsty. If he loses four quarts, he probably will become sick. A loss of eight to nine quarts probably will cause death from dehydration. You should drink extra water when you are in conditions that cause you to perspire. A good rule is to drink enough water to prevent a decrease in body weight of more than one or two pounds. It usually is not crucial whether you drink plain water or such fluids as milk or juice.

You should avoid any fad diets that limit water intake. If you are interested in weight management remember that water is calorie-free, whereas other fluids are not.

Other Nutritional Concerns

In addition to the seven food categories just dicussed, there are other things about the American diet of concern to you. In committing yourself to health+, you must also consider the role of these in your diet.

Organics.

Even though they are often thought of as the same, organic and natural foods are not identical. Organic food is food grown without the use of commercial chemicals. The soil has been treated with organic matter, such as manure, vegetable, compost, or natural and mineral fertilizers. In addition, organic foods are not processed with the use of artificial food additives. Natural foods are neither refined nor processed, but they aren't necessarily organically grown. Honey, molasses, unpolished brown rice, and grains are examples of natural foods.

The fear of conventionally grown foods being inferior in nutritional content and contaminated by pesticides has created an interest in organic and health foods. In health-food and natural-food stores these foods sell for ten to two hundred percent more than do processed and fortified supermarket foods. Are these foods worth the high cost? The following facts may help you to reach a decision:

- Organic foods do not have a higher nutritional value. The nutritional content of food is influenced by the soil content and the genetic structure of the plant. Commercial or organic ferilizer does not affect the nutritional content.
- Organic fertilizers probably contain more pathogenic bacteria than do commercial fertilizers. If the food is eaten raw, this may be a genuine risk, but cooking the food kills the bacteria.

- The use of pesticides and insecticides on commercially grown foods can be dangerous. As insects become immune to a pesticide often another treatment is produced hastily without careful testing of its possible long-term effects, in particular its possible cancer-causing abilities. However, even organic foods are not always free of pesticides, bacteria, lead, and mercury. These foods may have been grown without the intentional use of commercial chemicals, but residues from fertilizers, pesticides, and herbicides have been found in almost all agricultural soils and irrigation waters. Many organic farms have been affected by the pesticides used in surrounding areas.

  It would be ideal if the country's farms could produce enough food for the American people without the use of pesticides and insecticides, but at this point it appears that insects would destroy too many of the crops to make this possible.

- Long-established labeling and inspection standards regulate the quality of conventionally grown foods, but the standards for the multimillion dollar organic food industry are very lax. Foods grown without pesticides probably have insect markings; damaged plants grown under ordinary conditions can easily be sold as organic.

  Furthermore, there are no laws requiring health food manufacturers to date their products and health foods are more perishable than commercially processed foods. Rancid foods can irritate the stomach and bowel linings, and spoilage destroys the nutritional value of the food.

- There is no difference between "natural" or "organic" vitamins and those manufactured by reputable pharmaceutical companies. Whether they are extracted from a natural source or made in a laboratory, vitamins function exactly the same way in the body.

  Whenever possible you should eat unprocessed foods rather than processed ones. Processing any food usually results in the loss of some food value, but are organic foods worth the additional expense? It's for you to decide.

Additives.

The use of additives in processed foods should be of concern to you. The average American consumes more than five pounds of chemical food additives each year. Various reasons are given for the wide use of these additives. Preservatives keep food fresh and prevent the growth of bacteria. Colorings (dyes) give food a more attractive appearance. Emulsifiers break up fats and oils into small particles and make food smoother. Bleaches give some foods better appearance and texture. Antioxidants prevent foods from oxidizing. Humectants keep food moist.

Thickeners change the texture of food. Artificial sweeteners reduce the caloric value of foods or make them acceptable for diabetics.

Many additives are useful and most are harmless, but some are not necessary. They are used to give the product more "selling power." In addition, even though it is difficult to establish clear-cut evidence, there are reasons to be uneasy about what some of these additives might do.

The use of sodium nitrate and sodium nitrite is one example. The food industry claims these substances are used in cured meats (bacon, ham, hot dogs, luncheon meats) to retard decay and prevent the growth of botulism. According to consumer groups, the additives are used mainly for color and flavor enhancement. The real concern is what nitrates and nitrites may do to your body. Once you have consumed the meat, these additives combine with amines (compounds resulting from normal decay of processed meats) to form nitrosamines, which are highly potent carcinogens in animals. The food processing companies claim that the amount of nitrosamines formed in this process is insignificant and poses no health threat.

Food consumer groups dispute this by pointing to the rate of stomach cancer in Japan. The Japanese have a high intake of smoked fish to which nitrates have been added. But the food companies claim that there is no conclusive evidence linking these additives to cancer. They also argue that the additives vaporize during cooking. Other studies suggest that the formation of nitrosamines is blocked by vitamin C; so drinking your orange juice with breakfast may prevent your bacon from contributing to the formation of nitrosamines. Incidentally, many beers contain these same nitrosamines.

The food companies are correct in claiming there is no conclusive evidence condemning nitrates and nitrites. Further research is needed, but the possibility does exist that there is some danger. The U.S. government has taken a compromise position, reducing the permissible levels of sodium nitrite and nitrate, but not banning their use.

There are other disagreements between consumer groups and the food industry. The processing companies state that many people fear anything they see as "chemical," but that there must be a balance of risks against benefits. For instance, an alternative to the use of the nitrates and nitrites would be more refrigeration; but this would result in an enormous energy drain. Other alternatives would require expensive equipment. Perhaps these are valid concerns. However, until doubt had been removed by further research, you might wish to limit your consumption of additives as much as possible.

Many food additives are useful and most are harmless, but some are not necessary.

Salt.

Sodium, present in sodium chloride (salt), is essential for cellular function. Only a small amount is needed by your body, however. Primitive herbivorous people probably consumed no more than 600 mg a day because plants contain very little sodium. Animal products, particularly dairy products, have a higher sodium content, but early meat-eating people still probably consumed a maximum of about 4,000 mg (four gm) of sodium a day. Even this amount is more than you actually need.

It is difficult to measure exactly how much salt we consume daily, but most estimates place it somewhere between 6 and 24 gm per day. Ten to 15 gm is about average for the majority of people. This is equivalent to about four to six gm of sodium. There are about five gm in a teaspoon, so we are generally consuming two to three teaspoons of salt per day.

Much of the salt we consume is found in processed food, invisible to us. Most processed and factory-made food is overdosed with salt. In foods such as bacon, hot dogs, and ham, salt is added to prevent spoilage. But it is added at levels substantially higher than would be necessary for dietary reason alone.

Processing often leaves food flat and tasteless; the addition of salt provides an enhancement of flavor. When we prepare our food, we tend to add even more salt. We thus acquire a taste for a high level of salt.

There is a major health problem associated with our consumption of salt. A strong correlation exists worldwide between the quantity of salt ingested and the prevalance of high blood pressure (hypertension) in a given population. Northern Japan, where very salted soybean paste is widely consumed, has the highest incidence of hypertension in the world. The Northern Japanese eat about 2½ times as much salt as we do, and the occurrence of hypertension is two to four times greater than it is in our nation. (Over 24 million Americans suffer from hypertension.)

Hypertension is almost unknown in the isolated countries of the world where a person consumes less than 500 mg of salt per day. They are able to maintain a stable blood pressure throughout their lives, as contrasted to the U.S. where blood pressure gradually rises with age. Also, populations who consume less than 1600 mg of salt per day have a relatively low incidence of hypertension. In several primtive cultures, high blood pressure became a problem only when salt and preserved foods were introduced to the people.

Other findings confirm the role of salt in hypertension. Obese people who adopt special low-salt diets reduce their blood pressure long before they reduce their body weight. And blood pressure returns to normal in many hypertensives who consume less than one gm of salt per day.

The way salt contributes to high blood pressure has been studied extensively. Apparently, it causes the body to retain fluid producing an increase in the volume of blood. This increased blood elevates the pressure within the blood vessels. The kidneys respond to this pressure by speeding up their work of eliminating excessive water and salt as urine. If the kidneys are able to perform under this increased load, there may not be any lasting elevation in the blood pressure. As people grow older, though, the kidneys tend to perform less efficiently, and higher blood pressure can result.

Decrease of Salt Intake.

Just as you acquire a taste for salt over a period of time, you can become accustomed to unsalted or lightly salted foods. Once this occurs, foods containing only moderate salt will taste too salty. There are several things you can do to limit your salt intake.

- Avoid the use of the salt shaker at the table. You still will have an ample intake of salt from the processed foods you consume.
- Instead of using salt, prepare foods with other seasonings and spices. Examples of such seasonings and spices are lemon, onion, pepper, parsley, vinegar, celery, tomato, mushroom, green pepper, dry mustard, curry, bay leaf, paprika, nutmeg, cinnamon, and ginger. If you prepare food for children this practice can be of benefit to them. A high salt intake during infancy may very well cause hypertension during later years.
- Limit your intake of foods that have a high salt content. Such foods include:
  - baking powder and soda
  - canned meats
  - canned sauces
  - canned soups
  - cheeses—natural, processed, and spreads
  - condiments—catsup, chili sauce, soy sauce, mustard, pickles (especially dill), olives, seasoning salts, and other convenience foods
  - cured meats—ham, bacon, sausage, frankfurters, luncheon meats, salt pork
  - peanut butter (regular)
  - salted crackers and snacks—potato chips, peanuts, popcorn, pretzels, etc.
  - salty fish

Sugar.

Most Americans consume about 125 pounds of sugar each year. We are hooked on it. In 1974, when the price of sugar increased 400%, our consumption of it decreased by only three percent. Three-fourths of this sugar intake is "invisible," being found in foods and beverages prepared outside the home. In 1909-1913 only 32% of our carbohydrate intake came from sugar and sweetners. The remaining carbohydrates (68%) came from starchy foods. Today sugar and sweetners make up almost 55% of our carbohydrate intake. Or, to put it another way, approximately one-fourth of our total calories come from sugar.

Sugar is not only found in sweet baked goods, frozen desserts, and softdrinks. Catsup, chili sauce, fruit drinks, salad dressings, cured meats, some canned and frozen vegetables, fruit yogurt, and breakfast cereals also contain sugar. We create the desire for sugar in our children early, as it is present in many baby foods as a flavor enhancer. Many children prefer sugar and sweets over nutritious foods by the time they are one year old. The average American child annually consumes over 20 pounds of candy, nearly 400 cans or bottles of soft drinks, and 200 pieces of sugary chewing gum.

The body needs sugar, but it is best obtained from the carbohydrates found in vegetables, fruits, and bread. Refined sugar does provide calories. However, it provides no protein, fat, vitamins, or fiber.

There are significant health problems associated with a high sugar intake. It certainly is related to the most widespread disease in the Western world—tooth decay. A study in the 1960's by a U.S. government agency compared the findings of more than 100 international surveys for the prevalence of tooth decay in different populations. Apart from the flouride content found in the drinking water, sugar intake bore the only consistent positive relationship between nutrition and tooth decay. The lower the sugar consumption in a given society the lower the incidence of tooth decay.

Excess weight is another consequence of high sugar consumption. An annual intake of 125 pounds of sugar is equivalent to an intake of over 500 calories per day. If these 500 calories are in excess of what you really need for energy, you will gain 50 pounds of fat a year.

Diabetes mellitus (sugar diabetes) can occur in adults as a result of excessuve consumption of refined sugar. With this type of diabetes, the usual near normal level of insulin is apparently not enough to cope with the demands of the high blood sugar.

Even though it is not necessary for most people to elimiante all sugar intake, it probably would be wise for all of us to limit our intake. There are several ways to reach this health+ goal.

- Rely more on fruits, vegetables, grain flours, cereal, and skim milk to provide your necessary carbohydrates.
- Limit your consumption of sweets and soft drinks.
- Read labels of processed foods to determine whether some type of sugar is listed as one of the first two or three ingredients. You may find names such as sucrose, glucose, dextrose, fructose, maltose, lactose, corn syrup, or honey rather than the word sugar. Some of these substances (such as fructose) may not provide as many calories per gm as sugar, but they too have no nutritional value.

You should limit your consumption of sweets and soft drinks.

Caffeine.

Being a stimulant, caffeine is used medically in several ways. It is used as a stimulus for the central nervous system and kidneys (diuretic) in dosages ranging from 100 to 500 mg. Moreover, it is found in pain relief, cold, premenstrual and stay-awake tablets.

The average American consumes over 500 mg of caffeine daily through coffee, tea, and soft drinks. This caffeine increases your alertness, but it also raises your heart rate and blood pressure. Studies have suggested a relationship between caffeine and heart disease, but the evidence is inconclusive. Caffeine is, however, directly related to other health problems. It is a stomach irritant, which can be a problem to someone with an ulcer. It also can cause an irregular heartbeat, nervousness, and irritability.

While there is lack of agreement about the additive characteristics of caffeine, it is known to be habituating. Immediate, total withdrawal from caffeine can cause headache, irritability, sleepiness, and depression. If you have a high intake of caffeine and wish to decrease your consumption, or cease your intake entirely, do so gradually. Slowly taper off to the level at which you wish to be.

Sources of Caffeine

	mg
chocolate bar	25
coffee, brewed (6 oz)	100 to 150
coffee, decaffeinated (6 oz)	2 to 4
coffee, instant (6 oz)	86 to 99
cocoa (6 oz)	50
cola drinks (12 oz)	
Coca Cola	65
Diet Dr. Pepper	54
Diet RC	33
Dr. Pepper	61
Mountain Dew	58
Pepsi-Cola	43
RC Cola	34
Tab	49

In general, fast foods contain too many calories, too much fat, sugar and salt, and too little fiber and vitamins.

Fast Foods.

According to a recent Gallup poll, 33% of this nation's adults eat out every day, and 28% of those adults eat at fast-food establishments. This percentage is expected to increase during the coming years. Eight years ago there were 30,000 fast-food places; today there are approximately 140,000.

Are we consuming nutritional food from these fast-food establishments? Fast foods really don't differ significantly from the food eaten in the average American home. That is to say, we are making the same mistake with these foods that we do in preparing meals in our home. They contain too many calories, too much fat, sugar and salt, and too little fiber and vitamins.

Consumer's Union of United States, Inc., analyzed various selections available at fast-food establishments and presented the following findings:

Fast food hamburgers supply more than one-half of the protein recommended daily allowance (RDA) for a female. A Big Mac, milk shake, fried potatoes, and an apple pie provide more protein than is needed daily by the average male.

High-protein foods are often high-fat foods, and fast-foods are no exception. Since fats contain more than twice the number of calories per 45% fat. This is above the recommended 25% to 30% daily intake of fat calories.

Most fast-food meals have an excessive salt content (1000 to 2000 mg). It is often a key ingredient in the preparation of chicken, fish, potatoes, onions, and sauces. The salt in these meals may be too much for individuals on salt-restricted diets, or for people concerned about the risks of high salt intake.

Fast foods are generally low in vitamin A, iron, and some of the B vitamins. Most have at least one-quarter of a female's RDA for thiamine, riboflavin, vitamin B_{12}, niacin, phosphorus, and zinc. Calcium, magnesium, and vitamins A, B_6, and C are provided in amounts less than one-quarter of the female's RDA.

The majority of fast foods provide very little fiber. Mexican fast-food selections with beans provide some fiber.

Obviously, fast foods are high in calories, fat and sodium. It would be a mistake to include them routinely in your diet, but if eaten infrequently and as part of a well-balanced diet, they don't have to be avoided entirely. If you do find it necessary to eat fast food often, you might do well to avoid the fried potatoes and milk shakes. This will decrease your fat, sugar, and salt intake.

CALORIC AND NUTRITIONAL VALUES OF FOODS

	Cal	Fat Cal & % of Total Cal*	Carbo Cal & % of Total Cal	Protein Cal & % of Total Cal	Sodium (mg)
HAMBURGERS					
Burger Chef					
Big Chef	542	316 (58%)	144 (26%)	94 (17%)	—
Cheeseburger	304	158 (52%)	98 (32%)	57 (19%)	—
Hamburger	258	118 (46%)	96 (37%)	44 (17%)	—
Burger King					
Cheeseburger	305	121 (40%)	116 (38%)	68 (22%)	—
Hamburger	252	81 (32%)	115 (47%)	56 (22%)	—
Whopper	660	381 (58%)	201 (30%)	78 (12%)	1083
Dairy Queen					
Big Brazier Delux	470	216 (46%)	143 (30%)	111 (24%)	—
Big Brazier Regular	457	205 (45%)	146 (32%)	106 (23%)	—
Big Brazier w/Cheese	553	271 (49%)	153 (28%)	129 (23%)	—
Jack-in-the-Box Jumbo Jack	538	260 (48%)	180 (33%)	98 (18%)	1007
McDonald's					
Big Mac	541	280 (52%)	156 (29%)	105 (19%)	963
Cheeseburger	306	118 (39%)	123 (40%)	65 (21%)	—
Hamburger	257	83 (32%)	121 (47%)	43 (21%)	—
Quarter Pounder	418	188 (45%)	129 (31%)	101 (24%)	—
Wendy's Old Fashion	413	205 (50%)	119 (29%)	89 (22%)	708
SANDWICHES					
Arby's Roast Beef	370	140 (38%)	148 (40%)	82 (22%)	869
Burger King Chopped Beef Steak	445	121 (27%)	205 (46%)	119 (27%)	966
Hardee's Roast Beef	351	158 (45%)	131 (37%)	62 (18%)	765
Roy Rogers Roast Beef	356	112 (31%)	139 (39%)	105 (29%)	610

*% will not always total 100 due to rounding off.

Blanks in columns indicate information not available.

Adapted from Fast-food chains. Consumer Report 44: 509, 512, September 1979 and Falls HB, Baylor AM, Dishman RK: Essentials of Fitness. Phildelphia, Saunders College, 1980, pp 297–300.

CALORIC AND NUTRITIONAL VALUES OF FOODS (Con't)

	Cal	Fat Cal & % of Total Cal*	Caarbo Cal & % of Total Cal	Protein Cal & % of Total Cal	Sodium (mg)
FISH					
Arthur Treacher's Original	439	251 (57%)	111 (25%)	77 (18%)	421
Burger King's Whaler	584	316 (54%)	205 (35%)	63 (11%)	968
Long John Silver's	483	251 (52%)	111 (23%)	121 (25%)	1333
McDonald's Filet-o-Fish	383	167 (44%)	156 (41%)	60 (16%)	613
CHICKEN					
Arthur Treacher's Original Chicken	409	214 (52%)	103 (25%)	92 (22%)	580
Kentucky Fried Chicken Snack Box	405	195 (48%)	66 (17%)	44 (11%)	728
PIZZA HUT					
Thin 'n Crisp/Cheese**	450	136 (30%)	216 (48%)	100 (22%)	–
Thick 'n Chewy/Cheese**	560	130 (23%)	285 (51%)	145 (26%)	–
Thin 'n Crisp Supreme**	506	114 (23%)	262 (52%)	130 (26%)	1281
TACO					
Jack-in-the-Box	215	121 (56%)	70 (32%)	24 (12%)	640
Taco Bell	186	72 (39%)	56 (30%)	60 (32%)	–
FRENCH FRIES (3½ oz servings)					
Arby's	351	–	–	–	213
Arthur Treacher's	269	–	–	–	31
Burger Chef	275	115 (42%)	143 (52%)	17 (6%)	–
Burger King	314	132 (42%)	163 (52%)	19 (6%)	78
Hardee's	287	–	–	–	306
Jack-in-the-Box	349	–	–	–	207
Long John Silver's	320	157 (49%)	150 (47%)	13 (4%)	128
McDonald's	304	140 (46%)	146 (48%)	18 (6%)	88
Roy Rogers	320	–	–	–	141
Wendy's	270	–	–	–	105

**Based on serving size of ½ of 10" pizza.
According to Consumer Report, the high fat content of the french fries may be due to frying the potatoes in fat or oil that is not hot enough.

Supplementation.

You are now aware of the primary concerns in a health+ diet. The question can be asked—should you include vitamin and mineral supplements in your diet?

The ideal way to obtain all the necessary nutrients is to include a wide variety of good-quality fresh foods in which acceptable proportions of carbohydrates, fats and proteins are included. By consuming well-balanced meals of meats, cereals, vegetables, fruits, and milk you will take in the needed vitamins and minerals. Even if you are extremely active, a diet of this type will provide the necessary nutrients; you will probably consume more food if you are active.

However, there are other factors to consider. Because of our lifestyle, most of us don't always maintain a balanced diet. Moreover, our diet includes a significant amount of processed food that has lost some of its nutritional content. Finally, the need for vitamins and minerals vary from person to person. The right amount of vitamins for one person may not be enough for someone else.

SUGGESTED NUTRITIONAL SUPPLEMENT

Vitamin	Supplement	Mineral	Supplement
Vitamin A	7500 units	Calcium	250 mg
Vitamin C	250mg	Phosphate	750 mg
Vitamin D	400 units	Magnesium	200 mg
Vitamin E	40 units	Iron	15 mg
Vitamin K	2 mg	Zinc	15 mg
Vitamin B_1 (thiamine)	2 mg	Copper	2 mg
Vitamin B_2 (riboflavin)	2 mg	Iodine	0.15 mg
Vitamin B_6	3 mg	Maganese	5 mg
Vitamin B_{12}	9 mcg	Molybdenum	0.1 mg
Niacinamide	20 mg	Chromium	1 mg
Pantothenic acid	15 mg	Selenium	0.02 mg
Brotin	0.3 mg	Cobalt	0.1 mg
Folic acid	0.4 mg		
Choline	250 mg		
Inositol	250 mg		
P-aminobenzoic	30 mg		
Rutin	200 mg		

Considering these factors, it may be advisable for some individuals to take a vitamin-mineral supplement. But supplementation should be done wisely; some vitamins can be toxic when taken in large doses. Dr. Roger J. Williams, author of several chemistry, biochemistry, and nutrition books, has formulated a nutritional supplement plan designed to augment a balanced diet and provide for individual differences in nutritional needs. He lists items most likely to be helpful and to improve nutrition. Many of them may be taken through a multi-vitamin-mineral tablet or capsule. Remember, it is not necessary to pay exhorbitant amounts of money for your supplements. If all are from a reputable source, the tablets don't differ in quality, regardless of price.

Supplementation must not, however, be a substitute for your nutritional diet. Your diet should provide for your needs and not create health problems. As part of your health+ program, learn the sources of carbohydrates, fats, protein, vitamins, minerals, and fiber, and plan a diet with a balanced approach to their intake.

6

Weight Management

The continuous battle of the bulge.

You are overweight or obese when you have too much body fat. A man is overweight when his body fat is 16% to 20% of his total weight and obese when it is greater than 20%. A woman, who has a higher natural % body fat, is overweight when her body fat is 20% to 30% and obese when it is greater than 30%.

Some sources define obesity as weighing 20% or more above the desirable weight for a designated height and body frame. There are two major criticisms of this definition. (1) Most of those 20% above a specified weight for a particular height and frame are indeed fat, but it is possible to be less than 20% over and yet still be fat. (2) Weight charts do not typically provide for differences in frame size, and many individuals incorrectly estimate their frame size.

The problem of excess weight (overfatness) is truly a national one. Consider these statistics: 50% of American adults and 40% of all school children are overweight; 30% of the men and 40% of the women are obese. In a 1978 Louis Harris survey, an even higher percentage of Americans were found to be overweight. All respondents were asked to record their weight, height, and body frame (small, medium, or large). Their weight was then checked against the Standard Life Insurance industry tables of recommended heights and weights. On this basis, 62% of adults were found to be overweight. Harris acknowledged the criticisms of height-weight standard tables, but because people are more inclined to underestimate than to overestimate their weight, he reasoned that the survey was more likely to underestimate the number of people who are overweight than to overestimate it. Harris also found 42% among those aged 18 to 29 and 73% of those age 50 and over to be overweight.

With more people apparently being aware of good health practices, the incidence of excess weight should decrease. Tragically, this is not happening. Although we have grown taller, we have grown fatter even faster. Data from the National Center for Health Statistics indicate a five to seven percent increase in weight among Americans during the past decade. Surprisingly, this gain in weight has taken place despite a decreasing overall food intake. Even though we would like to believe so; a public commitment to weight management has not truly developed.

This lack of interest can be illustrated by another result of the Harris survey. Only one-third of all adults know the recommended weight for their height and body frame, and 62% of those who are overweight overestimate their recommended weight. Those who are not overweight are much more likely to know (or to underestimate their recommended weight).

Estimation of Overfatness

There is no simple, objective, and absolutely accurate method for determining whether you are overweight or obese. Body type, body measurements, total weight, and percentage of body fat are four criteria often used to estimate abnormal body weight.

Most tables of desirable weights classify body types according to frame size and designate weight ranges by height and body frame. For these purposes the small-frame individual usually has a slender body with small arms and legs, a long neck, and little definition of muscle tissue. The medium-frame individual has more of an athletic-looking body with broad shoulders, narrow hips, and definition of muscle tissue. The large-frame individual has a thick body with rounded arms and legs, about the same size chest and waist, and a thick neck. A practical method of estimating your body frame is to measure the ankle girth at the smallest point above the ankle, with the tape as tight as possible. Compare your measurement with the following standard:*

	Small Frame	Medium Frame	Large Frame
Male	Less than 8 in.	8 to 9.25 in.	More than 9.25 in.
Female	Less than 7.5 in.	7.5 to 8.75 in.	More than 8.75 in.

*Adapted from Johnson, P.B.; Updike, W.; Schaefer, M.; et al: *Sport, Exercise and You.* New York City, Holt, Rinehart, and Winston, 1975, p. 57

DESIRABLE WEIGHTS FOR MEN AND WOMEN

According to Height and Frame, Ages 25 and Over

Height (in shoes)	Weight in Pounds (in Indoor Clothing) *		
	Small Frame	Medium Frame	Large Frame
MEN			
5' 2"	128-134	131-141	138-150
3"	130-136	133-143	140-153
4"	132-138	135-145	142-156
5"	134-140	137-148	144-160
6"	136-142	139-151	146-164
7"	138-145	142-154	149-168
8"	140-148	145-157	152-172
9"	142-151	148-160	155-176
10"	144-154	151-163	158-180
11"	146-157	154-166	161-184
6' 0"	149-160	157-170	164-188
1"	152-164	160-174	168-192
2"	155-168	164-178	172-197
3"	158-172	167-182	176-202
4"	162-176	171-187	181-207
WOMEN			
4'10"	102-111	109-121	118-131
11"	103-113	111-123	120-134
5' 0"	104-115	113-126	122-137
1"	106-118	115-129	125-140
2"	108-121	118-132	128-143
3"	111-124	121-135	131-147
4"	114-127	124-138	134-151
5"	117-130	127-141	137-155
6"	120-133	130-144	140-159
7"	123-136	133-147	143-163
8"	126-139	136-150	146-167
9"	129-142	139-153	149-170
10"	132-145	142-156	152-173
11"	135-148	145-159	155-176
6' 0"	138-151	148-162	158-179

* Indoor clothing weighing 3 lbs. for women and 5 lbs. for men
** Shoes with 1-inch heels

Source: 1979 Build Study; Society of Actuaries and Association of Life Insurance Medical Directors of America, 1980   Courtesy of the Metropolitan Insurance Company

Acceptable body weight ranges for body types can be misinterpreted, however, if the percent of fat tissue is not known. A range of 10% to 15% body fat for men and 15% to 20% for women is generally desirable.

Individuals possessing a highly developed athletic body are sometimes incorrectly judged overweight even though they have a low % body fat. It is not uncommon for such individuals to have less than 5% body fat, and yet weigh more than the upper limit of a specified range in a height-weight table. The total body weight is high due to their large amount of lean tissue (primarily muscle and bone tissue).

The % body fat can be estimated by underwater weighing or by measuring the fat located beneath the skin with skinfold calipers. Underwater weighing is the more accurate of the two methods, but it requires the use of expensive laboratory equipment. Measurement with skinfold calipers involves pinching a fold of skin between the thumb and forefinger, pulling the fold away from the underlying muscle, and applying the calipers to the fold. Muscle tissue is not included, so the thickness of the fold reflects the % body fat. Skinfold measurements are usually taken in several of the following areas: at the front and back of the upper arm, below the shoulder blade, above the crest of the hip, in the chest and abdominal areas, and the front of the upper leg. The % body fat then can be estimated through the appropriate formula. If you are interested in knowing your skin fold measurements, it may be possible to have them taken at a YMCA, YWCA, or physical education department of a college or university, or a high school physical education teacher or a local physician may be able to perform the measurements.

Knowing your % body fat enables you to determine how much weight in body fat you should lose. However, if you are unable to have this percent estimated, stand in front of a full-length mirror while undressed. Be realistic. If you look fat, you probably are fat. A weight-reduction program should change your fat appearance.

Risks and Dangers of Being Overfat
Despite attempts by many psychologists to rationalize overfatness as an alternative lifestyle, the risks and dangers of obesity offer an unhappy substitute for a healthy lifestyle. And not only does obesity influence the quality of life, it affects the length of your life. According to one estimate, eliminating all deaths from cancer would add two years to the average lifespan, but removing all deaths related to obesity would increase the average lifespan five years. Excessive body fat places a burden upon circulation, respiration, and the kidneys, making obese persons more prone to develop disorders of these organs and systems.

Obesity is related to the prevalence of high blood pressure and atherosclerosis. When the effects of age and blood pressure are taken into consideration, body weight is revealed as a definite risk factor in the development of heart disease. In addition, individuals with a higher body mass index (weight divided by height squared) who experience a heart attack have a greater risk of subsequent sudden death.

More recent research suggests a strong relation between body fat and breast cancer. The relation does not stop there, however. Overweight women have a substantially lower rate of recovery from breast cancer than do lean women.

Fat people have lower exercise tolerance, greater difficulty in normal breathing, and a higher frequency of respiratory infections than do people of normal weight. Other problems associated with obesity are impaired carbohydrate and fat metabolism, joint, bone, and gall bladder disease, diabetes, and asthma. And individuals experiencing a significant gain in body fat often undergo changes in personality and behavior patterns manifested as depression, withdrawal, self-pity, irritability, and aggression.

Weight Gain

Normally every food you eat can be utilized by the body. When utilized, this food produces heat. The potential of food to produce heat is measured in calories. These calories are kilocalories, or large calories which produce 1000 times more heat than the calorie used to measure heat in chemistry and physics. Your body burns calories to perform all its necessary functions—heart contraction, breathing, brain function, and so on. When you perform physical activity you burn addditional calories.

When the amount of food you consume equals your body's need, your weight remains constant. Consuming more than you need results in weight gain. If over a period of time, you take in 3500 calories more than you need, you add one pound of fat to your weight. This period of time may be days, weeks, or months. Converting conversely, in order to lose one pound of body fat you must have a deficit of 3500 calories.

Changes in body fat usually parallel those in body weight. In the bulk of the population, weight gain and excess fat go hand-in-hand, and most people can bring their % body fat down to acceptable levels simply by reducing to the recommended weight for their frame size.

You accumulate body fat in two ways. One way is by enlarging or filling existing fat cells with more fat (fat cell hypertrophy). Another way is by increasing the total number of fat cells (fat cell hyperplasia).

Childhood Obesity.

Obesity of infancy and childhood involves both processes. There appear to be three critical periods when the number of fat cells increases significantly—the last trimester of pregnancy, the first year of life, and the adolescent growth spurt. Once they are formed, the number of fat cells cannot be reduced, but it is possible that the number of fat cells produced can be influenced through some form of intervention during these critical periods of life. It is important for expectant mothers to avoid an unusually large weight gain during the last trimester of pregnancy and for parents to monitor the diet and exercise patterns of children to try to prevent the formation of unwanted fat cells.

Ravelli demonstrated the importance of the expectant mother's diet by surveying the birthplaces and birthdates of Dutch boys 19 years after an acute catastrophic famine during the closing days of WW II. He found that boys whose mothers suffered severe famine in the first trimester of pregnancy had a significantly greater likelihood of being obese than the boys of mothers who avoided the famine. In contrast, the sons of mothers who experienced the famine during the last trimester were noted to have a significantly increased likelihood of being underweight. By avoiding large weight gains during the last three months of pregnancy, the expectant mother may help the unborn child avoid the formation of an abnormal number of fat cells. By analogy, the mothers who go on crash diets during the first trimester of pregnancy may inadvertently subject their child to conditions which program the developing brain to respond to life as if it is starving.

Adult Obesity.

After age 20, many Americans gain an average of one or two pounds a year. Generally, they begin to be overweight by about 30, but they don't acknowledge it for another 10 years. Consequently, we are among the heaviest people in the world.

The excess fat carried by the adult is the result of filling existing fat cells with more fat, rather than of producing new fat cells. This acquisition of fat takes place for three basic reasons. (1) We eat "just a bit more" even when our stomach feels full. (2) We decrease our physical activity. (3) Our basal metabolic rate declines during the aging process.

Overeating is practiced and learned at various times in an individual's life. How many times have you failed to cease eating even though you realized that you had eaten enough? When you take in more calories than the body needs, you will gain weight. It doesn't matter whether the calories are from steak or ice cream; your body does not distinguish the sources. For many adults, a daily caloric excess equivalent to one-half a slice of bread or one-half a glass of beer can result in a weight gain of more than 40 pounds within ten years. An intake of just 100 calories more per day than you need will result in a weight gain of 10 pounds during one year. Many American adult males consume as many as 3,300 calories a day. This is the amount required for an active 190 pound man, which is certainly more than average. "Creeping obesity" is the way most people gain weight.

In addition to eating more than we should, we decrease our physical activity as we grow older. In this modern age of mechanical convenience and conveyance, many people engage in so little physical activity that just eating to the point of feeling satisfied means consuming excess calories. If our intake of food continued to decrease as our physical activity decreased, we probably would gain less weight. However, decreasing physical activity below a certain point will no longer be accompanied by a decrease in the appetite. Given the present standard of sedentary living for most Americans, it is almost impossible to avoid obesity unless exercise habits are integrated into one's lifestyle. When we are active enough we can safely consume more food. Many Olympic athletes consume over 5,000 calories per day and do not gain weight because of their physical training.

We also tend to gain weight because of the decline with age in our basal metabolic rate. A considerable amount of energy must be utilized to maintain certain vital functions—respiration, heart contraction, glandular secretiions. This release of energy is called basal metabolic rate (BMR) and is measured when you are awake, reclined, and relaxed. The number of calories required for basal metabolism varies with your age, weight, stature, hormone production, and sex.

Normal basal metabolism utilizes about one calorie per hour for each kilogram (2.2 pounds) of body weight. Another method for estimating the necessary calories for a male's BMR is to multiply his weight by 11. The female's requirement is equal to her weight multiplied by 10; her BMR is approximately 10% lower than a male's. The average adult male needs approximately 1400 to 1800 calories a day for his basal metabolism, whereas the average adult female needs approximately 1200 to 1400.

ESTIMATED BASAL METABOLIC RATES FOR ADULTS

| Height | | Weight | | BMR |
Inches	cm	lb.	kg	calories/day
		MEN		
64	163	133 ± 11	60 ± 5	1630
66	168	142 ± 12	64 ± 5	1690
68	173	151 ± 14	69 ± 6	1775
70	178	159 ± 14	72 ± 6	1815
72	183	167 ± 15	76 ± 7	1870
74	188	175 ± 15	80 ± 7	1933
76	193	182 ± 16	83 ± 7	1983
		WOMEN		
60	152	109 ± 9	50 ± 4	1399
62	158	115 ± 9	52 ± 4	1429
64	163	122 ± 10	56 ± 5	1487
66	168	129 ± 10	59 ± 5	1530
68	173	136 ± 10	62 ± 5	1572
70	178	144 ± 11	66 ± 5	1626
72	183	152 ± 12	69 ± 5	1666

Adapted with permission of the National Academy of Sciences

In proportion to body weight, BMR is highest during childhood and gradually decreases throughout life. The decline begins during late adolescence, and the slope takes form at about the age of 25 in men and a little earlier, at about 22, for women. With increasing age, there is a gradual reduction in the number and size of functional cells. Muscle cells become fewer and the amount of fat in the existing fat cells increases. The rate of decline in BMR is usually between five and seven percent for each decade of life. The significance of this fact is that even if you are able to maintain the same weight throughout the years, your % body fat will still increase. Even if you are active, your % body fat may still increase.

In proportion to body weight, BMR is highest during childhood and gradually decreases throughout life.

Habits Leading to Obesity

Some uncontrollable factors may cause obesity. In some instances heredity influences the number of fat cells possessed by an individual. Sex hormones also influence the amount of body fat; female hormones tend to increase fat levels, whereas increased levels of male hormones tend to decrease them. Another factor related to adult obesity is eating patterns developed in childhood. It is conceivable that excessive eating during childhood has a long-term effect on weight by influencing the "satiety center"—that part of the hypothalamic area of the brain that helps to regulate eating. If this "thermostat" is pushed higher by child-hood eating patterns, the adult may feel the need for greater food intake. But there are also many manageable factors that influence eating habits and weight gain.

State of Mind.

Daily events unrelated to food itself often trigger the urge to eat. Depression, frustration, boredom, anxiety, guilt, sadness, or anger can be linked to excessive food intake. If consumption of food provides pleasurable sensations or relief from these states, then the disturbed person will be encouraged to eat often. A habit eventually develops linking these unpleasant events with food intake. These events will come to be signals for eating, and often are reinforced for many years.

Frequency of Eating.

Excess weight is more common among individuals who eat irregularly or eat fewer meals than among those with regular eating habits, especially those who eat several meals a day. Furthermore, many people who eat two large meals a day gain weight, while people eating the same number of calories spread over several portions throughout the day do not gain weight. In a study of 1000 men and 1000 women, ages 35 to 39, the % body fat decreased when they increased their number of meals from two to six per day.

This finding was supported in a study of genetically identical groups of rats. One group was allowed to eat as much and whenever they wished, producing a stable weight pattern. A second group pf animals was given the same number of calories of chow, but through a stomach tube, with only two feedings per day. The second group accumulated a significantly larger amount of fat tissue than did the first group.

Another study with identical infant rat litters reached the same con-clusion. One group of rats was allowed free access to food throughout the 24-hour day. A second group had access to food only during two hours per day. These rats gulped their food and soon outgained their litter mates, becoming obese. The abnormal feeding pattern and obesity persisted into adulthood long after free access to food was established. Eating just one or two large meals a day probably makes you more prone to accumulate fat tissue, especially if one of these meals is eaten prior to retiring for the night.

High Density Caloric Foods.

A preference for high density caloric foods can result in obesity. Eating foods high in sugar content produces a rapid rise in blood glucose, triggering the release of insulin. The insulin causes the blood glucose to drop just as rapidly, serving to make you hungry again. When you eat a breakfast high in sugar content, you probably feel the need for a mid-morning snack (again high in sugar), satisfying you until lunch. The mid-afternoon snack then satisfies you until dinner. If you snack on low calorie nutritious foods, your snacking is probably not bad for you; but most of us eat snack foods loaded with sugar.

Foods high in fat content are also considered to be high density caloric foods. When allowed free access to food containing a balance of fat, carbohydrate, and protein, rats maintain a stable weight. On the other hand, when given a diet rich in fat, certain strains of rats are unable to reduce their total food intake to compensate for the increased caloric intake (fats have 9.3 calories per gram). As a result, they develop gross obesity. Human beings generally have the same problem with a fat-rich diet.

Diets to Lose Weight.

America is a nation of dieters, as the popularity of fad diets and books on weight control indicates. Almost one in every six American adults (16%) are presently on a diet, and another 31% have been on a diet at some time in the past. As a nation we spend over $10 billion a year trying to lose weight. Sadly, 90% to 95% of those who lose weight through an unsupervised program gain it back within a very short time. Those who participate in supervised weight-reduction programs are not much more successful; only 15% to 20% reduce and stay that way for at least two years.

There are numerous diets promising startling results in an incredibly short period of time. Every new diet has its magic formula—a pill to break habits, a chemical reaction, a fat-burning trick. Some of these diets are unworkable, others are dangerous to health, and almost all will be replaced by others with even more unbelievable claims. Unfortunately, the public often believes such diets are based on real nutritional discoveries, and that if they are condemned by any scientific group, it is because of prejudice and jealousy.

Even more incredible is the number of people who, after losing weight with a particular diet, revert to their old eating habits, not believing they will gain weight. For some reason they fail to realize that it was the amount of food they ate before that kept them fat; that eating less reduced their weight; and that eating more will make them fat again. They miss the obvious; once they have reached their desired weight they can eat more than they did when on their diet; but if they want to keep their weight down, they will forevermore have to eat less than they did before. You can lose weight by reducing your caloric intake. But the goal is to keep it off and that usually means eating less.

Liquid Protein.
On occasion unsafe diets have become popular, and people have followed them without proper medical supervision. The liquid protein diet is one such example. In 1978, an estimated 98,000 women between ages 24 and 45, most of whom were overweight, used pre-digested protein products as their sole or principle source of nourishment for at least one month. About 70% of these women had no medical supervision, and at least one-third failed to take supplemental potassium, thus greatly increased the hazards of the diet. At least 58 deaths were associated with liquid protein diets.

Fasting and Starvation.
Advocates of fasting (not eating for an extended period of time) claim it to be a way of losing weight, getting rid of chemicals in the body, burning off old and diseased tissues, rejuvenating and revitalizing the body, and in general helping a person to feel better. Fasting is supposedly different from starving. A fasting body uses its own tissue reserves, with fat being used before muscle. If it leads to starvation, however, fasting can be dangerous.

Starvation dehydrates the body and produces weight reduction in the form of loss of protein, glycogen, potassium, sodium, phosphorus, sulfer, ribonucleic acid, enzymes, minerals, trace elements, and other important cell constituents. At least 50% of the weight loss induced by total starvation involves fat-free protoplasm. The tissues losing this protoplasm are those active in protein synthesis, such as the liver, pancreas, small intestine, and muscle. The depletion occurs because with sudden starvation there is no dietary protein to meet daily requirements.

Once you reach your desired weight, you can eat more than you did on your diet; however, if you want to keep your weight down, you will have to evermore eat less than you did before.

Some individuals use "modified fasting" diets, taking protein, vitamin and mineral supplements. The protein supplement is supposed to lessen some of the side effects of fasting by preventing the body from utilizing the protein in its own cells. If the protein supplement is of poor quality, however, this approach is dangerous too.

With or without protein supplements, any prolonged fast may be accompanied by side effects such as hair loss, muscle weakness, dizziness, nausea, headaches, constipation, and even nervous disorders. Because of the change in body metabolism, even greater potential danger exists for dieters who may be predisposed, often with no prior knowledge, to liver, kidney, heart, or gastrointestinal problems.

Likewise, semistarvation coupled with a diet low in carbohydrates could produce abnormal amounts of ketone bodies (ketosis). These substances are normal products of fat metabolism, and their concentration in the blood usually remains quite low. But when the body must rely on fat and muscle tissue for energy because of the absence of cellular glucose, fat is used in excess by the liver. Ketone bodies then accumulate in the blood. Should the concentrations of these ketone bodies rise to a high enough level, the blood becomes acidic. Moreover, the probable loss of too much water from the body adds to the individual's distress.

Fasting or starvation results in rapid weight loss, but this is not due entirely to the loss of fat. Water and muscle tissue are lost as well. Furthermore, this method does not incorporate an effort to permanently change eating behavior.

Low-Carbohydrate Diet.
Carbohydrates retain three times their weight in water. When you eat less than 60 mg of carbohydrates a day, you will lose weight—in water. Loss of water is not loss of fat. And you will regain this weight when the body begins to store water again to prevent dehydration.

However, if you stick with it you probably can experience some fat loss with a low-carbohydrate diet. This is so for several reasons.

- By excluding a whole food category, your total caloric intake automatically decreases.
- You become bored eating the same foods, so you eat less.
- By excluding carbohydrates, you eliminate the primary source of between-meal snacks.
- By excluding a whole category of food, you also exclude a lot of another category of food. You eliminate desserts, snacks, bread, potatoes, and movie food. Without bread, potatoes, or pasta you don't consume butter, sauce, or sour cream and the fats found in them. All

of these are eliminated without your worrying about portion size. There are two major weaknesses in the low-carbohydrate diet.

1) You probably will tire of the limited menu eventually and return to your old eating habits. The weight you lost will then quickly return.

2) You need food with all types of nutrients—including carbohydrates—to maintain good health. This is the most important reason for avoiding a low-carbohydrate diet.

Effective Weight Reduction

Many Americans are attempting to lose weight, but as indicated by Harris, 44% of those who are overweight have never attempted to lose weight. Everyone who is overfat should seek to reduce their body fat. It is possible for the majority of overweight people to reverse the process of obesity, and once they do so, to maintain % body fat at an acceptable level. With a reduction in excess body fat, diabetes and hypertension often disappear, blood lipid levels decrease, and there is less burden on the circulatory and respiratory systems. Moreover, the lower the body fat, the greater the body's ability to utilize oxygen. When obese people lose and keep off excess fat, according to data from life insurance companies, their life expectancy rises to what it would have been had they never been obese.

Most people give the same reasons for failure to lose weight when dieting—lack of self-discipline and the desire to eat more than should be eaten. There is another very prominent reason many fail. They have a punitive attitude toward their weight; self-blame, self-punishment, and guilt for their weight contribute to a negative self-image, which inhibits weight loss.

If you wish to succeed in a weight reduction program, you must maintain a positive self-image. Your self-image may very well improve as you lose weight, but initially you must not be overwhelmed by a negative body-and self-image. Don't emphasize your weight as a major factor in your interaction with others; concentrate on your worthwhile traits and abilities. Successful interactions with others depend on many qualities other than your weight.

Developing Your Program.

The first step in developing your weight-reduction program is to determine your target goal for acceptable % body fat and/or weight. A % body fat goal is preferable, but if you are unable to have your % body fat estimated, objectively appraise your body frame and state your target weight in relation to your body frame. Remember, it is possible to be heavy and even overweight according to height-weight charts, but not have too much body fat. Likewise, it is possible to weigh no more than what is expected for your height and frame and yet be overfat. You must be realistic about the appearance of your body fat. The body frame does not change, and if you are inactive, weigh more than you did at 22 years of age, and wear larger size of clothing, you are probably overfat.

The second step is to estimate your daily caloric requirements. This is determined by two factors: your minimal resting energy requirements (BMR), and your energy expenditure (daily physical activities). The amount of energy you need to perform functions other than basal metabolism varies in relation to your activities. An inactive individual may need only a few hundred additional calories, whereas a large, active man may need as many as 2000 or more. If you are not maintaining an exercise program and do not hold a physically demanding job, your body probably requires only 20% or 30% more calories beyond your basal needs. Of course, for an extremely inactive person this percentage will be even lower. Remember, when a diet is nutritionally sound, for weight management it isn't important what is eaten, but how many calories are consumed. Weight reduction will occur when intake of calories is less than the number expended during each day.

ENERGY NEED IN ADDITION TO BMR

Activity	Energy Need (Calories per kg of body weight)	
	Men	Women
Very Light	1.5	1.3
Light	2.9	2.6
Moderate	4.3	4.1
Heavy	8.4	8.0

*Multiply energy need factor by weight in kg.
Adapted with permission of the National Academy of Sciences

The third step in your program is to maintain a record of your food intake (including calories), eating behavior, and physical activity for at least a seven-day period. This procedure is essential if you are to experience behavior modification and reach your ultimate goal—to develop permanent eating and activity habits which result in weight reduction and lifetime maintenance of your desired weight.

The record of your eating behavior should include:
- When and where meals are eaten
- What is your mood, feeling, or psychological state during eating
- Time spent with each meal
- Other activities engaged in while eating (watching television, driving a car, etc.)
- What and how much food is eaten

You must be honest with the record of what and how much you eat. It probably is not necessary to measure and weigh the food, but do so if your wish. Labels on cans and boxes usually list the number of calories found in servings.

Labels on cans and boxes usually list the number of calories found in servings.

The fourth step is to design your own diet, remembering that the bottom line is compliance. Do not reduce your daily caloric intake to an unrealistic level which is virtually impossible for you to follow. Depending on the total number of calories you have been taking in, you probably should not decrease the number by more than 500 to 750 calories. If you undertake a physical activity program at the same time, you don't have to decrease your food intake as much.

Your diet should adhere to the nutritional principles previously discussed. Here are a few additional guidelines:
- Look for means to increase the use of fruits, vegetables, and whole grain cereals in your meals. Eat one vegetable meal daily, red meat only once or twice weekly, and add more fish and poultry. There have been few diets that make vegetables the main component, or even put them on a par with meat, fish, and eggs. Yet calorie for calorie, more vitamins, minerals, fiber, and protein are found in vegetables than in any other food.
- Limit your sugar intake. Don't allow more than 25% to 30% of your total carbohydrates to be sugar.
- Limit your beer, wine, and hard liquor intake.
- Attempt to keep your diet as close as possible to your tastes and habits of eating.
- Don't evaluate foods strictly on the basis of their caloric value. You may inadvertently exclude very nutritious foods.
- Develop a diet that protects you from between-meal hunger, gives you a sense of well-being, and does not make you feel tired.
- Develop a diet that enables you to eat both at home and away from home without feeling out of place.
- Develop a diet that you can live with for the rest of your life.

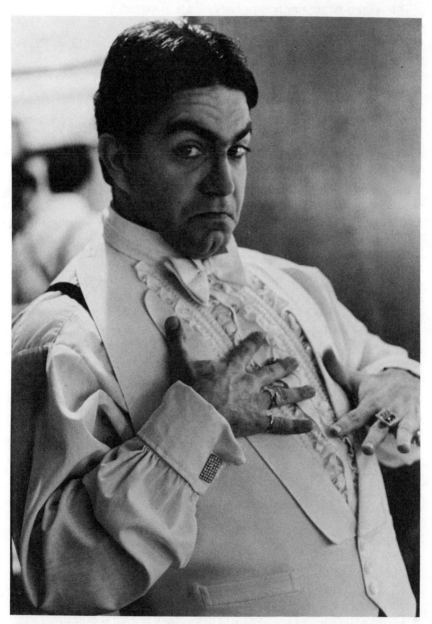

Behavior modification procedures for treating overweight people are more effective when they concentrate on changing the individual's eating and activity patterns, instead of focusing on the number of pounds lost.

Eating Behavior and Weight

Behavior modification procedures for treating overweight people are more effective when they concentrate on changing the individual's eating and activity patterns, instead of focusing on the number of pounds lost. Adhering to all or some of the following techniques can help you successfully reach that goal.

- Make the act of eating a ritual; eat at the same time and place and only eat enough food for a balanced meal.
- Avoid "family style" eating. Most of us tend to stuff ourselves in this type of atmosphere.
- Use small plates and prepare foods that can be placed directly on your plate and served in small portions.
- Don't follow the practice of always cleaning your plate.
- A second helping should require you to expend the effort of getting up from the table and preparing another serving of food. Make it as difficult as possible to obtain an extra serving of food.
- Remove food from locations in your home other than the kitchen.
- Reduce the availability of foods that can be eaten without preparation.
- If you eat snacks while watching television, substitute projects requiring the use of your hands for the time you would spend in front of the television—write letters, paint, sew, work with hardware tools, etc.
- If you eat snacks while driving, substitute singing or games that can be played while driving.
- If you feel hungry at mid-morning or mid-afternoon, go for a walk. When at work, take a water break and walk around instead of having the soft drink and crackers or candy.
- Rather than eating after being upset, take a walk.
- Eat slowly and take small bites. It takes about 20 minutes for the stomach to signal the brain that it is full. By eating too fast you get stuffed before the stomach can tell you to stop. Some individuals count the mouthfuls eaten and place their eating utensils on the table for a short time after every three or four bites.
- If you finish eating before others do, leave the table and return later for dessert (if you must have any). You may be tempted to eat more if you sit at the table waiting for others to finish their meals. This may also occur when a group remains at the table to talk after the meal.
- If you are responsible for the grocery shopping, strictly adhere to the shopping list and avoid doing the shopping when hungry. You may buy more high calorie foods when you are hungry.
- Avoid buying high calorie foods that may be eaten when watching television.

- Avoid weighing often. You may wish to weigh once a week on the same day and time. Regularly stepping on the scales and seeing little change in weight after being faithful to your program may disappoint you. Remember, in seeking to change your eating and activity habits with a gradual and realistic approach, you will not lose weight rapidly. You are, however, more likely to keep your weight down permanently.
- Establish a reward-penalty system for such things as eating balanced meals at regular intervals, eating small portions, eating low calorie snacks between meals, engaging in daily exercise, etc. Give yourself one point for each appropriate behavior and establish the number of points required to earn you the right to participate in a gratifying experience. Again, be realistic with your goals.
- Include others who are significantly active in your social environment. Do not overemphasize their role or expect them to be responsible for your behavior, but a little encouragement and aid is always beneficial.

You now may be saying, "If it is necessary to monitor my behavior to this extent, it is not worth the effort." Reexamine the list. There really isn't anything on the list demanding much effort and time. Remember, the goal is to change your eating behavior.

Physical Activity and Weight

It has been indicated by studies with rats that if an exercise program is followed during growth, a significant reduction in total body fat occurs. The reduction is in both the size and number of fat cells. There are also fewer fat cells in later life in animals that exercise during their growing periods.

In all likelihood, exercise and weight management started early in life and maintained thereafter can be effective in lowering total body fat. Prevention, starting early in childhood, is probably the most effective way to curb the high incidence of obesity that predominates in this nation.

Physically mature individuals should include activity in their weight reduction and management programs also. The calories expended during physical exercise are just as important as the calories eliminated from the diet. Many adults fail to include exercise in their weight-reduction programs because they believe these two fallacies:

(1) Exercise always increases the appetite and, therefore, results in no weight loss;

(2) Exercise expends only a small number of calories, hence only an exhaustive program can be of benefit.

Don't be misguided by these misconceptions!

Exercise and Appetite.

The truth is that overweight persons who undertake an exercise program usually make better use of food intake and utilize stored fat for energy. This means that the appetite does not increase,and it even decreases in some instances. There are several studies to support this claim. One such study involved 22 middle-aged women who took part in a 17-week exercise program. The women began with a twice weekly 20-minute session of vigorous walking and easy jogging preceded by 10 minutes of light calisthenics. By the end of the 17-week program they were running a full 20 minutes. Prior to the program, the women had rarely exercised and averaged close to 40% body fat. In addition, they had failed to lose weight through many methods of dieting. Because of a definite increase in energy level most of the women expanded their program to include additional walking, bicycling, and other activities. Making only slight changes in their diets, they averaged a loss of 19 pounds, a decrease of five percent in body fat, and lowered blood pressure.

Another study with 23 males college students had similar results. Through a walking, jogging, and running program, the students expended 500 to 600 calories per session. With no change in their diets, the obese achieved a significant reduction in body weight. This reduction occurred only through a loss of fat tissue, as there was an increase in lean tissue.

A study with overweight college women reached the same conclusions. The women walked and ran, expending 500 calories per exercise session. They did not alter their diets, but their total fat decreased while lean tissue increased.

Zuti and Golding compared three weight-reduction programs involving diet modification, exercise, and a combination of the two. Twenty-five women between 25 and 42 years of age and from 20 to 40 pounds overweight took part in a 16-week program study. The diet group reduced their daily intake by 500 calories; the exercise group increased their caloric expenditure by 500 calories but did not change their diet; and the combination group reduced their intake by 250 calories and utilized 250 calories through exercise. All three groups experienced a significant weight reduction (more than 10 pounds), but the diet group lost both fat and lean tissue. The other two groups lost fat tissue and weight, but experienced an increase in lean tissue.

Studies with men undergoing intensive physical training for the military support these findings. It is possible to lose body fat without following any special diet. Exercise is associated with the mobilization and utilization of fat and does not increase the appetite of the overweight individual. It in fact represses the appetite of many individuals for a short period of time; hence, exercising before your biggest meal may reduce food intake. Additionally, exercise protects against lean tissue loss, whereas weight reduction through diet alone results in a decrease in lean tissue. Incidentally, lean individuals usually do increase their appetite through exercise. Apparently, the obese body is ready to lose extra weight through exercise, whereas the thin body preserves its limited fat store.

Exercise and Caloric Expenditure.

Mild exercise programs do not expend a large number of calories during one particular exercise session, but there is a cumulative effect over all the exercise sessions. Expending 250 calories per exercise session at a frequency of five days per week would utilize 1250 calories. Since 3500 calories equal one pound of body fat, this exercise results in the loss of, or the avoidance of gaining, 18½ pounds in a year's time.

As previously stated, a daily caloric excess equivalent to one-half a slice of bread or one-half glass of beer can result in a weight gain of more than 40 pounds within 10 years. In other words, taking in only 40 to 50 more calories a day than is required causes "creeping obesity." A daily 10-miute walk can prevent this weight gain.

An organized exercise program is not the only way to increase your caloric expenditure. Any time you ride the bus to work, get off a few blocks ahead of your stop and walk the remaining distance. When you go to the grocery store, leave your car in the outer area of the parking lot. You can walk back to your car and drive it to the loading area for the groceries. (Have you ever noticed how the parking spaces close to a shopping center are always filled, but the ones on the perimeter aren't?) You can walk up the stairs rather than ride the elevator. If it is many levels to your destination, get off several levels below it and walk the remaining stairs. You can walk to mow your lawn rather than ride. There are many ways to increase your caloric expenditure if you wish to do so.

Diet and Exercise Combination.

An extreme reduction in caloric intake can lead to malnutrition and hunger pangs. Increasing your caloric output through physical activity has the advantage of allowing you to consume more calories and a more nutritious diet. Consider the following example of a 135-pound female whose daily average consumption is 2400 calories and who wishes to lose 15 pounds. (Remember, 3500 calories= 1 pound of body fat.)

300 calories—deducted from diet
<u>200</u> calories—utilized in exercise
500 calories—deficit

15 x 3500 = 52,500 calories
52,500 + 500 = 105 days (15 weeks)

This program takes 15 weeks to produce a loss of 15 pounds. It may actually require more days, due to the decreasing difference between total caloric demand (for BMR and physical acitvity) and intake as weight is lost.

Weight reduction at this rate may appear slow to you, but it is a sensible approach. It doesn't require starvation or extremely hard exercise. Abstaining from soft drinks, most desserts, and other high caloric foods with little nutritional value will eliminate 300 calories. If this female were to walk for 45 minutes at a 17 minute/mile pace, she would utilize 201 calories. Furthermore, this walking would not have to be performed in 45 continuous minutes for this number of calories to be expended. It could be done several times throughout the day for a total of 45 minutes. There are other forms of exercise that can be used, but a gradual approach using both exercise and diet modification will increase your chance of long term behavior modification and permanent loss of excess fat.

ENERGY EXPENDITURE
FOR VARIOUS PHYSICAL ACTIVITIES

Activity	Cal/min/lb
Bicycling (level road)	
12:00 min/mi	0.0250
11:00 min/mi	0.0291
6:20 min/mi	0.0455
6:00 min/mi	0.0500
5:00 min/mi	0.0708
4:30 min/mi	0.0720

ENERGY EXPENDITURE
FOR VARIOUS PHYSICAL ACTIVITIES

Activity	Cal/min/lb
Hiking	0.0420
Jogging/Running	
13:30 min/mi	0.0630
12:00 min/mi	0.0667
11:00 min/mi	0.0711
10:00 min/mi	0.0790
8:30 min/mi	0.0933
8:00 min/mi	0.0844
7:00 min/mi	0.1031
6:00 min/mi	0.1066
5:00 min/mi	0.1311
Rope Skipping	
80-turns/min	0.0757
Stationary running	
70-80 counts/min	0.00780
140 counts/min	0.1622
Skiing	
12 min/mi	0.0770
Swimming	
Back stroke (25 yd/min)	0.0252
Back stroke (35 yd/min)	0.0454
Breast stroke (20 yd/min)	0.0319
Breast stroke (40 yd/min)	0.0639
Crawl (45 yd/min)	0.0580
Crawl (55 yd/min)	0.0706
Walking (level ground)	
26:26 min/mi	0.0233
18:45 min/mi	0.0313
17:09 min/mi	0.0332
13:25 min/mi	0.0524
13:03 min/mi	0.0551
11:35 min/mi	0.0627
10:21 min/mi	0.0756

Adapted from Consolazio CF, Johnson RE, Pecora, LJ: Physiological Measurements of Metabolic functions in Man. New York City, McGraw-Hill Book Company, 1963, pp 331-332. To determine the number of calories expended in an activity, multiply the number of calories per minute per pound by your weight and by the number of minutes you perform the activity.

Spot Reducing

Attempts at spot reducing are not very productive. Much money has been spent on devices which supposedly promote spot reducing, but scientific evidence does not support their effectiveness. Exercising any group of muscles leads to mobilization of fatty acids from fat deposits throughout the body. A study in which 11 obese women progressively increased periods of walking each day demonstrates this concept. The women experienced a loss of fat over the arms through exercise of leg muscles. The site from which fat was lost was unrelated to the particular muscles exercised.

A comparison of the circumference and thickness of subcutaneous fat at specific sites over arms of both tennis players and non-tennis players also demonstrates that spot reducing does not occur. The tennis players played regularly for at least six hours per week for two or more years. They had a significantly larger dominant arm; the non-tennis players did not. However, neither group showed any significant difference in the amount of fat over the muscles of the arm involved in one exercise as compared with the arm receiving less exercise. In other words, the arm constantly moving and hitting the tennis ball did not have less fat than the other arm.

Do not believe that you can lose weight around the waist, hips, or legs by wearing some special type of garment or device. Neither will performing special exercises for designated areas of the body promote spot reducing. It is possible to increase muscle firmness in areas through these exercises, but they will not "melt" away fat. Spot reduction does not take place.

Commitment to Manage Your Weight

You can manage your weight by eating and exercising sensibly but you must make the commitment to do it for the rest of your life. You must commit yourself to a new lifestyle of healthy eating habits and physical activity. If you are overweight, it may be difficult to motivate yourself to be active, but if you truly want to succeed, you will search for ways to increase your physical activity.

Remember, reducing your weight and your % body fat will not cure you of your obesity. You will experience a shrinkage in fat cell size, but there will be no change in cell number. Returning to your former eating and exercise habits will result in the regaining of weight and fat.

Finally, if you do undertake a weight-reduction program, proceed ever so gradually. Allow time for behavior modification to take place, and you will succeed.

7

Stress Management

For every emotional reaction there usually is an opposite and stronger reaction.

Stress is the response of our body to any demand made on it. It is in every experience and activity we encounter; it takes place whenever our body must adapt or readjust to maintain normalcy. Any change in our physical or psychological environment causes some stress, and usually anything that happens for the first time causes stress. It is our body's physical, mental, and chemical reaction to circumstances that frighten, excite, confuse, endanger, or irritate us. It can be caused by good, bad, happy, or unhappy events (called stressors) such as weddings, births, changes in lifestyle, personal loss, illness, injury, new job responsibilities, money problems, family problems, ethical decisions, and retirement.

Dr. Hans Selye, a Canadian physician, endocrinologist, and pioneer in stress studies describes three stages of a stressful experience. He refers to these stages as the General Adaptation Syndrome (G.A.S.).

Alarm Reaction
Chemical changes and adaptations take place within the body during this stage. Several of these adaptations are due to the brain's instructions to the adrenal glands to secrete the stress hormones, adrenaline (epinephrine) and noradrenaline (norepinephrine). Adrenaline accelerates the rate and increases the strength of heart contraction, dilates coronary and skeletal muscle blood vessels, and constricts blood vessels in the skin, kidneys, and most internal organs. Thus, it elevates blood pressure and redirects blood flow to areas with increased energy needs. Noradrenaline aids in the constriction of small blood vessels and also plays a role in the increased strength of cardiac pumping.

Other adaptations take place, some of which are caused by additional hormones secreted by the adrenal glands.
- Energy-rich sugar is placed in the blood. The blood's clotting ability is increased.
- Muscle tension is increased.

- The breakdown of adipose tissue is increased.
- Protein is broken down into amino acids.
- The unneeded digestive system goes into temporary inaction.
- Hormones which have strong anti-inflammatory effects and which help the body cope with infection are put into action. (Cortisone, used to treat certain types of arthritis, is one of these hormones.) In fact, almost every known hormone can be influenced by stress.

Resistance
Hopefully, during this state we are able to deal with the stress and function effectively. The alarm stage adaptations should disappear. If the alarm is not quieted and we become overwhelmed by the stress, we enter into the third stage.

Exhaustion
When the stress continues too long, we are unable to maintain our normal functioning and the signs of the first stage reappear. Our blood pressure stays up, hormone depletion continues, insomnia takes place, and even a very small amount of additional stress can cause a breakdown. Unless the stress is relieved, physical disorders, or possibly even death can result.

Stress: Good Bad?
We tend to think of all stress and the response to it as harmful. However, these responses are not only normal but essential. Without them we would not live very long. These responses provide a "call to arms" of the body's defenses and enhance our chance of survival during a stressful experience. They gear up the body for effort and seek to protect it from harm. The harm results in what follows, or fails to follow, once these body adaptations take place. In other words, how we cope with stress determines whether our health will be affected.

Consider the dilemma of prehistoric human beings. When faced with emotionally exciting and physically demanding situations, such as the approach of a wild animal, these people had to be prepared to fight for their lives or run to save themselves. Either choice required action and placed demands on the body. The cardiovascular and respiratory systems worked harder to supply oxygen and nutrients to the cells and remove waste products. The increase in blood sugar and blood fats, and the breakdown of body protein not only provided energy but made them able to forego eating for a long period of time, if necessary, during times of danger. In addition, the amino acids liberated by the breakdown of protein provided a source of raw materials for tissue repair when injury occurred. The body was prepared for action, to fight or flee; and physiological adaptations were what prepared them.

These body changes continue to take place when we are confronted with stress today. However, wild animals have been replaced for the most part by psychological conflicts. In many instances, the wild tiger is now the "paper tiger." But our body does not make a distinction between emotional crisis and physical crisis. When we encounter an emotional conflict brought on by the many turmoils of our present society, our glands prepare the body for a stressful experience as if we were face-to-face with a wild animal. We are prepared for action. However, present-day civilization often makes it impossible to relieve the tensions within our body. We do not have the opportunity or social approval to perform the vigorous, physical action needed to neutralize the hormone secretions. Even though our body's response to stress is the same, modern society has made the fight or flight practice obsolete, and more people are experiencing emotional and physical problems because of their inability to cope with stress.

Not all stress is bad, however. If treated in a positive way, it can motivate us to grow, adapt, and find solutions to the problems we encounter. Some individuals thrive on stress and actually rise to the occasion to function better mentally and physically. Many top executives of major businesses fall into this category. They learn to deal with stress and use it creatively to better fulfill their responsibilities. Each stressful experience actually strengthens them for the next encounter. Those individuals who cannot cope with the stress do not make it to the top, or they do not last very long once they reach that level. Successful athletes enjoy the intense pressure of competition and perform well during such experiences. On the other hand, some individuals do not react very strongly during emotional experiences; they appear to remain calm. If they truly are calm within, they probably will not suffer from stress-related diseases or disorders. If they are calm only on the outside but in turmoil within, they are very likely to suffer from stress-related disorders.

Stress Related Diseases and Disorders

According to the 1978 Harris survey referred to in previous chapters, 34% of all American adults or someone in their family have experienced an emotional problem, nervous condition, stress or anxiety which has affected their physical health. They have allowed stress to get out of hand, to control them. When this occurs, some obvious signs are nervousness, trembling, dizziness, pounding of the heart, troubled breathing, and sweaty palms. However, there is a long list of more serious detrimental effects that may take place:

- insomnia
- indigestion, acid enters the stomach and leads to ulcers
- colitis and/or constipation
- back, neck, chest, and stomach pains due to muscle tension
- headache, fuzzy vision
- loss of appetite
- depression
- increased levels of fatty acids and serum cholesterol
- hypertension
- decreased time of blood coagulation
    (blod clots more easily internally)
- heart disease
- kidney disease
- endocrine gland disorders
- weakening of other organs of the body
- use of drugs, alcoholism, excessive smoking
- suicide

Indeed, as indicated by Selye's theory of stress, almost any disease can be caused by emotional stress.

The Type of Personality

In the 1970's Drs. Meyer and Friedman, two cardiologists, and Ray H. Roseman suggested that excess stress may be the most significant risk factor in the development of heart disease. They categorized individuals as showing either Type A behavior or Type B behavior. The Type A individual was described as aggressive, ambitious, competitive, and time conscious. The doctors concluded that the consequences of this stressful behavior—elevated blood pressure, increased levels of serum cholesterol and fatty acids, stimulation of blood clotting, and overproduction of various hormones—made these people more susceptible to heart disease. Type B behavior was described as more relaxed, though not necessarily less ambitious or successful. Other researchers have questioned Friedman's and Rosenman's lack of emphasis on the role of diet and exercise in heart disease, but there are supporting studies, and it is generally agreed that stress is a risk factor in heart disease.

In one study, 94 men, prior to undergoing diagnostic coronary testing, were asked to respond to tests for coronary-prone behavior pattern anxiety, depression, and neuroticism. The men with the greatest amount of atherosclerosis scored significantly higher on all four scales of the test for the Type A coronary-prone behavior pattern than did those with less disease. Other scientists in the U.S., the Netherlands, Australia, and

Israel have independently reported empirical studies comparing individuals with coronary disease and individuals without coronary disease. Consistently, the patients with heart disease exhibited the Type A personality.

Are You Type A?

According to Friedman and Roseman, you can be described as a Type A personality if you are:

- excessively competitive
- always strive for achievement
- are overly aggressive
- exhibit time urgency
- think of or do two or more things simultaneously
- restless
- feel "challenged" upon meeting another Type A person
- hyperalert
- have explosiveness of speech and amplitude
- struggle against the limitation of time and the insensitivity of the environment
- almost always feel guilty when you relax
- do not have the time to spare to become the things worth being because you are preoccupied with obtaining the things worth having
- have certain nervous characteristics (frequently clench your fist, tight facial muscles, bang your hand on the table, etc.)
- no longer observe the more important or interesting things in the world
- pretend to listen but really remain preoccupied with your own thoughts when you can't steer the conversation your ways

Stress Management

A recent American Management Association survey of 6,000 people reported that the four most stressful on-the-job conditions are:

(1) unrealistic deadlines coupled with heavy workloads

(2) the difference between what you have to do and your personal goals

(3) the general political atmosphere of the organization

(4) the lack of evaluative feedback on job performance.

Respondents then were asked to reveal how they attempted to relieve job stress. The most highly recommended technique was: analyze the stress producing situations and decide what aspects are worth worrying about and which ones are not. An attempt should be made to forget the "unimportant" problems. In other words, react only after thinking things through. The second most popular technique was: spread the load. Do not be a loner; seek help, information, or corner-cutting aid from fellow employees. There are exceptions, but usually your fellow employees are experiencing the same stress and would welcome the opportunity to help and be helped. The third recommended approach was to set priorities for each month, week and day. Each day perform tasks in their order of importance. This technique should prevent the occurrence of any high-stress, day's end panic because the most important task of the day has not been completed. Other listed tehcniques were: have regular sleep and good health habits, keep work and non-work life separate, withdraw physically from a stressful situation, and maintain an exercise program.

Dr. Thomas Tutko, a professor of psychology, lists nine positive ways to manage stress:

1. Be aware of stress. Attempt to know what types of stress affect you. Many individuals deny they are under stress or refuse to recognize it as significant.
2. Be objective—not emotional. It is important for you to separate facts from feelings and think objectively.
3. Have a general plan. Stress increases when you feel helpless and do not know how to react. A plan gives you direction. Plan for the unexpected and include alternate plans.
4. Collect facts and information. It is necessary to collect as much information as possible to support your plan. Knowledge produces confidence and objectivity. You will not fear the stress.
5. Be organized. Organize your plan and your facts so that dealing with stress becomes routine. Organization helps to make events predictable and enables you to gain and maintain control. To manage stress you must be in control.
6. Develop a variety of stress-reduction techniques. Relaxation techniques and physical exercise are excellent ways to reduce the effects of stress.
7. Be assertive. This does not mean "tell-someone off." Rather, it means, make your feelings clear without being cruel or destructive. Foster an exchange of feeling between you and the other individuals involved. Your anxiety only increases when you wait for something to happen. You must make things happen. Your plan, facts, and organization should give you confidence to assert yourself. By being assertive you work off energy and act rather than react.
8. Use mental techniques. Make visualization, imagery, and/or mental rehearsal a part of your plan. During a time of relaxation, imagine stressful occasions. Imagine yourself remaining in control rather than reacting with tension. In addition, analyze the stressful event into

components and practice your response for each part separately, step-by-step, and then link them together. Finally, imagine your reward for coping with the event. The more you mentally practice the event, the more it will become automatic.

9. Get feedback. Try to discover your strengths and weaknesses and what you might do to improve. Observe others; ask them how they cope with stress.

Two additional techniques for the mangement of stress should be considered.

(1) Always work to strengthen your self-image. You are more likely to handle successfully and benefit from stressful experiences if you like yourself.

(2) Learn to say "no" when asked to perform too much. The feeling of having too much to do in too little time is often a self-created problem. Feeling that "nobody can get this done except me," ambitious individuals too often accept, create, or volunteer for extra responsibilities. To make matters worse, they then set up or accept unrealistic deadlines. You must know how to say "no."

Relaxation
Relaxation is a conscious release of muscular tension. To perform a relaxation technique you must be aware of the presence of tension. Many people are not aware of how often they tense muscle groups, such as the face, neck, shoulders, and back; they then have difficulty in relaxing the muscles if they do become aware of the tension. But if you can achieve relaxation of tense muscles, your chances of relaxing your mind are good.

Various relaxation techniques have been reported to be successful in the release of tension. Herbert Benson, a cardiologist, proposed the following technique:

- Sit quietly in a comfortable position with the eyes closed.
- Beginning at the feet and progressing to the head, relax all the muscles.
- Breathe through the nose. Each time you breathe out, silently say the word one, or some other one syllable word. Breathe easily and naturally.
- Continue for 10 to 20 minutes. You may occasionally check the time (avoid this if possible), but do not use an alarm. Upon finishing, sit quietly for several minutes.
- Maintain a positive attitude and allow relaxation to occur at its own pace. When distracting thoughts intrude, try to ignore them by not dwelling upon them, and continue to repeat the word one.

Present clinical and experimental evidence overwhelmingly supports the view that physical activity is associated with a decrease in stress anxiety.

Practice this technique once or twice daily, but not within two hours after any meal. The digestive process seems to interfere with the success of this technique.

Other techniques promote relaxation by intentionally increasing and decreasing tension in muscle groups. Either sitting or lying in a quiet, comfortable setting, contract and release various muscles in this sequence: toes, feet, lower legs, upper legs, buttocks, stomach, chest, hands, lower arms, upper arms, shoulders, neck, face, and scalp.

Various forms of meditation also can be used to help you relax. Most of these techniques involve sitting quietly for 15 to 20 minutes once or twice a day while concentrating on a word or image and breathing slowly and rhythmically. This is similar to Benson's technique. As your mind concentrates on the word, image, or breathing, it frees itself from worries and problems. As your mind relaxes, the muscles relax.

It is not necessary for you to invest a large sum of money to develop a relaxation technique. With practice, you can be successful in one or more of the above techniques, or you may instead wish to develop your own technique.

Physical Activity and Stress

The present clinical and experimental evidence overwhelmingly supports the view that physical activity is associated with a decrease in stress anxiety. By providing a mild type of stress, exercise helps to condition and fortify the adrenal glands, enabling them to manage severe stresses more effectively. Exercise seems to cause the formation of greater reserves of steroids, which are used by the body to counteract stress. In addition, regular exercise decreases the uptake of adrenaline and noradrenaline by the trained heart, making it a more efficient heart during stress.

Herbert deVries, exercise physiologist, states that rhythmic exercise, such as walking, jogging, cycling, and bench-stepping, with a duration of 5 to 30 minutes and intensities of 30% to 60% of maximum heart rate significantly promotes relaxation in the tense individual. In addition, in a study of elderly persons with symptoms of anxiety tension, deVries found that exercise in single doses works better than tranquilizers as a muscle relaxant.

Hans Selye, through his research on stress, demonstrated that regular physical exercise can make animals less vulnerable to experimentally induced heart attacks and subsequent stress. He believes that through reasonable amounts of progressive exercise, the body develops an efficient response to stress, and the exhaustion stage is avoided. Also, the individual who exercises regularly should be better prepared to resist other stressors, and stressful experiences are not as dangerous to the physically conditioned person as they are to the sedentary one.

Studies with mentally ill patients support the role of physical activity in the release of tension, and an experimental study at Duke University resulted in the modification of Type A behavior through a regular exercise program. Through behavior modification, the individual can decrease his chances of getting "uptight" during a stressful event.

Competitive games provide important physical and emotional outlets for natural aggressive drives. Anger, hate, and frustration, often excluded from open expression by society, can be transformed in sports participation. Through concentration on the game and on the opponent, participants in tennis, racquetball, handball and similar activities find a mental diversion that provides their worried minds with a new and different set of problems to solve—problems whose solutions can be found in a short space of time. Worry and anxiety are temporarily forgotten, and tension is released.

For those individuals who prefer noncompetitive physical exercise, activities such as jogging, swimming, walking, and bicycling offer the opportunity to think about things which cannot be thought about while on the job. Hopes, dreams, and aspirations may be an important part of the exercise session, as well as plans of how to cope with an anticipated stressful event. But for a truly relaxing session, it is best to think only of pleasant things and not to allow any disturbing thoughts to linger in your mind. In fact, if you are a Type A personality and have any hopes of behavior modification, you should approach physical activity in a noncompetitive way.

Whatever program you choose to follow, regular exercise can help you manage stress, and can help you avoid stress-related diseases.

Comparison of Relaxation, Meditation, and Exercise

In a study of 75 adult men, Bahrke and Morgan compared the reduction of anxiety by three different treatments. Twenty-five men exercised for 20 minutes at 70% of their maximum; 25 practiced Benson's Relaxation for 20 minutes; and 25 rested quiety in a "Lazyboy" chair for 20 minutes. All three techniques were equally effective in reducing anxiety. Possibly, for the treatment of stress, the diversional aspects of these activities are just as important as any physiological changes which may take place. In other words, just "getting away from it all" may be the best prescription for coping with stress. According to the researchers, however, the anxiety reduction following exercise may be sustained for a longer period than that of the other two treatments.

You Can Manage Stress

The only way to avoid stress totally is to select an atmosphere (home, job, climate, social life, etc.) which is always in line with your preferences. Only then can you eliminate the need for constant adaptation. Of course you realize this is impossible. Stress cannot be avoided; it always will be a part of your life. No matter what you do, where you go, or what happens to you, there will be the need to resist and adapt to changing external influences. There is no absolute freedom from stress short of death.

The key to the management of stress is to have personal control. You cannot stop the flow of paper work on your job, but you can perform to the best of your abilities and control how much you worry about the workload. You cannot plan the lives of others, but you can control your life. You can control the progress you make toward your own life's goals. You can find your own stress level, and you can learn to make the most out of stress, to meet its challenge.

If you are a Type A personality, try to alter your behavior. Make stress management a part of your health+ program. As with the other goals in your program, this goal will take time to reach. Do not attempt to alter your behavior too fast. Do not allow this goal to create stress.

8

Aging and Physical Activity

To me old age is always
fifteen years older than I
am.
    Bernard Baruch

The aging process has predictable effects on your body, but some of these changes don't have to occur as rapidly as they do. Some typical changes associated with aging are:

- increase in body weight
- increase in blood pressure
- reduction in cardiac output
- decline in maximal oxygen uptake, that is, the amount of oxygen extracted from the blood during exercise
- decrease in flexibility
- decrease in muscular strength and endurance
- bone loss

Research shows that physical activity can slow down the rate at which these changes occur. For example, maximal oxygen uptake generally falls about 35% to 45% from age 30 to 70. It starts declining about 1% a year somewhere between the ages of 20 and 25 in sedentary individuals. This decline is primarily the result of the heart's decreasing ability to deliver enough blood and oxygen to the working muscles and other tissues of the body. This failing ability of the heart can be seen in the decline of the maximum number of times the heart will contract in a minute (maximum heart rate), a loss of strength in the heart's contractions, and an increase in the resistance to blood flow of the small arteries. All of these changes cause a decline in the maximal oxygen uptake, forcing the heart to work harder. In many older individuals the maximal oxygen uptake declines to the point that it is insufficient to meet the demands of daily living. In a sustantial proportion of women in their seventh decade of life, activities requiring an energy expenditure of only 3.5 to 4.0 calories per minute consume more than 50% of their available maximal oxygen uptake. (A 120 pound female will expend this amount of energy walking one mile in 19 minutes.)

Physical activity can forestall the decline in maximal oxygen uptake. Kasch and Wallace followed the maximal oxygen uptake of 16 active men, with an initial average of 44.6 years, for a 10-year period. The men ran or swam at an intensity of 60% of their maximal oxygen uptake. The runners averaged 15 miles per week, and the one swimmer averaged 6 miles per week. From age 45 to 55 the maximal oxygen uptake generally declines 9% to 15%, but for these men it went essentially unchanged during the 10-year period.

In another study, Kasch followed three groups of middle-aged men through 6, 7, and 10 years of controlled and documented physical training. The men through running and swimming prevented a decrease in their maximal oxygen uptake and maximum heart rate and did not undergo any rise in blood pressure.

Sidney worked with men and women, age 60 to 83 years, and found an improvement in maximal oxygen uptake as a result of physical activity. The total caloric expenditures for the 50 to 60 minute sessions was increased progressively in the course of the study from about 180 to as much as 300 calories. The men and women worked to reach a pulse rate of 120 to 130 beats per minute during the active phase which consisted of warm-up calisthenics and brisk walking.

Men who participate in Masters Athletic Competition (40 years of age and older) appear to be more fit than their contemporaries in the general population. In addition to experiencing a slower decline in maximal oxygen uptake, they show less accumulation of body fat, a better preservation of lean tissue, a lower resting blood pressure, and greater work performance at a given target heart rate.

Decreased flexibility also is observed in the elderly. It is believed that change in connective tissue causes this decrease. Sedentary individuals undergo this decrease faster, and much of the decline in flexibility can be prevented through physical activity. The rate of decline in muscular strength and change in bone composition also can be altered through organized physical activity.

Motivation of the Older Population to be Active

Being spectators rather than participants is a way of life in our nation that is carried over into later adulthood. Continuation of physical activity is uncommon beyond age 30. To compound the problem, we are conditioned to the belief that at retirement we should "slow down" and "enjoy

Physical activity can forestall the decline in maximal oxygen uptake.

a well-earned rest." In additon, we maintain an attitude of overprotection toward the older population. Because of fears about physical exertion, we encourage older people to reduce their physical activities to the point where problems of disuse occur.

Many older people do not have a realistic view of their need for physical activity. In a study of men and women 60 years of age and older, Sidney and Shephard found that many believed they were active enough already, that their weight was normal, and even that their fitness was above average. Tests did not confirm these beliefs. Further, when asked to select a frequency and intensity of physical training, the obese tended to select a low frequency and low intensity. Many of the group were embarrassed to be seen in a T-shirt and gym shorts at their age. They worried about the degree of exercise needed to maintain an acceptable physical condition.

According to Sidney and Shephard, the main motivators for the elderly to exercise seem to be the availability of facilities and the anticipated gains in health and mood. Interest is maintained when they are shown gains in health and mood through periodic repetition of simple fitness tests and psychological assessments. It is essential that negative impact be avoided in programs for the elderly. Negative impact can occur as loss of health (through excessive fatigue and minor injuries), or loss of self-image (through a discrepancy between expectations and actual achievements).

The National Association for Human Development (NAHD).* a non-profit organization started in 1974 by cardiologists Theodore G. Klumpp and Don W. Wenger, is seeking to change our attitudes and habits concerning aging and exercise. The NAHD conducts workshops to show community leaders and others who work with senior groups how to organize health education programs and regular exercise programs. The programs are designed to get the sedentary into a more active lifestyle. They emphasize the "overload principle," getting individuals to perform continuous rhythmic exercise for periods long enough to cause the circulatory and respiratory systems to increase their efficiency.

It's Not Too Late

Almost everyone needs more information about exercise and how it should fit into their daily schedule. The elderly need to be convinced that

* 1750 Pennsylvania Avenue, N.W.
  Washington, D.C. 20006

Many older people do not have a realistic view of their need for physical activity.

age is no barrier to exercise. They must believe that they can rise above their limited physical expectations, that they can have a beneficial and enjoyable exercise program without running extremely long distances or dedicating long periods of time. At the same time they should realize that they can devote long hours and achieve high goals if they choose to. Consider the 70 year-old man who took up running in his early 60's and worked up to marathon distance. Another example of it "never being too late" is the 73 year-old man who had been inactive for nearly 40 years. He began a walking program at 63 and first attempted jogging at 68. He had difficulty completing 100 yards, but over a 10-month period, he developed the ability to jog almost 10 miles a day. In less than five years he had jogged more than 10,000 miles.

Here are some guidelines for an exercise program to improve maximal oxygen uptake:

- Any older individual should certainly have medical clearance before initiating an exercise program.
- The exercise should be a mild, continuous, rhythmic activity such as walking, swimming, or bicycling.
- Short distances should be attempted first.
- For several weeks it is probably best to exercise only every other day.
- If you are a heavy smoker and/or obese, progress toward a predetermined goal should be slower.
- Cardiovascular and othopedic problems should be avoided.
- All participants should learn to count their pulse rate.
- Exertion that produces chest pain (or in fact, any pain), a marked shortness of breath, and persisting fatigue should be avoided.
- All participants should feel better 5 to 10 minutes after completing their exercise session than they did before.
- If it is necessary to stop exercising for a period of time, progress back gradually.
- If the weekend is the only opportunity for exercise, don't exercise at all. This type of program involves great risk.
- Flexibility and mild rotation exercises for the trunk and extremities should be included in the program.
- For the person in very poor condition, a variety of sit-down exercises may be performed.
- If a jogging program is desired, all participants first should be able to walk a brisk mile; then the distance that is jogged should be increased gradually.
- Time goals (how fast a specified distance can be run, swum, etc.) should be avoided. A target heart rate goal should be emphasized (see the chapter on exercise prescription).

There are about 44 million people over 55 years of age in this nation. Most of this group can and should be physically active. They can feel better, look better, and therefore, better enjoy life.

9

Flexibility

You can bend without breaking.

Flexibility is the ability to move your body joints through a maximum range of motion without undue strain. It is not a general factor but is specific to given joints and to particular sports or physical activities. If you have good flexibility in the shoulder you may not necessarily have good flexibility in the hip. Flexibility depends more on the soft tissues (muscles, ligaments, and tendons) of a joint than on the bony structure of the joint itself. However, the bony structure of certain joints does place limitations on flexibility. For example, extension of the elbow or knee is limited by the design of the bones in these joints.

Flexibility is also related to sex, age, and activity. As a general rule women are more flexible than men. Anatomical differences in and/or differences in regular physical activity between the sexes may account for these flexibility differences.

During the early school years flexibility increases, but a leveling off or decrease begins in early adolescence. Even though older people are less flexible than the young, seniors can benefit from flexibility training. It is very probable that dramatic loss of flexibility in the aging process is due to failure to maintain an active program of movement through the years.

Active individuals tend to be more flexible than inactive individuals. The soft tissues of the joints tend to shrink and thus lose extensibility when the muscles are maintainied in a shortened position, as can happen in a sedentary lifestyle. Considering all influences, flexibility is related more to activity habits than to age and sex differences.

Flexibility and Health+

Flexibility is an important part of your health+ program. The lack of it can create several disorders or functional problems.

In the U.S. as many as 75 million people have back problems. Medical records indicate that low back pain is one of the most prevalent health complaints in our country. Many of these problems can be avoided, since more than 50% of all lower back disorders are due to poor muscle tone, poor flexibility of the lower back, and inadequate abdominal muscle tone.

The loss of joint flexibility is due to the shortening of connective tissue on one side of a joint and the lengthening of the muscles on the opposite side of the joint. The condition of round shoulders in which shortened tendons and ligaments in the upper chest cause the muscles to pull the shoulders forward is an example of such a problem.

Short muscles also limit work efficiency, and become sore when they are exerted. Athletes who stretch regularly appear to experience fewer muscle pulls and less soreness than those who fail to do so. Anytime you take part in a physical activity program, you should stretch before and after participation to avoid muscle soreness and injury.

There is support for the belief that some cases of painful menstruation (Dysmenorrhea) can be prevented or at least reduced in severity through stretching of the muscles and connective tissues in the pelvic area. Finally, there are psychological benefits associated with good flexibility. When you are able to move freely without stiff, restricted movement, you look and feel better.

Development of Flexibility

It is impossible to say exactly how much flexibility is desireable, but everyone should strive to prevent loss of flexibility during the aging process. No special physical skill is necessary, so it is possible for everyone to learn to stretch. In addition, you can stretch anytime and usually anywhere you feel like it. You should always stretch before and after physical activity, but you may also stretch:

- in the morning upon rising from bed
- at work
- while watching television or listening to music
- after sitting or standing for some time
- to release nervous tension

It has been demonstrated that both slow, sustained stretching exercises (static stretch) and active, bouncing exercises (ballistic stretch) are effective in developing flexibility. However, the use of a fast, forceful, bobbing type of stretching can cause problems.

Your muscles are protected by a mechanism called the stretch reflex. Suddenly stretching the muscle fibers too far (either by bouncing or overstretching) activates a nerve response which signals the muscles to contract. The purpose of this reflex is to keep the muscle from being injured due to overstretching. Therefore, when you stretch too far, you tighten the very muscles you are trying to stretch. In addition, by forcing a muscle to overstretch when it is undergoing reflex contraction, you can cause microscopic tearing of muscle fibers. This tearing creates pain and leads to the formation of scar tissue, with a gradual loss of elasticity.

When you are able to move freely without stiff, restricted movement, you look and feel better.

Static stretch is less likely to evoke the stretch reflex, and there is less danger of accidentally overstretching a muscle. This type of stretching also can provide relief from muscle soreness. On occasion, both types of stretching can be performed. The static stretch should precede the active stretch, and any bouncing should be done in a slow, gentle manner.

Improvement in flexibility is most likely to result when sets of stretches for each specific area of flexibility are performed throughout the day, instead of in one massed, concentrated effort. Daily exercise is recommended; five days per week. Once the desired flexibility is attained, three days of stretching per week are probably sufficient to maintain it. The most important areas to consider are probably neck and shoulder flexion, back extension, trunk and hip flexion (including lower back and posterior upper-leg muscles), and posterior lower-leg extension (ankle flexion).

Guidelines for Development of Flexibility

Flexibility exercises should be a part of your health+ program. By following these guidelines you can increase your flexibility.

- Spend 20 to 30 seconds in gentle, static stretch with each exercise, and perform each exercise two or three times.
- The extent of the stretch should be increased gradually and progressively with full extension, flexion, or both being placed on the joint.
- Breathe slowly, rhythmically and under control.
- Stretch to the point that only a slight stretch pain is felt; you must stretch beyond the normal length of the muscle but do not cause even moderate pain.
- Practice regularly; perform the exercises several times per day.
- Perform flexibility exercises before strength and circuloresiratory endurance work-outs to prevent strains and other muscle injuries. Perform them after the workout to prevent soreness and loss of flexibility. For example, the lower back and posterior leg muscle may shorten as the result of a jogging program.
- Flexibility is highly specific to each joint and activity. Therefore flexibility exercises should be performed for each joint in which increased flexibility is desired.
- Always stretch the back and legs in straight lines; observe the placement of your feet.
- When stretching the posterior leg muscle, pull the toes back toward the body. This action will stretch the muscles more.

Flexibility exercises should be a daily part of your health + program.

The Flexibility Program

The following exercises are designed to develop flexibility throughout the body. You probably should perform at least one exercise for each area of the body. Some of the exercises are easier to perform than others. You should perform the exercises that only create a slight stretch pain. Remember: slow and gentle.

Neck

- Place your hands behind your head. Gradually press down and hold. Your posterior neck muscles should feel stretched.
- Slowly rotate the neck in a large circular pattern.

Shoulder and Upper Chest

- Stand in a doorway and grasp the doorjamb above the head. Lean forward through the doorway until stretch is felt.
- Stand with feet shoulder-width apart and lock your hands behind your waist. Straighten your arms behind you, raise and hold.
- Extend your arms overhead and interlace your fingers with the palms facing upward. Push upward and slightly backward.
- Interlace your fingers in front of you at shoulder height with the palms away from you. Extend your arms forward.
- Bring your right hand over your right shoulder to your upper back and reach down as far as you can. Bring your left hand under your left shoulder to your upper back. Grab fingers and hold. If you are unable to grasp the fingers together, hold a towel between them. Gradually move your left hand up the towel. Reverse hand positions and repeat.

Back

- Lie on your back with your arms above your head, knees bent, and feet flat on the floor. Move one knee as far as you can toward your chest and at the same time straighten out the other leg. Return to the original position and repeat the exercise, switching legs.
- Lie on your back with arms at your sides, knees bent, and feet flat on the floor. Pull in the stomach and bring your knees up to the chest. Grasp your knees and pull them toward your chest. Keep your knees together and your shoulders flat on the mat. Press your lower back to the floor.
- Sit on a hard chair with your arms folded loosely in front of you and feet about 24 inches apart. Bend forward, with your arms, shoulders and head between your knees.
- Sit on the floor with legs crossed and arms at your sides. Tuck your

chin and curl forward. Slide your hands forward on the floor, allowing your back to be rounded.

- Lie flat on your back with arms at your side. Draw your knees to your chest and slowly roll back, placing hips and back in a vertical position. Extend your legs and feet beyond your head. It may be necessary to keep your hands on your hips for support and control of the stretch. If you are unable to touch the floor behind you with your toes, find a comfortable position with knees bent. If you are fairly flexible, you may reach back and touch your toes.

Trunk
- Stand with your feet shoulder-width apart and toes pointed straight ahead. Extend both arms overhead; grasp your left hand with your right hand and bend slowly to the right. Pull the left arm over your head and down toward the ground with your right hand. Bend to the left, reversing your hand positions.
- Stand with your feet shoulder-width apart. Bend at the elbows, touch your fists in front of your waist, then raise your arms so that they are parallel to the ground. Turn as far as you can to the right and hold. Repeat in the opposite direction. This exercise may also be performed while sitting on the floor with legs crossed.
- Lie on your stomach with hands in the push-up position. Extend your arms fully to raise the shoulders and upper back. Keep the pelvis and legs on the floor.
- Stand with your right side toward a wall, feet together and about 18 inches from the wall. Place your right hand and forearm against the wall at shoulder level and the heel of your left hand on your left hip. Push your hips toward the wall with your left hand. Reverse sides and repeat.

Posterior Hip and Upper Leg (Also Involves the Lower Back)
- Stand with feet slightly apart. Bend your knees and bend forward at the waist until you can place the palms of your hands flat on the floor. You should be almost in a squat position. Keep your palms on the floor as you slowly attempt to straighten your legs. Do not overextend. As your flexibility improves, allowing you to reach maximum stretch, change your hand postion to holding on to your ankles, and pull your head as close to the floor as you can.
- Sit on the floor with legs straight in front of you and feet together. Bend forward at the waist (do not round the back; keep it straight) and grasp the outsides of your legs as far down as possible. Try to place your chest on your thighs and grasp the outer borders of the feet.

Keep your toes pointed back to stretch the posterior lower leg muscles. If you have trouble finding a position where you can stretch and relax, use a towel. Place the towel around your feet, grab it by the ends and pull yourself forward from the hips. Work your hands down the towel, until you can feel the stretch.

- Place a straight leg on a footstool, locking the knee. Keep the other leg straight and bring your head toward the knee of the extended leg. Keep your hands on your hips. Keep your toes pointed back to stretch the posterior lower leg muscles. Repeat with the opposite leg. Progress to the use of a chair and finally a table as you improve.

Anterior Hip and Thigh
- In a standing position, draw one knee up to your chest and pull it tightly to the chest with your hands. Repeat with the other knee.
- Stand on either leg. Bend the other knee and grasp your ankle behind you. Pull up on the leg as you lean forward slightly. Repeat with the opposite leg. You may perform this exercise while lying on your side by grasping the foot of the top leg and slowly pulling it back.
- Squat with the bent knee of one leg forward and the other leg extended behind you. Push forward until the knee of the front leg is directly over the ankle. The knee of the backward extended leg should be resting on the floor. Without changing the position of the legs and feet, lower the front of your hips downward to create an easy stretch. Reverse the position of the legs and repeat.

Groin Area
- Sit on the floor. Put the soles of your feet together and grasp your toes. Gently pull yourself forward, bending at the hips.
- Sit against a wall, or anything that will give support. With your back straight and the soles of your feet together, gently push down on the inside of your thighs with your hands.

Posterior Lower Leg
- Sit on the floor with one leg straight and the other in a comfortable position. Use a towel around the ball of the foot of the extended leg and pull your toes toward your knee. Reverse legs and repeat. If you are flexible enough, you may use your hands to pull your toes toward your knee.
- Facing a wall, stand approximately three to four feet from it. Lean forward and place your palms against the wall at arm's length and shoulder height. Keep your feet flat and your body in a straight line.

Allow your elbows to bend and lean forward more. Don't allow your heels to rise off the floor.

● Assume the same position as described in the previous exercise. Perform the same routine but also bend at the knees. Don't allow your heels to rise off the floor. You should feel the stretch in the area closer to your heel (Achilles tendon).

● Stand on a step facing the stairway. Lower your heels over the edge of the stair and hold. You may perform this exercise with a thick piece of wood or similar object placed under the front portion of the foot, if you prefer.

● Step forward with either leg. Keep the other leg straight with foot pointed straight ahead and heel on the floor. Bend the front leg to stretch the back leg. Step farther ahead with the front leg to gradually increase the distance between the feet and provide additional stretch.

Foot and Ankle

● Kneel, sitting on your feet with toes and ankles stretched backward. Balance with both hands on the floor just behind your hips. Raise your knees slightly from the floor. Don't allow your feet to flare out to the side. This exercise also stretches the anterior upper legs.

● Stand with feet apart. Touch the floor with the backs (upper side) of the toes of one foot. Press down until you feel the stretch. Repeat with the other foot.

10

Muscular Strength and Endurance

All growth depends upon activity.
There is no development physically
or intellectually without effort,
and effort means work.
    Calvin Coolidge

Strength is the ability of a muscle to exert force. The force may produce motion (dynamic contraction), or it may not produce motion (static contraction). It is best measured by tests which require one maximum effort. Strength is related to power, which is the speed at which force can be applied. Muscular endurance is the ability of a muscle group to resist fatigue and to make repeated contractions against a defined resistance, or to apply strength and hold it in a fixed position.

Strength

If muscles are used, they increase in size (hypertrophy) and strength; thus, strength-developing exercises increase the size of muscles. However, differences in hormones between men and women affect the extent of this growth. Muscular development is less pronounced in women, and increased strength seldom causes a "bulging muscle" appearance. When muscles are not used, they decrease in size (atrophy) and lose strength.

Strength is essential for high level performance in many sports, but it also is essential for health+, for the following reasons:

- Stronger muscles help protect the joints, making them less susceptible to sprains, strains, and other injuries.
- Strength is necessary for good posture. Such postural problems as sagging abdominal organs, round shoulders, and low back pain may be prevented.

- Strength will enable you to perform routine chores (household and occupational) more efficiently and to avoid end-of-day fatigue.
- Strength will enable you to experience more satisfaction from leisure sport participation.

Strength Development Principles

The amount of strength you wish to have beyond that of quality health depends upon your personal needs and interests. But to develop strength, three basic principles must be applied.

Overload.

The fundamental principle of strength development is overload. You must place a stress on the muscles above the level they normally encounter; they must work harder than usual. You may overload by increasing the load, increasing the number of times or repetitions an exercise is performed, increasing the speed at which the exercise is performed, or by various combinations of these. The extent of the overload will vary among individuals.

Progression.

As your muscles become stronger, it takes a proportionally greater stress to continue improvement; you must gradually increase the overload.

Specificity.

The development of strength is highly specific. If you wish to increase the strength in a particular muscle, you must exercise that muscle. Leg exercises develop the legs, and arm exercises develop the arms.

Types of Muscular Exercise

During exercise the muscle shortens, lenghtens, or maintains a static position. All three types of contraction may be used to increase strength, but there are advantages and disadvantages to each.

Isotonic.

In isotonic exercise the muscle shortens and lengthens, and work is performed. Isotonic programs traditionally involve the use of dumbbells, barbells, and weight pulleys, but exercises such as push-ups, sit-ups, and chin-ups are isotonic contractions also. During isotonic contraction, the same muscles that lift the weight or body (shortening process) also lower the weight or body (lengthening process). For example, when you bend your arms during push-ups (lowering your body), the posterior, upper arm muscles (triceps) still have tension, but they undergo a gradual lengthening. The anterior, upper arm muscles (biceps) undergo the same type of contractions when you perform chin-ups. Training benefits occur during both the shortening (concentric contraction) and the lengthening (eccentric contraction) of the muscles.

Advantages of Isotonic Exercise
- There is development of strength through the entire range of motion.
- Muscular endurance is developed, and recovery from muscular fatigue is faster in muscles that have been trained isotonically.
- Muscle size is increased to a greater extent through isotonic contractions. If increased muscle size is not a desired outcome, it may be limited through the amount of overload applied.
- If performed through the entire range of motion, isotonic exercises can improve flexibility.
- You are able to see the work being accomplished.

Disadvantages of Isotonic Exercise
- If equipment (such as barbells and dumbbells) is used, it can be expensive.
- If the equipment is kept at your home, you will need ample space.
- After the initial contractile force of the muscle overcomes the inertia of the weight, the weight is moved with little additional work by the contracting muscles. Because of this momentum, some investigators claim that the muscle is working as little as 30% of the time in a pure isotonic movement.
- The amount of weight lifted is limited to what can be moved at the weakest point in the range of motion. This means that relatively little resistance is placed on the muscle in the remaining range. To overcome this disadvantage, many manufacturers of isotonic equipment now sell equipment which varies the resistance through the range of motion (they call this "dynamic variable resistance").

Isometric.
During isometric exercise, muscle contraction occurs, but the length of the muscle remains the same and no mechanical work is performed. Isometric contractions are produced when a weight lifter tightens the grip on the bar before lifting. Pushing and pulling against an immovable object also produces isometric contraction.

Advantages of Isometric Exercise
- It can be used effectively in rehabilitation programs to exercise the muscle when a range of motion cannot be produced. This can prevent reduction in muscle size and strength.
- No special equipment is required.
- Little time is required.
- Little fatigue is experienced after exercising.
- It can be performed anywhere.

Disadvantages of Isometric Exercise
- There is no positive feedback. Because you do not know how much improvement has taken place, there may be a lack of motivation.
- Isometric exercises can be dangerous for anyone who has coronary heart disease and/or hypertension or who has experienced a stroke. When performing isometric exercises, the individual typically takes a deep breath, holds it, and forcefully compresses the air in the abdomen and chest. This action restricts the return of the blood to the heart, increases blood pressure, and reduces the amount of blood flowing to the heart and brain.
- Strength gain is limited to the specific joint angle at which the isometric contraction occurs. There must be contractions at various joint angles to develop strength throughout the entire range of motion.
- There is little development of flexibility.

Isokinetic.
A third type of muscular exercise is called isokinetic. The muscular contractions are all concentric in this type of exercise. You push and pull against a lever which moves at a fixed rate and resistance. The device adjusts automatically to control resistance and speed. In other words, the resistance is adjusted throughout the range of motion to match or accomodate the maximal possible force that you can apply. If you are motivated to apply maximum force throughout the entire range of motion, you can do so.

Advantages of Isokinetics.
- The equipment allows the muscle to exercise through a full range of motion with varying degrees of resistance. Maximum strength is applied for each angle of contraction. This is not true when lifting a dumbbell or barbell.
- The equipment is less expensive than barbells and can be stored, carried, and set up anywhere.
- They can be used safely in rehabilitation programs.

Disadvantages of Isokinetics.
- Special equipment is necessary.
- Isokinetic devices do not inform you as to how much resistance you are applying. The figures on the cylinders are only estimates.
- There is no eccentric contraction. This may not be a serious disadvantage, however, since you do not use eccentric contractions very often.

In view of the advantages and disadvantages, isotonic and isokinetic exercises appear to be preferable to isometric exercises. Because of the danger of the increased blood pressure, isometric exercises are not recommended.

Endurance

Have you experienced occasions when it was necesary to "keep going" even though your arms, legs, or entire body felt too tired to do so? Perhaps your arms have felt this way when carrying the groceries from the car into the house. You had the strength to pick up the groceries, but they became heavier and heavier the farther you carried them. This can occur when pushing a stalled car, carrying a heavy suitcase, or performing any task which involves sustained muscular contraction (muscular endurance).

It is possible to have good strength but not have muscular endurance. Strength enables you to lift more, while muscular endurance enables you to lift for longer. It is necessary to have some strength, however, to develop endurance. For example, to develop abdominal muscular endurance through sit-ups, you must have the strength to perform at least one sit-up.

Even if you do not lift and carry heavy loads, you probably lift light loads repeatedly or lift and move your body throughout the day. If so, to avoid end-of-day fatigue, you need muscular endurance. You will be less apt to have backaches or muscle soreness and injury if you maintain good muscular endurance; it will also be easier to maintain good posture.

Endurance Development Principles

The principles of endurance are very similar to the principles of strength development. Again, the amount of muscular endurance you wish to develop depends upon your personal needs and interests.

Overload.
To develop muscular endurance you must contract the muscles many times against a weight or resistance. The key to muscular endurance is the number of repetitions; you must do more than your muscle is accustomed to doing.

Progression.
To avoid muscle soreness you should start slowly (with a low number of repetitions) and gradually increase the number of repetitions until you reach your goal.

Specificity.
You must work with the specific muscles that you want to improve. To develop arm endurance you must perform arm exercises. Some circulorespiratory fitness programs, such as jogging and swimming, also develop muscular endurance in the legs and arms.

Development of Muscular Strength and Endurance

The following exercises can be used to develop muscular strength and endurance. Even though some of the exercises require the use of home-made equipment, no expensive equipment is necessary. Several exercises are described for each area of the body. You may wish to perform at least one exercise for each area. Do not expect to develop circulorespiratory endurance through these exercises, however. Continuous, rhythmic movement is the best developer of circulorespiratory endurance. If you wish to use weights or an isokinetic apparatus, there are numerous books available that describe such programs.

To avoid extreme soreness or injury, these guidelines should be observed.

- Perform stretching and warm-up exercises before you attempt any muscular effort.
- Some exercises are more strenuous than others; perform the ones that provide a mild overload and gradually progress to the more difficult ones.
- Unless otherwise indicated, begin with 10 repetitions and add two or three repetitions each week until you reach the number you wish to maintain. But if you are unable to perform 10 repetitions without intense effort, begin with a lower number.
- Perform the exercises three to five days per week.

Jumping Jack
- Stand erect with feet together and arms at your sides.
- Swing your arms upward until they are overhead, and spread your feet apart in one movement; return to starting position without pausing.
- Repeat 15 to 20 times.

Posterior Upper Arm, Shoulders, Chest, and Upper Back

Wall Push-Up
- Face wall, arm's distance away. Place feet shoulder-width apart, heels flat on floor.
- Place palms, fingers up, against the wall at shoulder level.
- Bend arms until forehead touches the wall.
- Straighten arms and return to starting position.

Chair Push-Up
- Place hands shoulder-width apart with fingertips forward on chair or bench, with feet on the floor, weight supported on toes.
- Straigthen arms with chin up and chest forward.
- Bend arms and lower chest within two to three inches of chair.
- Push back into starting position.

Modified Push-Up
- Lie face down (prone position). Place palms flat on the floor, shoulder-width apart.
- Bend legs and keep knees on the floor (feet and lower legs will be off the floor).
- Straighten arms and support weight on hands and knees.
- Bend arms and lower chest to within two to three inches of floor. Keep chin up and body straight.
- Straighten arms and return to starting position.

Push-Up
- Lie face down (prone position). Place palms flat on floor, shoulder-width apart.
- Straighten arms and support weight on hands and toes.
- Bend arms and lower chest to within two to three inches of floor. Keep chin and body straight.
- Straighten the arms and return to starting position.

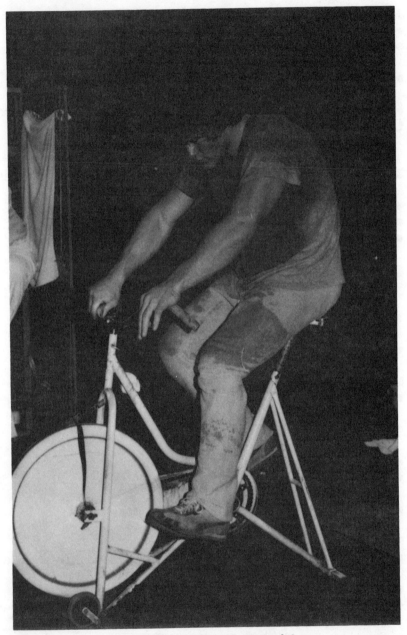

Chin-ups help to develop your upper body musculature.

Advanced Push-Up
- Assume same position as described in regular push-up but place feet on a bench or chair.
- Perform in same manner as described in regular push-up.

Press
- Fill two plastic milk or bleach bottles with equal amounts of water or sand. Tie a bottle to each end of bar or heavy stick which is approximately 36 to 40 inches long.
- To lift weight off floor bend at knees and keep back straight. Grasp bar with palms down, shoulder-width apart. Bring bar to resting position on upper chest with elbows down.
- Raise bar overhead by straightening arms until elbows lock.
- Lower bar back to chest position.
- Perform two sets of six to ten repetitions.

Anterior Upper Arm, Shoulders, Chest, and Upper Back

Modified-Chin-Up—A
- Placebar(orheavystick)acrosssupportssothatitisthreetofourfeethigh.
- Lie beneath bar and grip it with hands shoulder-width apart. Palms may be either up or down. The palms-down position makes the exercise more difficult.
- With body straight and heels on floor, pull up to bar until chest touches.
- Return to starting position.

Modified Chin-Up—B
- Place bar (or heavy stick) across supports so that it is approximately chin high.
- Hang from bar at 45° angle with hands shoulder-width apart and arms straight. Palms may be either up or down.
- With body straight and heels on floor, pull up until chin touches bar.
- Lower to starting position.

Chin-Up
- Place bar across supports at height that enables you to hang by hands without feet touching ground.
- Hang from bar with hands shoulder-width apart and arms straight. Palms may be either up or down.
- Pull up until chin is even with bar.
- Lower to starting position.

Chin-Up with Weight
- Fill two plastic milk or bleach bottles with equal amounts of water or sand. Tie a bottle to each end of a rope that is 24 to 36 inches long.
- Hang bottles around shoulders so that they are in front of the body. You may wish to place padding between rope and neck.
- Perform chin-up as described above.

Arm Curls
- Fill two plastic milk or bleach bottles with equal amounts of water or sand. Tie a bottle to each end of bar or heavy stick which is approximately 36 to 40 inches long.
- Stand erect with arms fully extended downward. Grasp bar with palms up and shoulder-width apart.
- Raise bar to chest by bending arms. Elbows should remain at sides and back should remain straight.
- Perform two sets of six to ten repetitions.

Abdomen
To perform these exercises, lie on your back with knees bent and feet flat on the floor.

Trunk Curl
- Clasp hands on top of head. Placing hands behind head may cause you to jerk the head forward, straining neck muscles.
- Roll head and shoulders forward and upward enough to feel tension in abdominal muscles.
- Return to starting positon.

Reverse Sit-Up
- Place arms at sides.
- Lift knees to chest, raising hips off floor.
- Return to starting positon.

Assisted Flexed Knee Sit-Up
- Place arms at sides.
- Put hands under thighs to help pull your upper body up to position where no resistance is encountered.

Flexed Knee Sit-Up
- Arms held at sides.
- Arms folded across chest.
- Hands clasped on top of head.

Sit-Up with Feet Elevated
- Same position as previous sit-ups but place feet on seat of chair, bed, etc. Knees remain bent.
- Arms and hands may be placed in any position.

Lateral Trunk

Side Bender
- Stand with feet shoulder-width apart and hands clasped behind head.
- Alternate bending to right and left while maintaining straight back and legs.
- Perform the same number of repetitions for each side.

Side Bender
Same as previous exercise but may be varied.
- Extend arms overhead.
- With arms extended at sides, hold a weight in each hand.

Lower Back and Buttocks

Back Tightener
- Lie face down with hands behind lower back.
- Raise head and chest. Tense lower back and buttocks muscles.
- Do not overextend. Only raise the head and chest slightly off the floor.

Leg Raise
- Support your body on your hands and knees.
- Extend and raise one leg behind your body.
- Perform the same number of repetitions for each leg.
- Wearing heavy shoes or adding weight to ankles will increase resistance.

Back Leg Raise
- Lie face down with hands clasped behind your head.
- Lift straight legs a few inches off floor. Hold head and chest down.

Back Extension
- Lie on a bench face down. Extend your body from the waist up over the edge of the bench. It will be necessary to strap your feet down, or have someone hold them.

- Clasp your hands behind your head. Lift head and trunk.
- Do not over extend.

Lateral Hip and Thigh

Side Leg Raise
- Lie on your right side with legs straight. Use your arms to maintain a balanced position.
- Lift left leg straight up from side as high as possible.
- Return to starting position.
- Perform the same number of repetitions with each leg.

Leg Raise
- Lie on your back with arms at your sides.
- Lift your legs until they are perpendicular to the floor.
- Open legs to a wide V-shape.
- Close the V, and return to starting position.

Upper Legs

Two-Leg Squat
- Stand with feet about 12 inches apart, arms extended in front, parallel to the ground.
- Squat until knees are bent at a 90° angle. Do not go beyond this point.
- Return to standing position.

Single Leg Knee Dip (With Assistance)
- Stand facing a partner. Hold right hands as if shaking hands.
- Squat down on right foot until right knee is at a 90° angle. Keep left leg straight. Your partner remains standing.
- Grab your partner's hand with both hands to lift yourself back up.
- Perform the same number of dips with each leg, but attempt no more than five dips when first performing this exercise. Do not go beyond a 90° angle.

Single Leg Knee Dip
- Same as previous exercise, but this time use your partner's hand only for balance.

Stride Jump
- Stand with right leg forward and left leg back.
- Place left arm parallel to the floor in front of you and right arm parallel to the floor behind you.
- Jump up moving left foot forward and right foot backward, switching the position of your arms at the same time. The opposite foot and arm should be forward.
- Keep feet at least 18 to 24 inches apart.
- Attempt to maintain rhythmic movement.

Lower Legs

Heel Raises
- Stand on a board, book, or something similar, with heels resting off the edge.
- Rise up onto toes; then return to starting position. Use your arms for balance.
- Hanging weights around your shoulders will increase resistance.

Jumps in Place
- With feet parallel and about 12 inches apart, jump in place.
- Maintain a steady pace.

11

Exercise Prescription

Sometimes slower is faster.

It should be apparent to you by now that key elements in your health+ program are exercise and fitness. In the words of the U.S. Public Health Service's "Forward Plan for 1977-1981",

> Habitual inactivity is thought to contribute to hypertension, chronic fatigue and resulting physical inefficiency, premature aging, the poor musculature and lack of flexibility which are the major causes of lower back pain and injury, mental tension, coronary heart disease and obesity. By contrast, studies have reported that regular exercise can lower serum triglycerides, reduce the clinical manifestations of heart disease, improve the efficiency of the heart and circulation and reduce blood pressure levels in individuals with hypertension.

Indeed, more and more scientific evidence demonstrates the value of regular exercise—people who live sensibly and keep physically fit are healthier and feel better. The Soviet Union has conducted extensive fitness research and found that working people who exercise regularly produce more, visit the doctor less frequently and are less prone to industrial accidents. Other studies have reached the following conclusions about individuals who exercise regularly:

- They feel better about their personal health.
- The overweight experience weight loss.
- They manage stress and tension better.
- They pay more attention to their diet.
- They sleep more soundly.
- Many either quit or reduce their smoking.
- They experience less fatigue and have improved physical work capacity.
- They have less absenteeism from work.
- They have a lower coronary risk profile.

There can be no doubt—regular exercise is basic to good health.

Physical Fitness

The following definition of physical fitness is endorsed by the American Academy of Physical Education.

Physical fitness is the ability to carry out daily tasks with vigor and alertness, without undue fatigue and with ample energy to engage in leisure time pursuits and to meet the above average physical stresses encountered in emergency situations.

Physical fitness is a positive and vital quality. It consists of the ability to meet the demands of your environment, manage stress, resist fatigue and have the energy to lead an abundant life. Even though the energy demands of daily tasks vary, physical fitness is necessary for anyone to function at their peak of effectiveness. Organic soundness, proper nutrition, and freedom from disease contribute to physical fitness, but these alone do not guarantee a desirable level of fitness. You could still be deficient in the four basic components of physical fitness: circulorespiratory endurance, flexibility, muscular strength, and muscular endurance. Exercises to develop flexibility and muscular strength and endurance have been described in previous chapters, and will not be repeated. These qualities are important, but usually it is not necessary to devote much time to their development and maintenance. In addition, exercise for these things can be performed in the home, whereas most circulorespiratory endurance exercises must be performed outside the home. As with all parts of your health+ program, the level of efficiency and fitness you wish to attain in each area is up to you. Your goals, however, should be in agreement with the guidelines we have discussed.

Circulorespiratory Endurance

Circulorespiratory endurance is developed through the moderate contraction of large muscle groups for relatively long periods of time, during which adjustments of the circulatory and respiratory systems are necessary. Activities of an endurance nature such as bicycling, swimming, walking, jogging, or hiking should be emphasized to achieve this.

Circulorespiratory endurance is also called aerobic endurance, which refers to your capacity to use oxygen. The aerobic limit, known as the maximum steady state, is the highest level at which you can breathe in, transport, and utilize oxygen. The maximum oxygen consumption that you can attain measures the effectiveness of your heart, lungs, and vascular system in the delivery of oxygen during heavy work. The higher your oxygen consumption, the more effective is your utilization of oxygen. You can increase your aerobic limit through exercise.

When you exercise beyond your maximum steady state, you begin exercising in an anaerobic state. This occurs because the oxygen demand is greater than your ability to utilize oxygen. You are able to continue exercising for a short period because of chemical changes in your body's metabolism which allow you to get the energy you need without oxygen. But anaerobic metabolism cannot go on indefinitely, and you undergo an oxygen debt which you must repay during recovery or rest.

Aerobic exercise is 19 times more economical than anaerobic exercise. The more intensely you exercise, the more quickly and less economically your body's energy is used, and the faster waste products accumulate in muscles in the form of lactic acid. This waste product increases cell activity and interferes with the activities of enzymes. You are limited in the amount of lactic acid that you can tolerate, which means you must at some point cease to exercise and recover. For these reasons, as well as others, you should stick to aerobic activities to develop circulorespiratory endurance.

Prior to undertaking an exercise program you should consider seven things: medical clearance, your initial level of fitness, type of exercise or activity, frequency of participation, duration of participation, intensity of participation, and your personal goals.

Medical Clearance.
If you have any known circulorespiratory problems or hypertension, diabetes, hyperlipidemia, significant obesity or a family history of any of these infirmities, it is especially important that you see a physician before undertaking an exercise program. In addition, the greater the number of years that you have been inactive, the more important it is for you to receive medical clearance. If cardiac disease is suspected as a result of your medical examination and tests, an exercise electrocardiogram (stress test) should be performed. Although there is some disagreement, many medical experts believe that an exercise stress test should be performed routinely on anyone over 35 (or certainly 40) who has been inactive and plans to begin an exercise program.

Stress Test.
A stress test usually consists of either riding a stationary bicycle or of walking or running on a treadmill. In both cases the intensity is gradually increased until either you can no longer continue or a predetermined target heart rate is reached or symptoms of cardiovascular disease are observed which indicate that the test should be terminated.

The test is time-consuming and expensive. A physician must be in attendance to monitor continuously the electrocardiogram (ECG), your reactions, blood pressure and heart rate. At the completion of the test, observations must be continued for up to 10 to 15 minutes or until your signs have returned to the baseline of your resting electrocardiogram. The record is then carefully analyzed to look for minor changes in the pattern and rhythm of the electrocardiogram. The major purpose of the test is to determine whether any parts of the heart muscle are being deprived of needed oxygen, an indication that the coronary arteries are clogged with fatty deposits and cannot provide the necessary nourishment.

The test does not always provide clear-cut answers. It may fail to show coronoary disease which has been demonstrated by other test. The test may also suggest that coronary disease is present when other tests are normal. In addition, changes in the electrocardiogram can be produced by drugs, hyperventilation, and other conditions.

A recent study of more than 2,000 suspected heart patients indicated that the exercise stress test adds little to the information a doctor needs to diagnose possible coronary heart disease. According to the study, the patient's medical history, the nature of the symptoms, and a resting electrocardiogram provide a fairly accurate diagnosis, which the added stress test rarely improves. Equally important, the test failed to indicate heart disease in a large portion of suspected heart patients, particularly males, who were later found to have clogged coronary arteries. Thus, a negative finding in an exercise stress test was of little help. Other studies concluded that the test is only 35 to 40 percent accurate in detecting heart disease during a routine check-up. For these reasons, some medical authorities do not believe the exercise stress test is necessary for individuals who otherwise seem to be healthy, such as those undergoing a routine annual health checkup.

However, other medical professionals do believe in the value of the stress test. Not only should the test be used to screen for underlying coronary disease, according to Dr. John D. Cantwell of the Emory University School of Medicine, but it should also be used to:
- Quantify your level of physical fitness. You may not be as physically fit as you believe you are.
- Assess exercise-related chest pain.
- Screen for exercise-related cardiac dysrhythmias and advise a safe exercise level.
- Screen candidates for cardiac rehabilitation programs.
- Evaluate exercise-related leg cramps.
- Detect unstable hypertension and assess antihypertensive therapy.
- Measure the response to medical surgical antihypertensive therapy.

Certainly you should have a thorough medical examination before initiating your exercise program. If possible, have your examination conducted by a doctor who is familiar with the stress test and seek advice as to whether you need the test.

Your Initial Level of Fitness.

If you have been inactive for some time, your present level of circulorespiratory endurance will probably be low. Prior to undertaking a high-intensity exercise program you should start with physical activity of a mild nature. It your goal is to take up a running program, start with a program of walking for several weeks. If you prefer swimming, perform swimming exercises of a mild intensity for several weeks. This procedure should be followed for any aerobic program. Trying to perform at too high a level too soon will only lead to injury, pain and discomfort, and you will be less likely to want to continue your program.

This guideline should be observed even if you plan to participate in a recreational sport. You should be in the physical condition needed to play that sport, rather than trying to use the sport to get into shape. As a general guideline, be able to expend 200 calories during one exercise session before attempting to intensify your program.

Type of Exercise or Activity

In general, activities with moderate to high energy cost, such as jogging/running, walking, swimming, bicycling, and cross-country skiing yield significant increases in circulorespiratory endurance and reductions in body weight and fat. By contrast, activities that are low in energy cost (below the intensity threshold), such as golf, bowling, and moderate calisthenics, yield no improvement. In addition, weight lifting will promote little or no change in circulorespiratory endurance.

Selection of an aerobic activity should be based upon your health, your interests, and your needs, and it should not cause financial burden or psychological strain. No single exercise will provide a complete program. For example, jogging is excellent for the development of circulorespiratory endurance, but it does not develop flexibility or strength. Thus, it should be supplemented with flexibility and resistance exercise if a complete physical fitness program is desired.

It is important to select an exercise or activity which you can enjoy. Why jog for 30 minutes and truly dislike it? You must be willing to pursue the activity. The circulorespiratory endurance benefits gained from tennis, racquetball and badminton are not as great as those gained from jogging, swimming, and bicycling for most people, but if you will make a commitment to such a program, do it. If your are willing to try, there surely is some endurance-type program you can enjoy. Many individuals combine an endurance program with a recreational program.

Monitoring your heart rate is the easiest technique you can use to determine the intensity of the exercise.

Frequency of Participation.
In the beginning you should limit your exercise to three days per week. This allows sufficient rest for your body between exercise sessions and decreases the likelihood of injury. As your level of fitness improves, you then can progress to four or five days per week. The benefits gained by exceeding five days per week are minimal and often increase the likelihood of injury. However, it you really feel good doing so and prefer to exercise more than five days, do it.

Your preferred exercise frequency may be determined by the number of calories utilized and the duration of each exercise session. Some individuals prefer to exercise 45 to 60 minutes per session, three days a week, while others exercise 30 minutes per session, five days a week. If you followed either program with the same intensity, the total caloric expenditure for the week would vary only a small amount. How frequently you participate is a personal decision, but try to allow no more than two days between exercise sessions, unless you are injured or sick.

Duration of Participation
The duration of each exercise session should be directly related to the intensity (heart rate and calories utilized per minute) and frequency of exercise. Cardiovascular benefits have been achieved by individuals in programs of moderately low intensity (65% to 75% of maximum) when the frequency was at least four days per week and the duration was sufficient to burn 300 or more calories. It appears that 20 to 60 minutes per day of exercise is optimal. Longer exercise sessions may result in greater improvement, but, as was the case with increasing frequency beyond a certain point, the gains are small in proportion to the time invested. Ideally, once you reach a level of fitness which allows you to do so comfortably, seek to expend a minimum of 300 calories each session.

Intensity of Participation
Determining the intensity at which you should exercise is probably the most difficult part of exercise prescription. Also, it is difficult to discuss intensity independently of duration. Circulorespiratory endurance can be developed as long as the intensity of exercise is above a minimal threshold level and a certain amount of total work is completed in an exercise session. In the beginning, your program certainly should be of the low intensity/long duration type. You can gradually increase the intensity during the weeks and months that follow.

Monitoring your heart rate is the easiest technique you can use to determine the intensity of exercise. You can count your heart rate by feeling your pulse in your chest, at the radial artery on the thumb side of your wrist, or at the carotid artery just in front of the large vertical muscle in your neck, next to the Adam's apple. The pulse at the radial artery is difficult to count after intense exercise, so this site is not usually used after hard work. If you use the carotid artery, place your first and second fingers very lightly at the pulse site. Too much pressure on the carotid artery may cause your heart rate to slow down by reflex action.

Because the heart rate begins to decrease immediately after you cease to exercise (usually within 15 seconds), the count should begin as soon as possible. Count the pulsations for 10 seconds and multiply that number by six to determine the number of beats per minute.

To make an accurate estimation of exercise intensity you need to know your resting and maximum heart rates. The best method for determining your maximum heart rate is by using the highest heart rate reached during a maximum graded exercise test (stress test in which you attempt to get your heart rate as high as possible). This method is preferred because there is considerable variation in maximum heart rate.

Another method is to count the heart rate after an all-out 12-minute run or 1.5 mile run. This method is not recommended for beginners or individuals suspected of having coronary problems. If you use this method, it should be only after medical clearance and after you have participated in your exercise program for two to three months.

A third and less accurate method is to subtract your age from 220 (maximum heart rate decreases with age). The inaccuracy of this method is due to the high variability of the maximum heart rate between individuals of the same age. However, even though this method provides only a rough approximation of your maximum heart rate, it is a practical method to use.

To decide at what intensity (target heart rate) you wish to exercise, you must calculate your maximum heart rate range. First find your resting heart rate by counting it in the early morning, just after rising, for 30 seconds, while sitting in a comfortable position, and before eating or smoking. Subtract this from your maximum heart rate. To determine your target heart rate, multiply this difference by a minimum of 50% to 65% and a maximum of 85% to 90%, and add the answer to your resting heart rate.

**To make an accurate estimation of exercise intensity you need to know
your resting and maximum heart rates.**

Example for an individual 42 years of age
220-42=178   Maximum heart rate
   -75   Resting heart rate
  103   Maximum heart rate range
 x.60   % Intensity
61.80   =62

75+62=137 target heart rate

Begin your program with an intensity level of no more than 50% to 60% for 20 to 30 minutes. This is classified as low work. The minimal threshold level for improvement in cardiovascular endurance is approximately 60% of the maximum heart rate range. Generally, a 60% intensity is at a heart rate of 130 to 150 beats for young individuals and 100 to 120 beats for unfit, middle-aged individuals. Thus, the threshold is lower for less-fit people. If after several exercise sessions you believe that you can tolerate a higher intensity, try it. But progress gradually. To avoid injury and unnecessary fatigue, you probably should not increase your intensity more than five percent at any one time. Once you can tolerate it, a 70% to 75% intensity is probably as hard as you will wish to work. You can maintain good cardiovascular endurance with this range of intensity and the appropriate duration. Eight-five percent intensity is the maximum rate at which you should work. Exercising at higher intensities will improve your cardiovascular endurance very little and may result in overwork or chronic fatigue.

During the first several weeks of your program, count your heart rate several times during each exercise session. At times this can be annoying, but you will probably avoid overwork and perform at the appropriate intensity if you follow this procedure. Be especially careful to check your heart rate on warm or hot days. An increase in temperature will, in most cases, cause a corresponding increase in the exercise heart rate. Infectious disease has a similar effect.

Exercise Guidelines

The following guidelines will help you plan a sound exercise program:
- There are individual differences in the ability to tolerate sustained exercise. Do not be discouraged if your progress is slower than that of your friends.
- For every decade of age after 30, it requires about 40% longer for participants to make visible progress in an exercise program. They adapt much more slowly to the exercise; therefore, they should

increase the intensity and duration of their exercise more slowly than should younger participants.

- There are no permanent effects of exercise on the body; your program must be maintained on a regular basis. A fifty percent loss of the improvements gained through exercise has been shown four to twelve weeks after ceasing to exercise.
- At a moderate work load about 50% of your energy comes from fat and about 50% from carbohydrate. With increasing work loads the muscles seem to prefer carbohydrate to fat. The metabolism of carbohydrate results in a greater accumulation of lactic acid. In addition, as glycogen stores are depleted, fatigue results. By working at a low intensity/long duration, you experience less fatigue and utilize more fat.
- Present evidence suggests that the total amount of work accomplished is the important factor in developing and maintaining circulorespiratory fitness. If the total energy cost of the exercise sessions are equal, improvement will be similar for activities performed at a lower intensity/longer duration as compared to higher intensity/shorter duration.
- There is a higher drop-out rate in high intensity programs. A low to moderate intensity for a longer period makes an exercise program safer and more enjoyable for most people. A steady diet of hurt, pain, and fatigue may cause depression.
- Do not place emphasis on the speed at which you can run, swim, bicycle, walk, etc., a certain distance. Remember, heart rate and the number of calories burned are the important considerations for exercise intensity. Do not judge the success of your program with a stopwatch.
- Allow a minimum of 12 to 15 weeks to observe any benefits of your program. You may see some benefits before that time but do not be impatient if you do not. Beginning at a low intensity and slowly progressing will not result in immediate, drastic improvements, but improvement will take place. You have the rest of your life to enjoy exercise, so take your time. And especially avoid the urge to compete with others.
- Low intensity/low duration programs have been shown to be beneficial when lifetime commitments are made. In a study of male runners and joggers between the ages of 35 and 66 years, Hartung and Squires found that for some men, jogging 11 miles per week resulted in dramatic increases in high-density lipoproteins. But, according to the researchers, these increases may take months or years to occur. Dressendorfer and Gahagen reached similar conclusions in a study of

male runners, 22 to 59 years of age. They found no significant differences in serum cholersterol and triglyceride levels between men who ran less than 12 miles per week and those who consistently ran over 28 miles per week. They concluded that running three miles per session, three times a week for several years may be enough to lower serum levels to acceptable levels.

- Other studies have concluded that your exercise program should utilize at least 2,000 calories a week. Individuals who expend this many calories are in the highest fitness category and have lower coronary risk profiles than their less fit colleagues.

- Many people do not enjoy their exercise sessions until 10 to 15 minutes have passed. It takes the body several minutes to adapt to the demands of the exercise, but there are probably other reasons for this initial lack of enjoyment. It may be because we are so time conscious, and it takes several minutes to dissociate from our mental calendar and timetable. As we get further into the exercise, we begin to forget our problems and frustrations.

By extending your exercise session to 30 minutes or more you can become more aware of the enjoyment that can result from the exercise and retreat from the emphasis on time and speed which is too pervasive in our society. This is especially important if you plan to use exercise to help you cope with stress and/or depression. The exercise time can be a chance to dream, relax, and experience mental freedom.

- Try to become "body conscious" and do what your body says. For the first few months it is important to monitor your heart rate but you can train yourself to be aware of effort and fatigue and know approximately what your heart rate is.

- Exercise can become addictive. This addiction can be used in a positive way for your health+ program if it is not carried to the extreme. Recognizing the importance of exercise and attempting to maintain a regular program is good, but do not allow the program to impair your judgment. Some people believe that they should never miss an exercise session. They ignore warning signs such as chest pains, and attempt to continue their program in spite of injury or illness. Often more serious problems occur because of their refusal to miss a few days of exercise. Your exercise should be a means to an end (health+) and not an end in itself. Control your exercise sessions; do not allow them to control you. Determine how much exercise provides you pleasure and benefits, and do not go beyond that point.

A related problem is overtraining. It is not always true that if a little bit of exercise is good then a great deal is much better. The competitive urge often causes people to overtrain. Many inexperienced runners make this mistake. If you experience such symptoms as persistant soreness, frequent mild colds and sore throats, swelling and aching in the lymph glands, excessive nervousness, depression, irritability, headaches and inability to relax or sleep, nagging fatigue and general sluggishness, unwanted loss of appetite or weight, diarrhea, unexplained drops in performance levels and disinterest in normally exciting activities—do not attempt to relieve them with more exercise. So what if you miss a few days of exercise? You will lose very little of what you have gained in your training by missing a few days. In fact, you probably will have more enthusiasm once you begin exercising again. Remember, however, the more days you miss, the more slowly you should progress back to your usual exercise routine. Perform a few sessions of lower intensity/shorter duration upon your return to the program.

- Do not exercise within two hours of a substanial meal, and replace the fluids you lose. Thirst cannot always be counted upon as a guide for the replacement of fluids. Weigh yourself before and after each exercise session. If you weigh a couple of pounds less after the exercise session and do not regain that weight prior to your next exercise session (and you are not attempting to lose weight), you probably are not replacing your fluids. It may be necessary to force yourself to drink more fluids.

- Reduce the intensity and duration of your program on hot days. This is especially important if the humdity is high. It may be necessary to exercise in the early morning or early evening to avoid the heat of midday.

- Always warm-up and cool-down. Your exercise session should begin with a 10-15 minute warm-up and muscle conditioning. This warm-up not only lessens the possibility of muscle and tendon injury, it also may prevent serious damage to the heart. Studies have confirmed that when sudden strenuous exercise is performed without prior warm-up, abnormal electrocardiographic changes and an abnormal increase in blood pressure may occur. The studies suggest that the adaptation of coronary blood flow to a rapid increase in cardiac work is not instantaneous, and that periods of inadequate blood flow may occur in hearts without apparent vascular obstruction. With proper warm-up these abnormal changes are less likely to take place. If on occasion you have less time for your exercise session, decrease your exercise time, don't forego the warm-up period.

In addition, always allow time to cool-down. Keep moving after any strenuous exercise. When you stop suddenly and remain in a vertical position, your muscles stop pumping blood back to the heart and ventilation no longer assists venous return. Consequently, the blood

pools in the legs, resulting in a drop in blood pressure and in adequate circulation to the brain. This will cause you to feel lightheaded and dizzy, and possibly to faint. Do not neglect to cool-down. Allow time for your cardiovascular system to slow down gradually to a state of equilibrium.
● Make your exercise session a pleasant time. Avoid unhappy thoughts. Look forward to your exercise.

Your Goals.
You now should be able to state your exercise goals. They may be related to self-image, depression, circulorespiratory endurance, weight management, stress, or any other considerations. It is important to establish realistic goals that you can fulfill and to consider sound exercise principles and guidelines when stating them. Remember, no goal can be too small, and it is important to recognize each of your achievements. With the inspiration of fulfilling your goals, you will remain more faithful to your program. Once you reach a satisfactory level of physical fitness and attain your major goals, the most important goal may be to maintain what you have. Make a lifetime commitment to your program.

Aerobic Activities
Five popular aerobic activities are aerobic dance, bicycling, jogging/running, rope skipping, and walking. There are other excellent activities such as cross-country skiing, hiking, and rowing, but they will not be discussed.

Aerobic Dance
This activity is rhythmic movement—walking, jogging, running, hopping, skipping, calisthenics—performed to music. Begun in 1969 under the leadership of Jacki Sorensen, aerobic dance classes are held throughout the U.S. The usual class consists of warm-up calisthenics, 30 to 35 minutes of vigorous aerobic movement, and five minutes of cooling-down activities. Heart rate is monitored during the sesion to determine the intensity of the exercise.

One study concluded that moderate-intensity aerobic sessions are comparable to ice skating at 9 mph, walking at 3½ mph, or bicycling at 30 mph, and that high-intensity sessions are equivalent to one half hour of vigorous basketball, cycling at 13 mph and swimming at 55 yards per minute. In caloric terms, another study found that the average size woman utilizes 3.96 calories per minute in a low-intensity routine, 6.28 calories per minute in a medium-intensity routine, and 7.75 calories per minute in a high-intensity routine. The average size man utilizes 4.17

calories in a low-intensity, 6.86 calories in a medium intensity, and 9.44 calories in a high-intensity workout.

Many different aerobic dance routines are available on records and tapes. Through the use of the records or tapes you can perform the routines in your home and at the intensity level of your choice.

Bicycling
Even though it is an excellent activity for all ages, bicycling is especially good for the overweight and very unfit who might have leg and foot problems with weight bearing activities. Most people enjoy bicycling and do not look upon it as work.

Perhaps such an attitude is the biggest disadvantage of this program. Because individuals do not look upon it as work, they often do not perform at a high enough intensity to promote cardiovascular benefits. It is necessary to pedal at a reasonably fast pace, use the gears to provide resistance, or pedal up hills to elevate the heart rate. However, a nice easy pace may be very beneficial for you mentally.

There are a few minor problems with this activity that you should consider. In addition to being limited by the weather on occasion, you may have some difficulty finding an appropriate place to cycle. Bicycling does not contribute to flexibility, so additional exercises should be included in your overall program. In fact, the posterior leg muscles may lose some flexibility if appropriate exercises are not performed.

Jogging/Running
Jogging is performed at a slower pace than running. For both activities the heart rate should be monitored to determine the intensity of the exercise. They are both excellent aerobic activities, they can be regulated very easily, and they can be done by almost anyone.

If you choose to undertake a running program, you should observe these guidelines:
- Walk for several weeks before you attempt to run.
- Do not attempt to run too fast or put in too many miles before you are ready. Progress slowly. Do not be out of breath when running; emphasize breathing more deeply rather than more often. The most common cause of running injuries is trying to progress too quickly.
- Monitor your heart rate. Run for a certain length of time at a target heart rate. This means you may run further on cool days than you do on hot days. If you choose to run a certain distance, emphasize the heart rate rather than the speed at which you can run the distance.
- Purchase good running shoes. Do not try to get by with cheap shoes; this can cause problems.

- Perform flexibility exercises for the back and legs before and after running. Running may cause a shortening of the posterior leg muscles.
- Listen to your body. Jog when you feel good, walk when you feel tired. Do not ignore pain. Pain that does not go away with rest should be treated. Pain does not have to be a part of the program.
- Use a comfortable running style.

Rope Skipping

Rope skipping can increase the heart rate substantially and be quite strenuous. In fact, it may be too severe for the average untrained adult starting a fitness program. A person should be able to walk briskly for two or three miles before beginning a skipping program.

When energy expenditure (calories burned per minute) comparisons are made at the same heart rate, jogging appears to be better for developing cardiovascular endurance because it involves more muscle mass than skipping in place. If you want physiological benefits from rope skipping, the intensity and duration should be at least as great as they would be if you were jogging. Do not be misled by claims that jumping rope for 10 minutes is equivalent to 30 minutes of jogging.

Warm-up and stretching exercises should be included in the program. Stretching exercises for the posterior lower legs, ankles, and feet are especially important. One major precaution: rope skipping, like running in place, is performed on the balls of the feet. Over long periods this can cause injury and pain to the feet. Be aware of how your feet are responding.

Walking

Done at progressively increasing rates and distances, walking can provide a sufficient stimulus to bring about circulorespiratory benefits, especially for poorly conditioned or older individuals. It reduces the likelihood of joint irritation and muscle soreness, and it is also a very low risk to the heart and blood vessels. Most walking participants will remain within the recommended guidelines. However, to promote circulorespiratory endurance, the minimum threshold intensity level must be reached. Flexibility exercises should be included in the program as well.

Sudden Death

Sudden death is defined as death from natural causes occurring in a person who was not restricted to home, hospital, or institution, and who during the preceding 24 hours was able to function in normal surroundings and activities. Most sudden deaths are heart related.

In spite of ample evidence that the overwhelming majority of heart attacks occur in bed, at rest, or during mild activity, many people fear that exercise will bring on a heart attack. Sudden deaths can occur in all types of physical activity; but more importantly, the victims are often individuals who have not felt well and have decided to take up exercise to feel better, who have continued to exercise despite such symptoms as "indigestion," weakness, shortness of breath, and other signs of heart disease. Thus, many sudden deaths occur because individuals ignore the symptoms and the advice of their physician, or fail to receive medical clearance before beginning their exercise programs.

The number of heart-related exercise deaths is very small relative to the number of people exercising and benefitting from their exercise. However, to decrease the risk of such an occurrence: get medical clearance before you initiate an exercise program, begin at a low intensity, progress slowly, and avoid the urge to be competitive.

12

Success With Your Health+ Program

*. . . the beginning of wise ambition lies in
a man's accepting himself as himself and not
as someone else, and in trying to make the
most and the best of that self and not of
another.*
   Henry Emerson Fosdick

Since 1960, the nation's total spending on health care has increased
from $27 billion a year to over $212 billion a year with the federal
government paying 43 cents of each dollar spent. In 1960, less than six
percent of the gross national product went to health care; today the
figure is nine percent. Despite significant advances in the health care
fields, death rates and life expectancies have improved little over the last
generation.

What is the solution to these health problems? Taking responsibility
for your own health! Your health is far more likely to be imperiled by your
own conduct than by any other factor. According to Dr. Richard E. Palmer
of the American Medical Association, "The medical system affects
about 10 percent of the usual factors that determine a patient's state of
health." The doctors have little or no control over the remaining 90
percent. In other words, your personal health decisions offer better hope
for your health than the medical system.

You now should have the knowledge to make changes in your lifestyle
and to plan an organized health+ program. Hopefully, you also have the
motivation to do so. The success of your attempt to achieve health+ is
directly related to your inner motivation. There are things you can do to
keep your motivation alive, and thereby assure your success.

● Value your health and be aware of the threats to it. The responsibility
   for your health rests with you, and health+ must be a lifetime pursuit.
   Treat your body with respect; it's the only one you have. You won't
   get a second chance if you fail to take care of it.

- You must not only recognize the threats to your health; you must also believe that there are ways to reduce or eliminate those threats.
- Believe in your ability to control the threats to your health. Believe in your ability to rise above any failure that you encounter along the way, and believe that success is possible. Have confidence in your ability to control the outcome of your efforts, and persist in your efforts.
- Seek to understand and accept yourself. Like yourself, don't put yourself down, and plan to become all you are capable of becoming.
- Have the courage to risk your self-image. Accept that without risks there are no challenges, and without challenges you will not grow psychologically.
- If you fail to reach a goal for some reason, aim for another one.
- Accept that things will not always go your way. Praise rather than gripe, and be adaptable. Be open-minded and seek alternative approaches. React aggressively and positively when a different approach must be followed.
- Be a self-starter, have a sense of direction, and dwell on your health+ goals. Know what you want to accomplish in your health+ program. Be capable of clearly stating and visualizing your goals. Plan to keep moving forward with your program.
- Be aware of how your time is used, and place your responsibilties and personal wants in a priority order. Schedule time for your health+ program. Recognize that the fulfillment of your health+ goals is necessary to help you better fulfill other goals in your life.
- Be prepared to make sacrifices when necessary to reach your health+ goals. If the "sacrifice" is in the interest of your health, it really is not a sacrifice.
- Gradually change your health habits and monitor your progress in terms of permanent behavior change. The positive changes you see will serve to provide inner motivation.
- Admit the difference between "can not" and "will not." Avoid having to look back one day and say, "I regret not having tried."

HEALTH+! GO FOR IT!

Appendix

CALORIC AND NUTRITIONAL VALUE OF FOODS*

Food Item	Measure	Calories	Fiber (gm)	Carbohydrate Calories	Carbohydrate Percentage	Protein Calories	Protein Percentages	Total Fat Calories	Total Fat Percentage	Saturated Fat Calories	Saturated Fat Percentage	Unsaturated Fat Calories	Unsaturated Fat Percentage	Cholesterol (mg)	Sodium (mg)
BEVERAGES															
Alcoholic															
Beer, 4.5% alcohol	12 oz	150	0	56	37 %	4	3 %	0	0	0	0%	0	0%	0	21
Daiquiri	3.5 oz	122	0	21	17	4	2.5	0	0	0	0	0	0	0	
Gin, Rum, Vodka, Whiskey															
80-proof	1.5 oz	95	0	T	0	0	0	0	0	0	0	0	0	0	T
86-proof	1.5 oz	105	0	T	0	0	0	0	0	0	0	0	0	0	T
90-proof	1.5 oz	110	0	T	0	0	0	0	0	0	0	0	0	0	T
94-proof	1.5 oz	117	0	T	0	0	0	0	0	0	0	0	0	0	T
100-proof	1.5 oz	126	0	1	0	0	0	0	0	0	0	0	0	0	
Martini	3.5 oz	140	0	T	.7	T		0	0	0	0	0	0	0	T
Tom Collins	10 oz	180	0	36	20	T		0	0	0	0	0	0	0	T
Wines															
Sweet, 18.8% alcohol	3.5 oz	140	0	32	23	T		0	0	0	0	0	0	0	5
Dry, 12.2% alcohol	3.5 oz	85	0	16	19	T		0	0	0	0	0	0	0	4
Common															
Club Soda	8 oz	0	0	0	0	0	0	0	0	0	0	0	0	0	59
Coffee, black	8 oz	5	0	3	60	1	20	1	20	0	0	0	0	0	2.3
Cola Drinks	12 oz	145	0	145	100	0	0	0	0	0	0	0	0	0	3
Fruit-flavored Drinks	12 oz	170	0	170	100	0	0	0	0	0	0	0	0	0	18
Diet Drinks	12 oz	T	0	0	0	0	0	0	0	0	0	0	0	0	
Ginger Ale	12 oz	115	0	115	100	0	0	0	0	0	0	0	0	0	18
Root Beer	12 oz	150	0	150	100	0	0	0	0	0	0	0	0	0	18
Tea, clear	8 oz	4	T	3.7	92	T	0	T	0	0	0	0	0	0	1.6

*Blank spaces indicate that analysis of the food for that nutrient is lacking; zero confirms the absence of a nutrient. Total percentages may not equal 100 due to rounding off of values. Adapted from Kirschmann JD (Director, Nutrition, Inc): Nutrition Almanac. New York City, McGraw-Hill Book Company, 1979 and Composition of Foods. Agriculture Handbook No. 8, Department of Agriculture.

BREADS, FLOURS, CEREALS, GRAINS, AND GRAIN PRODUCTS

Food Item	Measure	Calories	Fiber (gm)	Carbohydrate Calories	Carbohydrate Percentage	Protein Calories	Protein Percentages	Total Fat Calories	Total Fat Percentage	Saturated Fat Calories	Saturated Fat Percentage	Unsaturated Fat Calories	Unsaturated Fat Percentage	Cholesterol (mg)	Sodium (mg)
Bagel, egg	3" diam.	165		120	73%	25	15%	20	12%	5	3%	15	9%		6
Barley, pearled, light, uncooked	8 oz	790	.7	705	89	66	8	17	2	T	0	17	2		
Bran, wheat, raw	8 oz	121	5.2	83	69	16	13	22	18	3.5	2	15	8		5.13
Breads															
Biscuit, enr.	2" diam.	105	.1	52	50	9	8	44	42	9	9	27	26		175
Cornbread, whl grd	2" square	93	.2	52	56	13	14	28	30	7	8	20	22	283	283
Cracked wheat, enr.	1 slice	60	.1	48	80	7	12	5	8	1	2	4	7		122
French or Vienna	1 slice	58	T	45	78	7	12	6	10	1	2	4	7		116
Italian	1 slice	55	T	45	82	7	13	3	5	T		2	4		117
Pumpernickel	1 slice	70	.4	64	91	4	6	2	3						182
Raisin	1 slice	60	.2	48	80	6	10	6	10	2	3	4	7		84
Rye, American	1 slice	60	.1	50	83	7	12	3	5						128
White	1 slice	65	T	48	74	8	12	9	14	2	3	5	8	117	117
Whole wheat	1 slice	65	.4	44	67	12	18	9	14	1	2	4	6		121
Buns (hamburger, hot dog)	1 avg	120		86	72	13	11	21	18	5	4	15	13		202
Corn (hominy) grits; degermed	1 cup	125	.2	111	89	12	10	2	2	T	1	2	2		502
Corn meal, whl grd, dry	1 cup	435	1.2	363	83	30	7	42	10	4		25	6		1
Corn meal, degermed, ckd	1 cup	119	.2	106	89	8	7	5	4			3	3		T
Cornstarch	1 tbsp	29	T	28		T		T		T		T			.32
Crackers															
Graham, plain	1 large	55	.22	40	73	4	7	11	20	3	5	8	15	95	95
Rye wafers, whole-grain	2 avg	45	.3	38	84	7	16	T	T			7			111
Soda	1 avg	13		8	61	1	8	4	31	.1					31
Soup or oyster	10	33		21	64	3	9	9	27						83
Cream of wheat, ckd	1 cup	133	.1	113	85	17	13	3	2						3.7

CALORIC AND NUTRITIONAL VALUE OF FOODS (continued)

Food Item	Measure	Calories	Fiber (gm)	Carbohydrate Calories	Carbohydrate Percentage	Protein Calories	Protein Percentages	Total Fat Calories	Total Fat Percentage	Saturated Fat Calories	Saturated Fat Percentage	Unsaturated Fat Calories	Unsaturated Fat Percentage	Cholesterol (mg)	Sodium (mg)
Flour															
Buckwheat, dark, sftd.	1 cup	333	1.6	273	82%	39	12%	21	6%	4	1%	15	5%		1
Buckwheat, light, sftd.	1 cup	347	.5	315	91	22	6	10	3	2	1	7	2		1
Corn	1 cup	431	.8	369	86	34	8	28	6	3	1	22	5		3
Peanut, defatted	1 cup	223	1.6	77	34	100	45	46	21	10	4	33	15		5
Potato	1 cup	386	1.8	355	92	24	6	7	2						37.4
Rice, granulated	1 cup	479	.2	445	93	30	6	4	1						37.4
Rye, Dark, sftd	1 cup	419	3.1	329	78	62	15	28	7	4	1	8	2		1
Rye, light, sftd	1 cup	286	.3	253	88	26	9	7	2						1
Soy, full-fat, stirred	1 cup	303	1.7	91	30	92	30	120	40	21	7	89	29		1
Soy, low-fat, stirred	1 cup	356	2.5	149	42	151	42	56	16	9	3	41	12		1
Soy, defatted, stirred	1 cup	450	3.2	208	46	221	49	21	5						1
Wheat, all purpose, sftd	1 cup	400	.3	345	86	45	11	10	3	T					4
Wheat, whole, stirred	1 cup	400	2.8	323	81	57	14	20	5			17	4		1
Macaroni, enr, ckd	1 cup	160	.1	133	83	19	12	8	5						1
Muffins															
Plain	1 avg	118	.1	74	63	11	9	33	28	8	7	25	21	21	176
Bran	1 avg	104	.7	65	62	6	6	33	32	10	10	20	19		179
Corn meal, whl grd	1 avg	130	.2	78	60	12	9	40	31	19	15	18	14		223
Whole wheat	1 avg	103	.6	80	78	14	13	9	9						226
Noodles, egg, enr, ckd	1 cup	200	.2	154	77	26	13	20	10	8	4	8	4	50	3
Oatmeal (rolled oats), ckd	1 cup	132	.5	96	73	16	12	20	15	3	2	15	11		1
Pancakes															
Plain	4" diam	62	.1	39	63	7	11	16	26	4	6	11	18	115	
Buckwheat, from mix	4" diam	54	.2	26	48	7	13	21	39	7	13	13	24		125
Whole Wheat	4" diam	74		33	45	14	19	27	36						
Pasta, whole, wheat, dry	4 oz	400		320	80	72	18	8	2						
Pizza, cheese, 14" diam	1/8	153	.2	74	48	31	20	48	31	18	12	27	18		456
Popcorn, plain	1 cup	54	.3	43	80	5	9	6	11	T		5			T

Food Item	Measure	Calories	Fiber (gm)	Carbohydrate Calories	Carbohydrate Percentage	Protein Calories	Protein Percentages	Total Fat Calories	Total Fat Percentage	Saturated Fat Calories	Saturated Fat Percentage	Unsaturated Fat Calories	Unsaturated Fat Percentage	Cholesterol (mg)	Sodium (mg)
Pretzel, twisted	1 avg	62	.1	50	80%	6	10%	6	10%						269
Rice															
Brown, raw	1 cup	704	1.6	624	89	50	7	30	4	3	2%	8	5%		16
Brown, ckd w/salt	1 cup	178	.5	155	87	13	7	10	6	1		2	1		423
Instant, enr, ckd, w/salt	1 cup	180	.1	166	92	14	8	T		1	.5	2	1		450
Parboiled, enr, ckd w/salt	1 cup	186	.2	169	91	14	7	3	2						627
White, ckd w/salt	1 cup	223	.2	205	92	15	7	3	1	1	.5				627
Wild, raw	1 cup	565	.1	477	84	79	14	9	2						11
Rice, polish or bran	1 cup	278	2.4	145	52	24	9	109	39	20	7	78	28		T
Rolls															
Danish, enr	1 avg	179	T	78	43	12	7	89	50	29	16	59	32		156
Dinner, enr	1 avg	113	.1	81	72	12	10	20	18	5	4	13	12		192
Hard, enr	1 avg	156	.1	120	77	21	13	15	10	3	2	7	4		313
Whole wheat	1 avg	90	.6	69	77	13	14	8	9	T		3			197
Shredded Wheat, Biscuit	1 avg	89	.5	76	85	9	10	4	5			3	3		1
Spaghetti, enr, ckd	1 cup	155	.2	132	85	18	12	5	3						1
Tapioca, dry	1 cup	535	.15	529	99	3	.5	3	.5						5
Tortilla, yellow corn	6" diam	63	.3	54	86	4	6	5	8						
Waffles, plain, enr	5½" diam	209	.1	119	57	28	13	62	30	17	8	42	20		356
Wheat germ, raw	1 cup	363	2.5	178	49	96	26	91	25	16	4	68	19		3
Wheat flakes, fortified	1 cup	106	.5	89	84	11	10	6	6	1	1	4	4		310
Wheat, puffed, fortified w/o sugar, salt	1 cup	54	.2	44	81	8	15	2	4						1
Wheatmeal cereal															
Dry	1 cup	423	.75	340	80	60	14	23	5	3	3	8	7	45	3
Cooked	1 cup	110		88	80	16	15	6	5						T

CALORIC AND NUTRITIONAL VALUE OF FOODS (continued)

Food Item	Measure	Calories	Fiber (gm)	Carbohydrate Calories	Carbohydrate Percentage	Protein Calories	Protein Percentages	Total Fat Calories	Total Fat Percentage	Saturated Fat Calories	Saturated Fat Percentage	Unsaturated Fat Calories	Unsaturated Fat Percentage	Cholesterol (mg)	Sodium (mg)
DAIRY PRODUCTS															
Cheese															
American, pasteurized, processed	1 oz	107	0	2	2%	28	26%	77	72%	49	46%	25	23%	27	406
Bleu	1 oz	103	0	3	3	27	26	73	71	47	46	21	20	21	396
Brick	1 oz	103	0	3	3	27	26	73	71	47	46	21	20	27	159
Brie	1 oz	95	0	.5	.5	25	26	69	73					28	178
Camembert, domestic	1 oz	84	0	2	2	22	26	60	71	38	45	19	23	20	239
Cheddar, American	1 oz	112	0	1	1	29	26	82	73	53	47	26	23	30	176
Cheddar, American, grated, not packed	1 cup	455	0	6	1	120	26	329	72	209	46	103	23	119	701
Cheese spread, American, pasteurized, processed	1 oz	81	0	9	11	19	23	53	65	33	41	17	21	16	381
Colby	1 oz	112	0	3	3	29	26	80	71	50	45	25	22	27	171
Cottage, creamed, not packed	1 cup	217	0	22	10	112	52	83	38	53	24	26	12	31	850
Cottage, 2% fat, not packed	1 cup	203	0	32	16	132	65	39	19	24	12	12	6	19	918
Cottage, dry, not packed	1 cup	123	0	10	8	107	87	6	5	3	2	2	2	10	19
Cream	1 oz	105	0	2	2	10	9	93	89	52	50	32	30	31	70
Edam	1 oz	101	0	2	2	32	32	67	66	44	44	22	22	25	274
Gjetost	1 oz	132	0	47	36	12	9	73	55	48	36	22	17		170
Gouda	1 oz	101	0	3	3	30	30	68	67	44	44	21	21	32	232
Limberger	1 oz	93	0	1	1	24	26	68	73	42	45	23	25	26	227
Monterey	1 oz	106	0	1	1	30	28	75	71						152
Mozzarella	1 oz	80	0	4	5	23	29	53	66	33	41	18	23	22	106
Mozzarella, part skim, low moisture	1 oz	79	0	3	4	33	42	43	54	27	34	13	16	15	150
Muenster	1 oz	104	0	1	1	28	27	75	72	48	46	23	22	27	178
Parmesan, hard	1 oz	110	0	3	3	43	39	64	58	41	37	20	18	19	205
Parmesan, grated	1 tbsp	23	0	1	4	9	39	13	57	8	35	4	17	4	93

Food Item	Measure	Calories	Fiber (gm)	Carbohydrate Calories	Carbohydrate Percentage	Protein Calories	Protein Percentages	Total Fat Calories	Total Fat Percentage	Saturated Fat Calories	Saturated Fat Percentage	Unsaturated Fat Calories	Unsaturated Fat Percentage	Cholesterol (mg)	Sodium (mg)
Cheese (continued)															
Port du Salut	1 oz	100	0	1	2	29	29	70	70	42	42	25	25	35	151
Provolone	1 oz	100	0	2	2	31	31	67	67	43	43	20	20	20	248
Ricotta, whl milk	1 cup	428	0	30	7	118	28	280	65	179	42	87	20	124	207
Ricotta, part skim	1 cup	340	0	49	14	120	35	171	50	106	31	53	16	9	307
Roquefort	1 oz	105	0	2	2	26	25	77	73	48	46	24	23	26	513
Swiss	1 oz	107	0	4	4	35	33	68	63	44	41	21	20	26	74
Swiss, pasteurized, processed	1 oz	95	0	2	2	30	32	63	66	40	42	19	20	24	388
Cheese souffle, cheddar	1 cup	207	0	23	11	41	20	143	69	75	36	59	29	159	346
Cream															
Half and Half	1 cup	315	0	40	13	31	10	244	77	152	48	80	25	89	98
Half and Half	1 tbsp	20	0	3	15	2	10	15	75	9	45	5	25	6	6
Coffee or table	1 tbsp	29	0	2	7	2	7	25	86	16	55	8	28	10	6
Sour, cultured	1 cup	497	0	38	8	31	6	428	86	264	53	138	28	102	123
Whipping, lt	1 cup	699	0	27	4	22	3	650	93	406	58	209	30	265	82
Whipping, hvy	1 cup	821	0	26	3	21	3	774	94	482	59	252	31	326	89
Eggs															
Raw, ext lge	1	94	0	2	2	32	34	60	64	20	21	24	26	351	70
Raw, lge	1	82	0	2	2	28	34	52	63	17	21	21	26	312	61
Raw, med	1	72	0	1	1	25	35	46	64	16	22	19	26	274	54
Raw, sm	1	65	0	1	1	23	35	41	63	12	18	15	23	219	49
Raw, white	1 lg	17	0	T	6	16	94	0	0	0	0	0	0	0	48
Raw, yolk	1 lg	59	0	T	T	12	20	47	80	16	27	27	46	312	9
Fried (½ tsp fat & dash of salt)	1 lg	99	0	2	2	26	26	71	72	22	22	9	9	319	144
Hard cooked	1 lg	99	0	2	2	28	34	52	63	17	21	30	37	312	61
Omelet or scrambled (1½ tbsp milk, ½ tsp fat, & dash salt)	1 egg	111	0	6	5	31	28	74	67	25	23	30	27	314	164
Poached	1 lg	82	0	2	2	28	34	52	63	15	18	27	33	312	61
Dried, whole	2 tbsp	60	0	2	3	20	33	38	63	11	18	20	33	210	52

CALORIC AND NUTRITIONAL VALUE OF FOODS (continued)

Food Item	Measure	Calories	Fiber (gm)	Carbohydrate Calories	Carbohydrate Percentage	Protein Calories	Protein Percentages	Total Fat Calories	Total Fat Percentage	Saturated Fat Calories	Saturated Fat Percentage	Unsaturated Fat Calories	Unsaturated Fat Percentage	Cholesterol (mg)	Sodium (mg)
ggnog (8 oz whole milk, one egg, & 3 tsp sugar)	1 cup	342	0	128	37%	42	12%	172	50%	102	30%	59	17%	149	138
e cream, hard	1 cup	269	0	123	46	20	7	126	47	78	29	41	15	59	116
e milk, hard	1 cup	184	0	113	61	22	12	49	27	31	17	16	9	18	105
Milk															
Buttermilk	1 cup	99	0	45	45	35	35	19	19	12	12	6	6	9	257
Chocolate, whole	1 cup	208	0	100	48	34	16	74	36	46	22	25	12	30	149
Condensed, sweetened	1 cup	982	0	642	65	106	11	234	24	148	15	74	8	104	389
Dried, whole	1 cup	635	0	190	30	144	23	301	47	188	30	97	15	124	475
Dried, whole, instant	1 cup	527	0	155	29	118	22	254	48					65	425
Dried, nonfat	1 cup	435	0	242	56	102	42	4	2	3	1	1	.5	12	373
Dried, nonfat, instant	1 cup	244	0	137	56	102	42	4	2	3	1	1	.5	12	373
Evaporated, whole, unsw	1 cup	338	0	98	29	73	22	167	49	102	30	57	17	74	266
Evaporated, skim, unsw	1 cup	198	0	112	57	81	41	5	2	3	2	5	1	10	294
Goat, whole	1 cup	168	0	42	25	37	22	89	53	57	34	12	7	28	122
Human	1 oz	21	0	8	38	1	5	12	57	5	24	6	29	4	5
Low-fat	1 cup	121	0	45	37	35	29	41	34	26	21	13	11	18	122
Malted (8 oz whole milk, one egg, 3 tsp sugar)	1 cup	236	.13	103	44	46	19	87	37	52	22	30	35	37	215
Skim	1 cup	86	0	46	53	36	42	4	5	3	3	1	1	4	126
Whole	1 cup	159	0	47	29	36	23	76	48	45	28	23	9	33	120
Sherbet	1 cup	270	T	277	84	9	3	34	13	21	8	11	4	14	88
Whey, sweet, dry	1 tbsp	26	0	21	81	4	15	1	4	T	T	T	T	T	80
Yogurt															
Whole milk, plain	8 oz	139	0	41	29	33	24	65	47	42	30	20	14	29	105
Low-fat, plain, 12 gm protein	8 oz	114	0	62	43	51	35	31	22	20	14	9	6	14	159
Skim, plain, 13 gm protein	8 oz	127	0	67	53	56	44	4	3	2	2	1	1	4	174
Low-fat, fruit, 9 gm protein	8 oz	225	.27	163	72	39	17	23	10	15	7	7	3	10	121
Low-fat, fruit, 11 gm protein	8 oz	239	.27	164	69	47	19	28	12	18	8	9	4	12	147

DESSERTS AND SWEETS

Food Item	Measure	Calories	Fiber (gm)	Carbohydrate Calories	Carbohydrate Percentage	Protein Calories	Protein Percentages	Total Fat Calories	Total Fat Percentage	Saturated Fat Calories	Saturated Fat Percentage	Unsaturated Fat Calories	Unsaturated Fat Percentage	Cholesterol (mg)	Sodium (mg)
Apple or Brown Betty (enr bread)	1 cup	325	1.4	245	75%	12	4%	68	21%	18	6%	18	6%		329
Apple Butter	1 tbsp	33	.2	32	97	T	0	1	3						T
Boston Cream Pie, 1/8 cake	1 piece	311	0	202	65	22	7	87	28	27	9	45	14		192
Brownies, enr, 2x2x3/4	1 piece	146	.2	52	36	9	6	85	58	14	10	54	37	26	75
Cake															
Angel Food, 1/10 cake	1 piece	121	0	106	88	14	11	1	1						127
Chocolate, devils food, no icing, 2x3x2	1 piece	165	.1	87	53	9	5	69	42						132
Gingerbread, enr, 3x3x2	1 piece	371	T	242	65	18	5	113	30						277
Pound, old-fashioned, 3x3x1/2	1 piece	142	T	57	40	7	5	78	55						33
Pound, low-fat, 3x3x1/2	1 piece	123	T	65	53	8	6	50	41						53
Sponge, 1/10 cake	1 piece	149	0	107	72	16	11	26	17	9	6	9	6		84
White, no icing	1 piece	188	.1	106	56	10	5	72	38	18	10	45	24	123	162
Cake icing															
Chocolate	1 cup	1034	T	656	63	38	4	340	33	187	18	134	13		168
White, boiled	1 cup	297	0	291	98	6	2	0	0	0	0	0	0		134
Candied citron	1 oz	89	.39	88	99	T	0	1	1						82
Candy															
Caramel, plain or chocolate	1 piece	20	.01	14	70	1	5	5	25	3	15	2	10		11
Chocolate milk bar, plain	1 oz	147	.11	57	39	0	6	81	55	45	31	27	18		27
Chocolate, fudge	1 cube	84	.04	55	65	3	4	26	31	13	15	7	8		40
Mint patty, chocolate-covered	1-3/8 diam	45	T	33	73	1	2	11	24						20
Peanut brittle	1 oz	119	.13	90	76	6	5	23	19	4	3	16	13		9
Chocolate															
Bitter or baking	1 oz	143	.7	11	8	6	4	126	88	67	47	50	35		
Bittersweet	1 oz	135	.5	36	27	4	3	95	70						1
Semisweet	1 oz	144	.28	58	40	2	1	84	58	47	33	32	22		1

CALORIC AND NUTRITIONAL VALUE OF FOODS (continued)

Food Item	Measure	Calories	Fiber (gm)	Carbohydrate Calories	Carbohydrate Percentage	Protein Calories	Protein Percentages	Total Fat Calories	Total Fat Percentage	Saturated Fat Calories	Saturated Fat Percentage	Unsaturated Fat Calories	Unsaturated Fat Percentage	Cholesterol (mg)	Sodium (mg)
Chocolate syrup	1 tbsp	46	.1	40	87%	2	4%	4	9%	T	T%	T	T%		10
Cookies															
Chocolate chip, enr, 2-1/3 diam	1	51	T	24	47	2	2	25	49	8	16	17	33		35
Fig bar	1	50	.24	41	82	2	4	7	14	1	2	4	8		35
Gingersnap, 2" diam	1	29	T	23	79	1	3	5	17						40
Macaroon	1 med	67	.3	37	55	3	4	27	40	19	28	7	10		5
Oatmeal w/raisin, 3" diam	1	63	.1	42	67	3	5	18	28						23
Vanilla wafer	1	17	T	11	65	1	6	5	29						9.3
Custard, baked	1 cup	305	0	113	37	62	20	130	43	59	19	50	16	278	209
Doughnut															
Cake, plain	1 avg	125	T	66	53	6	5	53	42	8	6	33	26		160
Raised, plain	1 avg	124		49	40	8	6	67	54	15	12	48	39		70
Eclair, custard, chocolate icing	1 avg	239	0	91	38	27	11	121	51	33	14	67	28		82
Honey	1 tbsp	64	0	64	100	T	T	0	0						1
Jams, preserves	1 tbsp	54	.1	53	98	T	T	T	T						2
Jellies	1 tbsp	49	T	48	98	0	0	T	T						3
Molasses															
Blackstrap	1 tbsp	43		42	98	0	0	0							19
Light	1 tbsp	50		49	98	0	0	0							3
Pie															
Apple, 1/6 of 9" pie	1 piece	410	.6	238	58	13	3	159	39	42	10	104	25	156	482
Meringue, lemon, 1/6 of pie	1 piece	357	T	211	59	20	6	126	35	41	11	73	20	130	395
Pecan, 1/6 of pie	1 piece	668	.8	323	48	28	4	317	47						354
Pumpkin, 1/6 of pie	1 piece	317	.8	148	47	24	7	145	46	50	16	81	26	91	321
Piecrust, baked, enr, 9"	1	675	.3	262	39	32	5	381	56	100	15	251	37		825

Food Item	Measure	Calories	Fiber (gm)	Carbohydrate Calories	Carbohydrate Percentage	Protein Calories	Protein Percentages	Total Fat Calories	Total Fat Percentage	Saturated Fat Calories	Saturated Fat Percentage	Unsaturated Fat Calories	Unsaturated Fat Percentage	Cholesterol (mg)	Sodium (mg)
Pudding															
Bread w/raisins, enr	1 cup	496	.2	301	61%	59	12%	136	27%	67	14%	44	9%	170	533
Chocolate, cornstarch	1 cup	385	.2	268	70	15	4	102	26	59	15	33	9	30	146
Rice w/raisins	1 cup	387	.13	281	73	37	9	69	18	44	11	22	6		188
Tapioca cream	1 cup	221	0	118	53	33	15	70	32	33	15	25	11	29	257
Sugar															
Beet or cane, granulated	1 cup	770	0	770	100	0	0	0	0	0	0	0	0		2
Beet or cane, granulated	1 tbsp	46	0	46	100	0	0	0	0	0	0	0	0		T
Brown, packed	1 cup	821	0	821	100	0	0	0	0	0	0	0	0		66
Powdered	1 cup	462	0	462	100	0	0	0	0	0	0	0	0		T
Syrup															
Maple	1 tbsp	50	0	50	100	0	0	0	0	0	0	0	0		3
Corn	1 tbsp	57	0	57	100	0	0	0	0	0	0	0	0		3
FISH AND SEAFOOD[1]															
Abalone	1 lb	445	0	62	14	362	81	21	5	3	14	7	33		
Anchovy, canned	3 fillets	21	0	T	T	10	48	11	52	22	5	63	13		
Bass	1 lb	472	0	0	0	366	78	106	22						306
Bluefish	1 lb	531	0	0	0	396	75	135	25						336
Carp	1 lb	522	0	0	0	350	67	172	33	31	6	118	23		227
Catfish	1 lb	467	0	0	0	340	73	127	27	35	8	84	18		272
Caviar, sturgeon, granular	1 tbsp	42		2	5	18	43	22	52					30	220

[1]Values are for raw flesh only unless stated otherwise.

CALORIC AND NUTRITIONAL VALUE OF FOODS (continued)

Food Item	Measure	Calories	Fiber (gm)	Carbohydrate Calories	Carbohydrate Percentage	Protein Calories	Protein Percentages	Total Fat Calories	Total Fat Percentage	Saturated Fat Calories	Saturated Fat Percentage	Unsaturated Fat Calories	Unsaturated Fat Percentage	Cholesterol (mg)	Sodium (mg)
Clams															
Fresh	4 lg or 9 sm	82		5	6%	60	73%	17	21%					120	36
Canned	1 cup	104		23	22	68	65	13	13					240	318
Cod	1 lb	354	0	0	0	341	96	13	4					227	
Steamed	1 lb	422	0	9	2	335	79	78	18					453	
Canned, drained, packed	1 cup	162	0	7	4	119	73	36	22					161	1600
Eel	1 lb	1057	0	0	0	308	29	749	71	171	16%	271	26%	227	353
Flounder, sole, or sandabs	1 lb	358	0	0	0	324	91	34	9					227	354
Frog's legs	4 lg	73	0	0	0	70	96	3	4					40	55
Haddock	1 lb	358	0	0	0	354	99	4	1					272	277
Halibut	1 lb	454	0	0	0	405	89	49	11	8	2	25	6	227	245
Herring															
Fresh	1 lb	798	0	0	0	335	42	463	58					386	535
Canned	1 cup	416	0	0	0	170	41	246	59						1359
Lobster	1 lb	413	0	9	2	327	79	77	19					900	652
Mackerel															
Fresh	1 lb	866	0	0	0	368	42	498	58	99	11	248	29	431	
Canned, drained	1 cup	384	0	0	0	192	50	192	50					199	
Oysters															
Fresh	1 lb	299	0	62	21	163	54	74	25	18	11	18	11	227	331
Canned	1 cup	158	0	33	21	86	54	39	25					108	175
Perch															
White	1 lb	535	0	0	0	373	70	162	30					317	286
Yellow	1 lb	413	0	0	0	376	91	37	9						308
Pike, walleye	1 lb	422	0	0	0	373	88	49	12	7	2	19	5		231
Pollock, fillet	1 lb	431	0	0	0	394	91	37	9	5	1	22	5		218

Food Item	Measure	Calories	Fiber (gm)	Carbohydrate Calories	Carbohydrate Percentage	Protein Calories	Protein Percentages	Total Fat Calories	Total Fat Percentage	Saturated Fat Calories	Saturated Fat Percentage	Unsaturated Fat Calories	Unsaturated Fat Percentage	Cholesterol (mg)	Sodium (mg)
Salmon															
Fresh	1 lb	984	0	0	0%	436	44%	548	56%					272	217
Pink, canned	1 cup	310	0	0	0	193	62	117	38					77	851
Sockeye, canned	1 cup	376	0	0	0	191	51	185	49					77	1148
Sardines, canned in oil, drained	1 oz	58	0	0	0	29	50	29	50					20	233
Scallops (frozen, possibly brined)	1 lb	367		61	17	296	81	8	2					159	1155
Shad	1 lb	771	0	0	0	361	47	410	53						245
Shrimp															
Fresh	1 lb	413		28	7	352	85	33	8					680	635
Canned, drained	1 cup	148	0	3	2	132	89	13	9					192	80
Smelt	1 lb	445	0	0	0	360	81	85	19						
Snails	3.5 oz	90	0	8	9	69	77	13	14						
Snapper	1 lb	422	0	0	0	384	91	38	9	10	2%	26	6%		304
Swordfish	1 lb	535	0	0	0	372	70	163	30						
Trout, rainbow	1 lb	885	0	0	0	418	47	467	53	99	11	117	13	289	177
Tuna															
Canned in oil, drained	1 cup	315	0	0	0	197	63	118	37	43	14	58	18	104	1733
Canned in water (regular water pack with salt added)	1 cup	254	0	0	0	239	94	15	6						236
Whitefish	1 lb	703	0	0	0	367	52	336	48					126	
FRUITS AND FRUIT JUICES															
Acerola (Barbados cherry)															
Raw	10 fruits	23	.4	20	87	1	4	2	9						7
Juice	1 cup	56	.73	47	84	3	5	6	11						7
Apple															
Raw	1 med	96	1.8	87	91	1	1	8	8						2
Dried	1 cup	234	2.6	219	93	3	2	12	5						4
Juice, unsw	1 cup	117	.26	116	99	1	1	T	T						2

CALORIC AND NUTRITIONAL VALUE OF FOODS (continued)

Food Item	Measure	Calories	Fiber (gm)	Carbohydrate Calories	Carbohydrate Percentage	Protein Calories	Protein Percentages	Total Fat Calories	Total Fat Percentage	Saturated Fat Calories	Saturated Fat Percentage	Unsaturated Fat Calories	Unsaturated Fat Percentage	Cholesterol (mg)	Sodium (mg)
Apple sauce, unsw	1 cup	100	1.3	94	94%	2	2%	4	4%						5
Apricot															
Raw	3 avg	55	.7	49	89	4	7	2	4						1
Canned, hvy syrup	1 cup	222	1	214	96	5	2	3	1						3
Dried	1 cup	338	3.9	310	92	22	7	6	2						34
Nectar	1 cup	143	.5	137	96	3	2	3	2						T
Avocado, raw, pitted	1 avg	334	3.2	45	13	14	4	275	82						8
Banana, raw	1 avg	127	.8	119	94	5	4	3	2						8
Blackberries															
Raw	1 cup	84	5.9	67	80	6	7	11	13						1
Canned, hvy syrup	1 cup	233	6.5	214	92	7	3	13	5						3
Juice, unsw	1 cup	91	T	76	84	2	2	13	14						2
Blueberries															
Raw	1 cup	90	2.2	81	90	3	3	6	7						1
Canned, hvy syrup	1 cup	242	2.16	236	98	3	1	3	1						2
Frozen, sweetened, unthawed	1 cup	242	2	231	95	5	2	6	2						2
Boysenberries, frozen, unsw	1 cup	60	3.38	52	87	5	8	3	5						1
Cantaloupe, raw	¼ avg	30	.3	27	90	2	7	1	3						12
Casaba melon, raw	1/10 avg	38	1.2	33	87	5	13	T	T						17
Cherries															
Sour, raw, pitted	1 cup	90	.4	80	89	6	7	4	4						3
Sour, canned, hvy syrup	1 cup	119	.2	108	91	7	6	4	3						2
Sweet, raw	1 cup	82	.52	74	90	5	6	3	4						2
Sweet, canned, hvy syrup	1 cup	208	.2	196	94	8	4	4	2						3
Crabapple, raw	3.5 oz	68	.6	64	94	8	4	4	2						1
Cranberry, raw	1 cup	46	1.4	39	85	1	2	6	13						2

Food Item	Measure	Calories	Fiber (gm)	Carbohydrate Calories	Carbohydrate Percentage	Protein Calories	Protein Percentages	Total Fat Calories	Total Fat Percentage	Saturated Fat Calories	Saturated Fat Percentage	Unsaturated Fat Calories	Unsaturated Fat Percentage	Cholesterol (mg)	Sodium (mg)
Cranberry Sauce															
Home-prepared 91 lb cranberries and 2 cups sugar)	1 cup	493	1.94	484	98%	2	.5%	7	1 %						3
Canned	1 cup	404	.55	398	99	1	0	5	1						3
Currants															
Black, raw	3.5 oz	54	2.4	47	87	6	11	1	2						3
Red or white, raw	1 cup	67	4.5	59	88	6	9	2	3						2.7
Dates, pitted	10 med	274	2.3	263	96	7	2	4	1						1
Elderberries, raw	3.5 oz	72	7	59	82	9	12	4	6						
Figs															
Raw	2 lg	80	1.2	72	90	5	6	3	4						2
Canned, hvy syrup	1 cup	218	1.7	208	95	6	3	4	2						5
Dried	5 med	274	5.6	248	91	15	5	11	4						34
Fruit cocktail, canned, hvy syrup	1 cup	194	1	188	97	3	1.5	3	1.5						13
Gooseberries															
Raw	1 cup	59	2.9	52	88	4	7	3	5						2
Canned, hvy syrup	1 cup	180	2.4	175	97	3	2	2	1						2
Granadilla (passion fruit), raw	3.5 oz	90		77	85	7	8	6	7						28
Grapefruit															
Raw	½ med	41	.2	38	93	2	5	1	2						1
Canned in syrup	1 cup	178	.5	170	95	5	3	3	2						36
Juice, unsw	1 cup	98	T	91	93	5	5	2	2						38
Grapes															
American (slip skin), raw	1 cup	106	.9	86	81	7	7	13	12						5
European (adherent skin), raw	1 cup	107	.8	100	93	3	3	4	4						5
Thompson seedless, canned, hvy syrup	1 can	197	.4	190	96	4	2	3	2						10
Juice, unsw	1 cup	167	T	165	99	2	1	T	0						5

CALORIC AND NUTRITIONAL VALUE OF FOODS (continued)

Food Item	Measure	Calories	Fiber (gm)	Carbohydrate Calories	Carbohydrate Percentage	Protein Calories	Protein Percentages	Total Fat Calories	Total Fat Percentage	Saturated Fat Calories	Saturated Fat Percentage	Unsaturated Fat Calories	Unsaturated Fat Percentage	Cholesterol (mg)	Sodium (mg)
Guava, raw	1 med	62	5.6	54	87%	3	5%	5	8%						4
Honeydew, melon, raw	2" wide	49	.9	41	84	4	8	4	8						4
Kumquat, raw	1 med	12	.74	11	91	1	8	T	0						18
Lemon															
Raw, peeled	1 med	20	.4	16	80	3	15	1	5						1
Juice, unsw	1 tbsp	4	T	4	100	T	0	T	0						T
Peel, grated	1 tbsp	3		3	100	T	0	T	0						T
Lemonade, frozen concentrate, diluted	1 cup	107	T	107	100	T	0	T	0						1
Lime															
Raw	1 small	19	.5	17	89	1	5	1	5						1
Juice, unsw	1 tbsp	4	T	4	100	T	0	T	0						T
Loganberries, raw	1 cup	89	4	76	85	5	6	8	9						1
Loquats, raw	10 fruits	59	.8	55	93	2	3	2	3						
Lychees															
Raw	10 fruits	58	.45	53	91	3	5	2	3						3
dried	3.5 oz	277	1.4	254	91	13	5	2	3						3
Mango, raw	1 fruit	152	2.7	139	91	5	3	8	5						16
Nectarine, raw	1 avg	88	.6	85	97	3	3	T	0						8
Olives															
Green	2 med	15	.2	1	1	1	1	13	87						312
Ripe	2 large	37	.3	3	8	1	1	33	89						150
Greek (salt cured)	3 med	67	.3	6	9	2	3	59	88						658
Orange															
Raw	1 avg	64	.9	57	89	4	6	3	5						1
Juice, unsw	1 cup	112	.3	102	91	6	5	4	4						2
Juice, frozen concentrate, diluted, unsw	1 cup	122	T	114	93	6	5	4	4						2
Papaya															
Raw	½ med	58	1.8	54	93	3	5	1	2						2
Juice, canned	1 cup	120		117	97	3	3	0	0						4.

Food Item	Measure	Calories	Fiber (gm)	Carbohydrate Calories	Carbohydrate Percentage	Protein Calories	Protein Percentages	Total Fat Calories	Total Fat Percentage	Saturated Fat Calories	Saturated Fat Percentage	Unsaturated Fat Calories	Unsaturated Fat Percentage	Cholesterol (mg)	Sodium (mg)
Peach															
Raw	1 med	38	.69	35	92%	2	5%	1	3%						1
Canned, hvy syrup	1 cup	200	1	194	97	3	2	3	2						5
Dried	1 cup	419	5	393	94	17	4	9	2						26
Pear															
Raw	1 avg	122	2.8	110	90	5	4	7	6						4
Canned, hvy syrup	1 cup	194	1.5	188	97	2	1	4	2						3
Dried	1 cup	482	6.2	436	90	19	4	27	6						13
Persimmon															
Japanese, raw	1 med	77	1.6	72	93	2	3	3	4						2
Native, raw	1 med	127	1.5	121	95	3	2	3	2						1
Pineapple															
Diced, raw	1 cup	81	.5	76	94	2	2	3	4						2
Canned, hvy syrup	1 cup	189	.7	183	97	3	2	3	4						3
Juice, unsw	1 cup	138	.2	132	96	3	2	3	2						3
Plantain (baking banana), raw	1 large	313	1.4	294	94	10	3	9	3						13
Plums															
Damson, raw	2 med	66	.4	64	97	2	3	T	0						2
Prune type, raw	3 med	75	.4	70	93	3	4	2	3						3
Purple, canned, hvy syrup	1 cup	214	.8	208	97	3	1	3	1						3
Pomegranate, raw	1 large	97	.5	90	93	3	3	4	4						5
Pricklypear, raw	1 avg	42	1.6	39	93	2	5	1	2						2
Prunes															
Dehydrated, nugget type	1 cup	344	2.2	329	96	11	3	4	1						11
Dried, softenized	1 cup	411	2	392	95	11	3	8	2						13
Cked, unsw	1 cup	253	2	241	95	7	3	5	2						9
Juice, unsw	1 cup	197	T	191	97	3	2	3	2						5
Quince, raw	3.5 oz	57	1.7	55	96	1	2	1	2						4

CALORIC AND NUTRITIONAL VALUE OF FOODS (continued)

Food Item	Measure	Calories	Fiber (gm)	Carbohydrate Calories	Carbohydrate Percentage	Protein Calories	Protein Percentages	Total Fat Calories	Total Fat Percentage	Saturated Fat Calories	Saturated Fat Percentage	Unsaturated Fat Calories	Unsaturated Fat Percentage	Cholesterol (mg)	Sodium (mg)
Raisins, packed	1 cup	477	1.4	460	96%	14	3%	3	1%						45
Raspberries															
Black, raw	1 cup	98	7.7	76	78	7	7	15	15						1
Red, raw	1 cup	70	4	60	86	5	7	5	7						1
Frozen, sweetened, unthawed	1 cup	245	5.5	235	96	6	2	4	2						3
Juice, unsw	1 cup	49	T	49	100	T	0	0	0						
Rhubarb, diced, raw	1 cup	20	.7	17	85	2	10	1	5						2
Strawberries															
Raw	1 cup	56	2	46	82	3	5	7	13						2
Frozen, sweetened, unthawed	1 cup	278	2	270	97	4	1	4	1						3
Tangelo, raw	1 med	39		36	92	2	5	1	3						
Tangerine, raw	1 med	39	.5	35	90	2	5	2	5						2
Watermelon															
Slice	6"x1½"	156	1.8	136	87	10	6	10	6						6
Balls or cubes	1 cup	26	.3	22	85	2	8	2	8						1
MEAT AND POULTRY															
Beef[2]															
Chuck roast	1 lb	905	0	0	0	337	37	568	63	272	30%	257	28%	270	276
Club steak	1 lb	1443	0	0	0	252	17	1191	83	572	40	548	38	261	206
Corned, boneless	1 lb	1329	0	0	0	308	23	1021	77	487	37	469	35		5897
Dried, chipped	3 oz	173	0	0	0	124	72	49	28	23	8	23	8		3660
Flank steak	1 lb	653	0	0	0	418	64	235	36	112	17	107	16	261	343
Ground beef, lean	1 lb	812	0	0	0	401	49	412	51	198	24	189	23	295	
Ground beef, regular	1 lb	1216	0	0	0	347	29	869	71	433	36	397	33	307	

[2]Values are for raw meat only, unless stated otherwise.

Food Item	Measure	Calories	Fiber (gm)	Carbohydrate Calories	Carbohydrate Percentage	Protein Calories	Protein Percentages	Total Fat Calories	Total Fat Percentage	Saturated Fat Calories	Saturated Fat Percentage	Unsaturated Fat Calories	Unsaturated Fat Percentage	Cholesterol (mg)	Sodium (mg)
Beef[2] (continued)															
Heart	1 lb	490	0	12	2%	331	68%	147	30%	45	9%	70	14%	680	390
Kidney	1 lb	590	0	16	3	299	51	275	47	61	10	45	7	1700	176
Liver	1 lb	635	0	93	15	386	61	156	25					1360	136
Porterhouse steak	1 lb	1603	0	0	0	260	16	1343	84	640	40	613	38	261	213
Rib Roast	1 lb	1673	0	0	0	264	16	1409	84	676	40	648	39	261	216
Round steak	1 lb	863	0	0	0	378	44	485	56	235	27	226	26	261	310
Rump Roast	1 lb	1167	0	0	0	287	25	880	75	424	36	415	36	261	235
Sirloin steak	1 lb	1316	0	0	0	304	23	1012	77	469	36	415	36	261	249
T-bone steak	1 lb	1596	0	0	0	251	16	1345	84	560	35	712	45	261	207
Tongue	1 lb	714	0	5	1	240	33	469	66						252
Brains, all kinds	1 lb	567	0	14	2	201	35	352	62					320	567
Chicken[3]															
Back	1 lb	385	0	0	0	173	45	212	55	60	16	131	34	368	377
Breast	1 lb	94	0	0	0	316	80	78	20	23	6	47	12	239	377
Canned	1 cup	406	0	0	0	190	47	216	53	72	18	108	27		
Drumstick	1 lb	313	0	0	0	218	70	95	30	27	9	59	19	239	377
Gizzard	1 lb	513	0	12	2	390	76	111	22					658	295
Heart	10 med	157	0	6	4	88	56	63	40					170	79
Liver	1 lb	585	0	51	9	382	65	152	26	56	10	70	12	2517	318
Neck	1 lb	329	0	0	0	144	44	185	56	43	13	93	29	368	377
Thigh	1 lb	435	0	0	0	263	60	172	40	49	11	106	24	368	377
Wing	1 lb	325	0	0	0	176	54	149	46					368	377
Chili con carne w/beans	1 cup	339	1.5	119	35	80	24	140	41	68	20	68	20		1354
Corned beef hash w/potato	1 cup	398	1.25	90	23	83	21	225	57	99	25	99	25		1188
Duck, ready to cook	1 lb	1213	0	0	0	254	21	959	79	229	19	591	49	318	386

[2]Values are for raw meat only, unless stated otherwise.
[3]Whole chicken per lb contains 15 gms total fat, 5 gms sat. fat, and 9 gms uns. fat.

CALORIC AND NUTRITIONAL VALUE OF FOODS (continued)

Food Item	Measure	Calories	Fiber (gm)	Carbohydrate Calories	Carbohydrate Percentage	Protein Calories	Protein Percentage	Total Fat Calories	Total Fat Percentage	Saturated Fat Calories	Saturated Fat Percentage	Unsaturated Fat Calories	Unsaturated Fat Percentage	Cholesterol (mg)	Sodium (mg)
Frankfurter	1 lb	1402	0	32	2%	242	17%	1128	80%	440	31%	621	44%	295	4990
Goose, ready to cook	1 lb	1172	0	0	0	232	20	940	80	253	22	541	46		386
Lamb															
Leg	1 lb	845	0	0	0	289	34	556	66	316	37	216	26	265	237
Chops	1 lb	1146	0	0	0	272	24	874	76	490	43	341	27	270	223
Liver	1 lb	617	0	50	8	407	66	160	26	62	10	60	10	1361	236
Shoulder	1 lb	1082	0	0	0	252	23	830	77	469	43	325	30	270	206
Liver pate	1 tbsp	60	0	2	3	6	10	52	87						
Pheasant, ready to cook	1 lb	596	0	0	0	410	69	186	31	57	10	110	18		
Pork (lean meat)															
Bacon, sliced	1 lb	3016	0	28	1	164	5	2834	94	911	30	1615	54	999	3084
Bacon, canadian	1 lb	980	0	5	1	387	39	588	60	207	21	298	30		8578
Boston butt	1 lb	1220	0	0	0	280	23	938	77	334	27	478	39		231
Chops	1 lb	1065	0	0	0	261	25	804	75	289	27	406	38		214
Ham, cured	1 lb	1535	0	5	.5	285	19	1245	81	451	29	631	41	232	3415
Ham, deviled	1 cup	790	0	0	0	134	17	656	83	271	34	352	45	260	
Ham, minced	1 lb	1034	0	77	7	265	26	692	67	298	29	424	41	318	
Picnic	1 lb	1083	0	0	0	251	23	832	77	289	27	415	38	232	207
Spareribs	1 lb	976	0	0	0	167	17	809	83					232	137
Potted meat, all kinds	1 cup	558	0	0	0	168	30	390	70						
Rabbit, ready to cook	1 lb	581	0	0	0	320	55	261	45	99	17	117	20	295	154
Sausage															
Blood	1 lb	1787	0	5	.3	273	15	1506	84	458	26	585	33		5897
Bologna	1 lb	1379	0	19	1	234	17	1126	82	406	29	268	19		5897
Braunschweiger	1 lb	1447	0	40	3	288	20	1119	77						
Brown and Serve	1 lb	1783	0	49	3	262	15	1472	83						
Cervelat	1 lb	2046	0	30	1	478	23	1538	75	627	31	632	31		
Country-style	1 lb	1565	0	0	0	293	19	1272	81	460	29	649	41		

Food Item	Measure	Calories	Fiber (gm)	Carbohydrate Calories	Carbohydrate Percentage	Protein Calories	Protein Percentages	Total Fat Calories	Total Fat Percentage	Saturated Fat Calories	Saturated Fat Percentage	Unsaturated Fat Calories	Unsaturated Fat Percentage	Cholesterol (mg)	Sodium (mg)
Sausage (continued)															
Headcheese	1 lb	1216	0	16	1%	300	25%	900	74%	325	27%	460	39%		
Knockwurst	1 lb	1216	0	39	3	273	22	949	75	351	28	544	43		
Liverwurst	1 lb	1393	0	33	2	314	23	1046	75	370	27	581	42		
Polish-style	1 lb	1379	0	20	1	304	22	1055	77						
Pork, link or bulk	1 lb	2259	0	2	0	182	8	2075	92	749	33	1037	46		
Salami	1 lb	2041	0	21	1	461	23	1559	76	552	27	924	45		3357
Thuringer	1 lb	1393	0	29	2	361	26	1003	72						
Vienna, canned	7 saus	271	0	1	0	68	25	202	75						
Turkey															
Dark meat, ckd	1 lb	921	0	0	0	581	63	340	37	98	11	217	24	458	449
Light Meat, ckd	1 lb	798	0	0	0	637	80	161	20	46	6	102	13	349	372
Canned	1 cup	414	0	0	0	183	44	231	56	72	17	144	35		
Veal (calf)															
Breast	1 lb	828	0	0	0	279	34	549	66	264	32	253	31	254	230
Chuck	1 lb	628	0	0	0	301	48	327	52	153	24	153	24	320	246
Cutlet	1 lb	681	0	0	0	310	46	371	54	178	26	170	25	254	253
Liver	1 lb	635	0	72	11	371	58	192	30					1361	331
Rib Roast	1 lb	723	0	0	0	281	39	442	61	212	29	204	28		230
Rump Roast	1 lb	573	0	0	0	291	51	282	49	134	23	128	22	254	230
Sweetbreads (pancreas)	1 lb	426	0	0	0	344	81	82	19					1135	281
Venison (deer)	1 lb	572	0	0	0	408	71	164	29	99	17	45	8		318

CALORIC AND NUTRITIONAL VALUE OF FOODS (continued)

Food Item	Measure	Calories	Fiber (gm)	Carbohydrate Calories	Carbohydrate Percentage	Protein Calories	Protein Percentages	Total Fat Calories	Total Fat Percentage	Saturated Fat Calories	Saturated Fat Percentage	Unsaturated Fat Calories	Unsaturated Fat Percentage	Cholesterol (mg)	Sodium (mg)
NUTS, NUT PRODUCTS, AND SEEDS[4]															
Almonds															
Raw	1 cup	849	3.85	113	13%	92	11%	644	76%	52	6%	561	66%		6
Roasted and salted	1 cup	984	3.85	125	13	101	10	758	77	61	6	660	67		311
Almond Meal	1 oz	116	.64	33	28	39	34	44	38	3	3	38	33		2
Brazil nuts, raw	1 cup	916	4.2	62	7	69	8	785	36	157	17	580	63		1
Cashews, roasted	1 cup	785	1.96	166	21	84	11	535	68	16	2	413	53		21
Chestnuts															
Fresh	1 cup	310	1.66	273	88	15	5	22	7	4	1	17	5		10
Dried	1 cup	377	2.5	320	85	23	6	34	9						4
Coconut															
Fresh, shredded, not packed	1 cup	277	2.7	31	11	10	4	236	85	203	73	17	6		18
Dried, shredded, sweetened	1 cup	344	2.55	134	39	8	2	202	59						11
Milk (mixture of coconut meat and water)	1 cup	605	T	51	8	27	4	527	87	453	75	37	6		60
Water (liquid from coconuts)	1 cup	53	1.05	46	87	2	4	5	9						3
Hazelnuts (filberts), raw	1 cup	856		92	11	59	7	705	82	35	4	494	58		
Hickory nuts, dried	15 small	101	.3	8	8	7	7	86	85	8	8	74	73		T
Lychee nuts, dried	6 avg	45	.48	42	93	2	4	1	2						
Macadamia nuts, roasted	6 avg	109	.38	6	6	5	5	98	90	14	13	74	68		
Peanuts, roasted	1 cup	838	3.89	121	14	131	16	586	70	129	15	423	50		7
Peanut butter	1 tbsp	94	.33	12	13	14	15	68	72	13	14	51	54		18
Pecans, halves, raw	1 cup	742	2.3	64	9	34	5	644	87	45	6	534	72		T
Pine nuts, raw	1 oz	180	.31	24	13	13	7	143	79	17	9	118	66		
Pistachio nuts, shelled	30 avg	88	.3	11	13	10	11	67	76	9	10	54	61		
Pumpkin and squash seeds, dried, hulled	1 cup	774	2.66	85	11	141	18	548	71	22	3	427	55		

[4]All nuts and seeds are unsalted, unless stated otherwise. For salted nuts, the sodium content is approximately 280 mg/cup.

Food Item	Measure	Calories	Fiber (gm)	Carbohydrate Calories	Carbohydrate Percentage %	Protein Calories	Protein Percentages %	Total Fat Calories	Total Fat Percentage	Saturated Fat Calories	Saturated Fat Percentage	Unsaturated Fat Calories	Unsaturated Fat Percentage	Cholesterol (mg)	Sodium (mg)
Sesame seeds, dried, hulled	1 cup	873	3.6	108	12	95	11	670	77%	94	11%	536	61%		4
Sunflower seeds, dried, hulled	1 cup	812	5.5	118	15	120	15	574	71	69	8	476	59		2
Walnuts															
Black, chopped, raw	1 cup	785	2.13	75	10	90	11	620	79	38	5	516	66		
English, halves, raw	1 cup	651	2.1	64	10	51	8	536	32	38	6	414	64		
OILS, FATS, AND SHORTENING															
Bacon Fat	1 tbsp	126	0	0	0	T	0	126	100						
Butter	1 tbsp	102	0	.5	.5	.5	.5	101	99	55	54	36	35	35	140
Butter	1 cup	1625	0	3	0	6	0	1617	100	888	55	582	36	570	2240
Chicken Fat	1 tbsp	126	0	0	0	0	0	126	100			66	56	12	T
Lard	1 tbsp	117	0	0	0	0	0	117	100	44	38				
Margarine															
Regular	1 tbsp	102	0	.5	.5	.5	.5	101	99	19	19	81	79	0[5]	140
Whipped	1 tbsp	68	0	T	0	.5	1	67	99	13	19	54		0[5]	93
Oils															
Cod-liver	1 tbsp	126	0	0	0	0	0	126	100	12	10	97	77	119	T
Corn	1 tbsp	126	0	0	0	0	0	126	100	30	24	86	68	T	T
Cottonseed	1 tbsp	126	0	0	0	0	0	126	100	13	10	99	80	0	0
Olive	1 tbsp	124	0	T	0	T	0	124	100	21	17	90	73	T	T
Peanut	1 tbsp	124	0	T	0	T	0	124	100	10	8	104	84	T	T
Safflower	1 tbsp	124	0	0	0	0	0	124	100	18	15	87	70	T	T
Soybean	1 tbsp	120	0	T	0	T	0	120	100	17	14	93	78	T	T
Sesame	1 tbsp	124	0	T	0	T	0	124	100	21	17	78	63		T
Sunflower	1 tbsp	124	0	T	0	T	0	124	100						
Wheat germ	1 tbsp	111	0	T	0	T	0	111	100						0
Vegetable Shortening	1 tbsp	111	0	0	0	0	0	111	100						0

[5]Value for all vegetable fat; 2/3 animal fat and 1/3 vegetable fat has 7 mg/tbsp.

CALORIC AND NUTRITIONAL VALUE OF FOODS (continued)

Food Item	Measure	Calories	Fiber (gm)	Carbohydrate Calories	Carbohydrate Percentage	Protein Calories	Protein Percentages	Total Fat Calories	Total Fat Percentage	Saturated Fat Calories	Saturated Fat Percentage	Unsaturated Fat Calories	Unsaturated Fat Percentage	Cholesterol (mg)	Sodium (mg)
SALAD DRESSINGS AND SAUCES															
Barbecue Sauce	1 tbsp	14	.09	4	29%	1	7%	9	64%	1	7%	7	50%		127
Catsup, tomato	1 tbsp	16	.08	14	88	1	6	1	6						156
Chili Sauce	1 tbsp	16	.13	13	81	2	13	1	6						201
Hollandaise Sauce	1 tbsp	45		1	2	2	4	42	93						14
Horseradish, prepared	1 tbsp	6	.11	5	83	1	17	T	0						84
Mayonnaise	1 tbsp	101	T	1	1	1	1	99	98	18	18	70	69	10	195
Mustard	1 tbsp	15	.3	4	27	3	20	8	53						
Salad Dressings															
Bleu or Roquefort Cheese, regular	1 tbsp	76	T	4	5	3	4	69	91	14	18	48	63		164
Bleu or Roquefort Cheese, low calorie	1 tbsp	13	T	3	23	2	15	8	62	4	31	3	23		177
Caesar	1 tbsp	73	T	2	3	1	1	70	96	10	15	40	61		236
French, regular	1 tbsp	66		11	17	1	2	54	82	1	7	4	27		219
French, low calorie	1 tbsp	15	T	9	60	T	0	6	40						126
Green Goddess	1 tbsp	72	T	3	4	T	0	69	96						140
Italian	1 tbsp	83	T	3	4	T	0	80	96	14	17	58	70		314
Russian	1 tbsp	74		6	8	1	1	67	91	12	16	49	66		130
Thousand Island, regular	1 tbsp	80	.05	9	11	T	0	71	89	12	15	50	63		112
Thousand Island, low calorie	1 tbsp	27	.04	8	30	T	0	19	70	4	15	17	63		105
Soy Sauce	1 tbsp	12	.04	7	58	3	25	2	17						1319
Vinegar	1 tbsp	2	0	2	100	T	0	0	0						T
White sauce, medium	1 tbsp	27	0	6	22	3	11	18	67	9	33	6	22	2	59
Worcestershire sauce	1 tbsp	12	T	11	92	1	8	0	0	0	0	0	0		

SOUPS (diluted with water)

Food Item	Measure	Calories	Fiber (gm)	Carbohydrate Calories	Carbohydrate Percentage	Protein Calories	Protein Percentages	Total Fat Calories	Total Fat Percentage	Saturated Fat Calories	Saturated Fat Percentage	Unsaturated Fat Calories	Unsaturated Fat Percentage	Cholesterol (mg)	Sodium (mg)
Asparagus, cream of	1 cup	65	.8	40	62%	10	15%	15	23%	12	7%	35	21%		984
Bean and Pork	1 cup	168	1.8	90	54	28	17	50	30						1008
Beef															
Consomme or bouillon	1 cup	31	.14	10	32	21	68	0	0						782
Noodle	1 cup	140	.15	58	41	33	24	49	35	15	11	30	21		1872
Celery, cream of	1 cup	86	.84	34	40	8	9	44	51	8	9	33	38		955
Chicken															
Consumme or bouillon	1 cup	22	T	7	32	15	68	T	0						722
Cream of	1 cup	94	.3	30	32	12	13	52	55	8	9	39	41		970
Gumbo	1 cup	55	.1	28	51	14	25	13	24						950
Noodle	1 cup	62	.25	30	48	15	24	17	27						979
w/rice	1 cup	48	.12	22	46	15	31	11	23						917
Chili Beef	1 cup	168	1.1	92	55	34	20	42	25						1102
Clam Chowder															
Manhattan	1 cup	81	.4	49	60	9	11	23	28						938
New England	1 cup	130	.25	43	33	18	14	69	53						104
Minestrone	1 cup	105	.9	58	55	19	18	28	27						995
Mushroom, cream of	1 cup	134	.12	36	27	18	13	80	60	11	8	61	46		955
Onion	1 cup	65	.5	21	32	23	35	21	32						1051
Oyster Stew	1 cup	130	.1	32	25	26	20	72	55	8	6	15	10		512
Pea, split	1 cup	145	.5	86	59	32	22	27	19	26	23	18	16		941
Potato, cream of	1 cup	115	.45	51	44	14	12	50	43	4	5	14	16		1274
Tomato	1 cup	88	.7	60	68	7	8	21	24	7	9	16	20		970
Turkey noodle	1 cup	79	.12	34	43	18	23	27	34						998
Vegetable															
Beef	1 cup	78	.65	36	46	22	28	20	26						1046
Vegetarian	1 cup	78	.9	54	69	7	9	17	22						1046

CALORIC AND NUTRITIONAL VALUE OF FOODS (continued)

Food Item	Measure	Calories	Fiber (gm)	Carbohydrate Calories	Carbohydrate Percentage	Protein Calories	Protein Percentages	Total Fat Calories	Total Fat Percentage	Saturated Fat Calories	Saturated Fat Percentage	Unsaturated Fat Calories	Unsaturated Fat Percentage	Cholesterol (mg)	Sodium (mg)
Paprika	1 tsp	6	.44											0	T
Parsley, dried	1 tsp	1	.03											0	T
Pepper															
Black	1 tsp	5	.28											0	T
Red or cayenne	1 tsp	6	.45											0	T
White	1 tsp	7	.1											0	T
Poppy seed	1 tsp	15	.18											0	T
Poultry seasoning	1 tsp	5	.17											0	T
Pumpkin pie spice	1 tsp	6	.25											0	T
Rosemary, dried	1 tsp	4	.21											0	T
Saffron	1 tsp	2	.03											0	T
Sage, grd	1 tsp	2	.13											0	T
Salt	1 tsp	0												0	2132
Savory, grd	1 tsp	4	.21											0	T
Tarragon, grd	1 tsp	5	.12											0	T
Thyme, grd	1 tsp	4	.26											0	T
Turmeric	1 tsp	8	.15											0	T
VEGETABLES, LEGUMES, SPROUTS AND VEGETABLE JUICES[6]															
Artichoke, globe, boiled	1 avg	44	2.4	35	80%	7	16%	2	5%					0	30
Asparagus															
Cut pieces, raw	1 cup	35	.95	24	69	8	23	3	9					0	3
Spears, ckd	4 large	20	.7	13	65	5	25	2	10					0	1
Spears, canned, drained	4 avg	17	.4	10	59	5	29	2	12					0	189
Bamboo shoots, raw	1 cup	36	.93	25	69	8	22	3	8					0	
Beans															
Black, dry	1 cup	678		497	73	155	23	26	4					0	50
Black-eye peas, ckd	1 cup	178		121	68	46	26	11	6					0	2

[6]Most of the vegetables are cooked, unsalted, in small amount of water for a short time.

Food Item	Measure	Calories	Fiber (gm)	Carbohydrate Calories	Carbohydrate Percentage	Protein Calories	Protein Percentages	Total Fat Calories	Total Fat Percentage	Saturated Fat Calories	Saturated Fat Percentage	Unsaturated Fat Calories	Unsaturated Fat Percentage	Cholesterol (mg)	Sodium (mg)
SPICES AND HERBS															
Allspice, grd	1 tsp	5	.41											0	1
Anise seed	1 tsp	7	.31											0	T
Basil, grd	1 tsp	4	.25											0	T
Bay leaf, crumbles	1 tsp	2	.16											0	T
Caraway seed	1 tsp	7	.27											0	T
Cardamon, grd	1 tsp	6	.23											0	T
Celery seed	1 tsp	8	.24											0	3
Chervil, dried	1 tsp	1	.07											0	T
Chili Powder	1 tsp	8	.58											0	26
Cinnamon, grd	1 tsp	6	.56											0	1
Cloves, grd	1 tsp	7	.2											0	5
Coriander leaf, dried	1 tsp	2	.06											0	1
Coriander seed	1 tsp	5	.52											0	1
Cumin seed	1 tsp	8	.22											0	4
Curry powder	1 tsp	6	.33											0	1
Dill seed	1 tsp	6	.44											0	T
Dill weed, dried	1 tsp	3	.12											0	2
Fennel seed	1 tsp	7	.31											0	2
Fenugreek seed	1 tsp	12	.37											0	2
Garlic powder	1 tsp	9	.05											0	1
Ginger, grd	1 tsp	6	.11											0	1
Mace, grd	1 tsp	8	.08											0	T
Marjoram, dried	1 tsp	2	.11											0	T
Mustard seed, yellow	1 tsp	15	.22											0	T
Nutmeg, grd	1 tsp	12	.09											0	T
Onion powder	1 tsp	7	.12											0	T
Oregano, grd	1 tsp	5	.22											0	1

CALORIC AND NUTRITIONAL VALUE OF FOODS (continued)

Food Item	Measure	Calories	Fiber (gm)	Carbohydrate Calories	Carbohydrate Percentage	Protein Calories	Protein Percentages	Total Fat Calories	Total Fat Percentage	Saturated Fat Calories	Saturated Fat Percentage	Unsaturated Fat Calories	Unsaturated Fat Percentage	Cholesterol (mg)	Sodium (mg)
Beans (continued)															
Canned w/pork	1 cup	304	3.6	194	64%	53	17%	57	18%	20	7%	29	10%		1158
Canned w/o pork	1 cup	300	3.6	235	78	55	18	10	3						844
Chickpeas (garbanzos), dry	1 cup	720	10	498	69	142	20	80	11	8	1	69	10		52
Green, snap, raw	1 cup	35	1.1	28	80	5	14	2	6						8
Green, snap, ckd	1 cup	31	1.2	24	77	5	16	2	6						5
Green, snap, canned, drained	1 cup	32		25	78	5	16	2	6						319
Lentils, ckd	1 cup	212	2.4	158	75	54	25	T	0						
Lentils sprouts, raw	1 cup	104	1.1	72	69	29	28	3	3						4
Lima, ckd	1 cup	262	3	199	76	54	21	9	3						
Lima, canned, drained	1 cup	163		127	78	32	20	4	2						401
Mung, sprouts, raw	1 cup	37	.7	25	68	10	27	2	5						5
Pinto, dry	1 cup	663	8	493	74	151	23	19	3						19
Red Kidney, ckd	1 cup	218	2.78	160	73	50	23	8	4						6
Red kidney, canned	1 cup	230	2.3	172	75	50	22	8	3						8
Soybeans, ckd	1 cup	234	3	79	34	69	29	86	37						4
Soybeans, canned, drained	1 cup	153	2.1	44	29	47	31	62	41						354
Soybean curd (tofu)	3.5 oz	72	.1	10	14	27	38	35	49						7
Soybean milk	1 cup	75		20	27	27	36	28	37						4
Soybean sprouts, raw	1 cup	48	2.3	19	40	17	35	12	25						
Yellow wax, ckd	1 cup	28	1	21	75	4	14	3	11						
Yellow wax, canned, drained	1 cup	32	1	24	75	5	16	3	9						319
White, ckd	1 cup	224	3	164	73	51	23	9	4						13
Beets, diced															
Raw	1 cup	58	1.1	51	88	6	10	1	2						81
Cooked	1 cup	54	.94	47	87	5	9	2	4						73
Canned, drained	1 cup	63	.94	56	89	5	8	2	3						401

Food Item	Measure	Calories	Fiber (gm)	Carbohydrate Calories	Carbohydrate Percentage	Protein Calories	Protein Percentages	Total Fat Calories	Total Fat Percentage	Saturated Fat Calories	Saturated Fat Percentage	Unsaturated Fat Calories	Unsaturated Fat Percentage	Cholesterol (mg)	Sodium (mg)
Beet greens															
Raw	3.5 oz	24	1.3	16	67%	5	21%	3	13%						130
Cooked	1 cup	26	1.4	17	65	6	23	3	12						110
Broccoli															
Raw, 5½" long	1 piece	32	1.5	21	66	9	28	2	6						15
Cooked	1 cup	40	2	24	60	12	30	4	10						16
Brussels Sprouts															
Raw	9 med	45	1.6	30	67	12	27	3	7						14
Cooked	1 cup	56	2.1	35	63	16	29	5	9						16
Cabbage															
Common, sliced, raw	1 cup	17	.8	14	82	2	12	1	6						14
Common, sliced, ckd	1 cup	29	1	22	76	4	14	3	10						20
Red, sliced, raw	1 cup	22	1	17	77	4	18	1	5						18
Savoy, sliced, raw	1 cup	17	.5	12	71	4	24	1	5						15
Chinese, raw	1 cup	11	.6	8	73	2	18	1	9						17
Chinese, cooked	1 cup	16		9	56	6	38	1	6						17
Carrots															
Raw	1 large	42	1	37	88	3	7	2	5						47
Cooked	1 cup	48	1.5	41	85	4	8	3	6						51
Canned, drained	1 cup	47	1	40	85	3	6	4	9						366
Juice	1 cup	96		85	89	7	7	4	4						105
Cauliflower, flower buds															
Raw	1 cup	27	1	18	67	7	26	2	7						13
Cooked	1 cup	28	1.25	18	64	7	25	3	11						11
Celeriac root, raw	4 roots	40	1.3	32	80	5	13	3	8						100
Celery															
Raw	1 cup	20	.7	16	80	3	15	1	5						151
Cooked	1 cup	21	.9	16	76	3	14	2	10						132

CALORIC AND NUTRITIONAL VALUE OF FOODS (continued)

Food Item	Measure	Calories	Fiber (gm)	Carbohydrate Calories	Carbohydrate Percentage	Protein Calories	Protein Percentages	Total Fat Calories	Total Fat Percentage	Saturated Fat Calories	Saturated Fat Percentage	Unsaturated Fat Calories	Unsaturated Fat Percentage	Cholesterol (mg)	Sodium (mg)
Chard, Swiss															
Raw	3.5 oz	25	.8	16	64%	6	24%	3	12%						147
Cooked	1 cup	26	1	17	65	6	23	3	12						125
Chives, chopped, raw	1 tbsp	3	.1	2	67	1	33	T	0						T
Collards															
Raw	3 oz	40	.9	25	63	9	23	6	15						43
Cooked	1 cup	42	1.15	25	60	10	24	7	17						36
Corn															
Cooked	1 cup	137	1.16	110	80	13	9	14	10						T
Canned, drained	1 cup	139	1.1	117	84	11	8	11	8						389
Cream-style, canned	1 cup	210	1.28	183	87	14	7	13	6						604
Cress, sprigs															
Raw	5-8	4	.1	2	50	1	25	1	25						1
Cooked	1 cup	31	1.2	18	58	6	19	7	23						11
Cucumber, sliced, unprepared, raw	1 cup	16	.6	13	81	2	13	1	6						6
Dandelion Greens															
Raw	3.5 oz	45	1.6	32	71	7	16	6	13						76
Cooked	1 cup	35	1.3	25	71	5	14	5	14						46
Dock (sorrel), raw	3.5 oz	28	.8	20	71	5	18	3	11						5
Eggplant															
Raw	1 cup	50	1.8	41	82	6	12	3	6						4
Cooked	1 cup	38	1.8	30	79	5	13	3	8						2
Endive, raw	1 cup	10	.45	7	70	2	20	1	10						7
Garlic, raw	1 clove	4		3	75	1	25	T	0						1
Ginger Root, fresh	3.5 oz	49	1.1	37	76	4	8	8	16						6
Jerusalem artichoke, raw	4 small	67[7]	.8	60	90	6	9	1	1						6
Kale															
Raw	3.5 oz	38	1.3	21	55	10	26	7	18						75
Cooked	1 cup	43	1.4	24	56	12	28	7	16						47

[7]Values range from 7/100 gm for freshly harvested to 75 after long storage.

Food Item	Measure	Calories	Fiber (gm)	Carbohydrate Calories	Carbohydrate Percentage	Protein Calories	Protein Percentages	Total Fat Calories	Total Fat Percentage	Saturated Fat Calories	Saturated Fat Percentage	Unsaturated Fat Calories	Unsaturated Fat Percentage	Cholesterol (mg)	Sodium (mg)
Kohlrabi, diced															
Raw	1 cup	43	1.5	35	81%	7	16%	1	2%						12
Cooked	1 cup	40	1.5	31	78	7	18	2	5						10
Leeks, raw, 5 long	3-4	52	1.3	43	83	6	12	3	6						5
Lettuce															
Boston or bib, raw	1 cup	8	.25	5	63	2	25	1	13						5
Cos or Romaine, raw	1 cup	10	.35	7	70	2	20	1	10						7
Iceberg, raw	1 cup	10	.35	7	70	2	20	1	10						5
Looseleaf, raw	1 cup	10	.35	7	70	2	20	1	10						
Lotus Root, 1 segment	2/3 avg	69	.35	61	88	7	10	1	1						11
Mushrooms															
Raw	1 cup	20	.56	13	65	5	25	2	10						32
Canned, drained	1 cup	40	.42	25	63	10	25	5	13						32
Sauteed	4 med	78	.7	11	14	5	6	62	79						
Mustard Greens															
Raw	3.5 oz	31	1.1	20	65	7	23	4	13						3
Cooked	1 cup	29	1.82	18	62	8	28	3	10						3
Okra															
Raw	1 cup	36	1	27	75	6	16	3	8						
Cooked	1 cup	46	1.5	34	74	8	17	4	9						
Onions															
Raw	1 cup	65	1	56	86	7	11	2	3						17
Cooked	1 cup	61	1.2	52	85	7	11	2	3						15
Dehydrated, flakes	3.5 oz	350	4.4	315	90	24	7	11	3						88
Scallions, bulb and tops, raw	1 cup	36	1	30	83	4	11	2	6						5
Parsley, chopped, raw	1 cup	26	.9	18	69	5	19	3	12						27
Parsnips															
Raw	1/2 large	76	2	67	88	5	7	4	5						12
Cooked	1 cup	102	3	89	87	6	6	7	7						12

CALORIC AND NUTRITIONAL VALUE OF FOODS (continued)

Food Item	Measure	Calories	Fiber (gm)	Carbohydrate Calories	Carbohydrate Percentage	Protein Calories	Protein Percentages	Total Fat Calories	Total Fat Percentage	Saturated Fat Calories	Saturated Fat Percentage	Unsaturated Fat Calories	Unsaturated Fat Percentage	Cholesterol (mg)	Sodium (mg)
Peas															
Raw	1 cup	122	2.9	85	70%	32	26%	5	4%						3
Cooked	1 cup	114	3.2	79	69	30	26	5	4						3
Canned, drained	1 cup	150	3.9	116	77	28	19	6	4						401
Split, cooked	1 cup	230	.8	170	74	56	24	4	2						26
Peppers															
Green, sliced, raw	1 cup	18	1.12	14	78	2	11	2	11						10
Green, sliced, ckd	1 cup	24	1.89	18	75	3	13	3	13						12
Red, sliced, raw	1 cup	31		25	81	3	10	3	10						
Hot Chili, green, canned	1 cup	49	3	43	88	4	8	3	4						
Hot Chili, red, canned	1 cup	51		33	65	5	10	13	25						10
Pickles															
Dill	1 large	15	.5	11	73	2	13	2	13						1428
Sour	1 large	14	.5	10	71	2	14	2	14						1353
Sweet (gherkins)	1 large	51		49	96	1	2	1	2						
Pimientos, canned	3 med	27	.6	21	78	2	7	4	15						
Potato															
Raw, diced	1 cup	114		103	90	9	8	2	2						5
Baked in skin	1 large	145	1.2	132	91	11	8	2	1						6
Boiled in skin	1 med	76	.5	69	91	6	8	1	1						3
Dehydrated flakes, dry	1 cup	164	.5	152	93	9	5	1							40
Dehydrated flakes, prepared	1 cup	195		125	64	12	6	3	2						485
French Fries	10 pieces	137	.5	73	53	6	4	58	42	17	12%	34	25%		379
Fried from raw	1 cup	456	1.6	223	49	19	4	214	47						446
Hash Browns	1 cup	355	1.2	182	51	13	4	160	45						446
Mashed w/milk[8]	1 cup	137	.8	110	80	12	9	15	11						632

[8] Made with 6 tbsp milk and 3/4 tsp salt added to four medium potatoes.

Food Item	Measure	Calories	Fiber (gm)	Carbohydrate Calories	Carbohydrate Percentage	Protein Calories	Protein Percentages	Total Fat Calories	Total Fat Percentage	Saturated Fat Calories	Saturated Fat Percentage	Unsaturated Fat Calories	Unsaturated Fat Percentage	Cholesterol (mg)	Sodium (mg)
Potato (continued)															
Scalloped & au gratin w/o cheese	1 cup	255		144	56%	30	12%	81	32%	16	14%	50	44%	14	870
Scalloped & au gratin w/cheese	1 cup	355		133	37	52	15	170	48					36	1095
Potato Chips	10 chips	113	.3	41	36	3	3	69	61						—[9]
Pumpkin, canned	1 cup	81	3	69	85	6	7	6	7						5
Radish															
Red, raw	10 med	8	.35	7	88	1	13	T	0						8
Oriental, raw	3.5 oz	19	.7	16	84	2	11	1	5						
Rutabaga															
Raw	1 cup	64	1.4	59	92	4	6	1	2						7
Cooked	1 cup	60	2	54	90	4	7	2	3						7
Sauerkraut															
Canned	1 cup	42	1.6	32	76	6	14	4	10						1755[10]
Juice	1 cup	24	1	20	83	4	17	T	0						1905[10]
Shallots, chopped, raw	1 tbsp	7		6	86	1	14	T	0						1
Spinach															
Raw	1 cup	14	.3	8	57	4	29	2	14						39
Cooked	1 cup	41	1	23	56	14	34	4	10						90
Canned, drained	1 cup	49	1.6	26	53	13	27	10	20						484
New Zealand, raw	3.5 oz	19	.7	11	58	5	26	3	16						159
New Zealand, cooked	1 cup	23	1.1	13	57	7	30	3	13						166
Squash															
Summer, raw	1 cup	25	.75	20	80	4	16	1	4						1
Summer, cooked	1 cup	25	.8	19	76	4	16	2	8						2
Winter, baked	1 cup	129	2.6	113	88	9	7	7	5						2

[9] Sodium content is variable. May be as high as 200 mg per 10 chips.
[10] Amounts may vary significantly between brands.

CALORIC AND NUTRITIONAL VALUE OF FOODS (continued)

Food Item	Measure	Calories	Fiber (gm)	Carbohydrate Calories	Carbohydrate Percentage	Protein Calories	Protein Percentages	Total Fat Calories	Total Fat Percentage	Saturated Fat Calories	Saturated Fat Percentage	Unsaturated Fat Calories	Unsaturated Fat Percentage	Cholesterol (mg)	Sodium (mg)
Sweet Potato															
Baked	1 avg	151	1.8	149	93%	7	4%	5	3%						14
Candied, 2"x4"	2 halves	168	.6	138	82	4	2	26	15						42
Canned	1 cup	216	2	201	93	11	5	4	2						96
Tomato															
Raw	1 med	33	.8	26	79	4	12	3	9						4
Canned	1 cup	51	.8	40	78	7	14	4	8						3.3
Juice	1 cup	46	.4	39	85	5	11	2	4						486
Paste, canned	1 cup	215	.2	185	86	22	10	8	4						100
Puree, canned	1 cup	97	1	88	91	5	5	4	4						1000
Turnips															
Raw	1 cup	39	1.15	33	85	4	10	2	5						64
Cooked	1 cup	36	1.35	30	83	4	11	2	6						53
Turnip Greens															
Raw	3.5 oz	28	.8	19	68	7	25	2	7						10
Cooked	1 cup	29	1	19	66	8	28	2	7						
Vegetable Juice Cocktail	1 cup	41	.8	33	80	6	15	2	5						484
Water Chestnuts	4 avg	20	.2	18	90	1	5	1	5						5
Watercress, raw	1 cup	7	.35	4	57	2	29	1	14						18
Yams, cooked in skin	1 cup	210	1.8	194	92	13	6	3	1						
Yeast															
Bakers', dry (active)	1 oz	80	.1	40	50	36	45	4	5						15
Bakers', compressed	1 oz	24		13	54	10	42	1	4						5
Brewer's debittered	1 tbsp	23	.14	11	48	11	48	1	4						10
Torula	1 oz	79	.92	40	51	36	46	3	4						4

References

Alexander JK, Fred HL, Wright KE, et al: Exercise and coronary artery disease. Heart Lung 7:141-144, January-February, 1978.

Allon N: Self-perceptions of the stigma of overweight in relationship to weight-losing patterns. Amer J Clin Nutr 32:470-480, February 1979.

American College of Sports Medicine: The recommended quantity and quality of exercise for developing and maintaining fitness in healthy adults. J Phys Educ Rec 51:17-18, May 1980.

Anderson B: Stretching. Bolinas, CA, Shelter Publications, 1980.

Anderson JW, Chen WL: Plant fiber, carbohydrate and liquid metabolism. Am J Clin Nutr 32:346-363, February 1979.

Anderson R: Running—a road to mental health. Runner's World 14: 48-51, July 1979.

Bahrke MS, Morgan WP: Anxiety reduction following exercise and meditation. Cog Ther Res 2:323-333, April 1978.

Bailey RC: Self-concept differences in low and high achieving students. J Clin Psychol 27:188-191, February 1971.

Barnard RJ: The heart needs warm-up time. Physician Sportsmed 4:40, January 1976.

Barnard RJ, Grimditch GK, Wilmore JH: Physiological Characteristics of sprint and endurance Masters runners. Med Sci Sports 11:167-171, Summer 1979.

Barndt R, Blankenhorn DH, Crawford DW, et al: Regression and progression of early femoral atherosclerosis in treated hyperlipoproteinemic patients. Ann Intern Med 86:139-146, 1977.

Benson H: The Relaxation Response. New York City, William Morrow and Co, 1975.

Bentwegna A, Kelley EJ, Kalenak A: Diet, fitness, and athletic performance. Physician Sportsmed 7:98-105, October 1979.

Berg K: Exercise prescription: a practitioner's view. Physician Sportsmed 6:98-104, February 1978.

Bittker T: Runner's gluttony. Runner's World 12:10-11, June 1977.

Boileau RA, Buskirk ER, Horstman DH, et al: Body composition changes in obese and lean men during physical conditioning. Med Sci Sports 3:183-189, Winter 1971.

Bonney M: Self becoming as self growth. TIP 13:329-334, December 1974.

Bray G: The nutritional message must be spread. JAMA 241:1320-1321, March 30, 1979.

Briney KL: Cardiovascular Disease: A Matter of Prevention. Belmont, CA, Wadsworth Publishing Co, 1970.

Brody JE: 'Hidden fat' proves hard to cut from American diet. Wilmington Star News, Wilmington, NC, July 20, 1980.

Brown RS, Ramirez DE, Taub JM: The prescription of exercise for depression. Physician Sportsmed 6:34-45, December 1978.

Burch, BG, Danley WE Sr: Self-perception: an essential in staff development. NASSP Bulletin 62:15-19, April 1978.

Burkitt DP: The link between low-fiber diets and diseases, in Readings in Health 80/81. Guilford, CT, Dushkin Publishing Group, Inc, 1980.

Bypass the stress test. Runner's World 14:13-14, October 1979.

Caldwell F: The search for strength. Physician Sportsmed 6:82-88, January 1978.

Canfield J, Wells HC: 100 ways to enhance self concept in the classroom: a handbook for teachers and parents. Englewood Cliffs, NJ, Prentice-Hall, Inc, 1976.

Cantwell JD: Running. JAMA 240:1409-1410, September 22, 1978.

Cantwell JD: Stress testing indicated in a variety of complaints. Physician Sportsmed 5:70-74, February 1977.

Cantwell JD, Fletcher GF: Sudden death and jogging. Physician Sportsmed 6:94-98, March 1978.

Cantwell JD, Watt EW, Piper JH: Fitness, aerobic points, and coronary risk. Physician Sportsmed 7:79-84, August 1979.

Caplan RD, Jones KW: Effects of work load, role ambiguity, and type A personality on anxiety, depressions and heart rate. J Appl Physiol 60:713-719, June 1975.

Cathcart LM: A four year study of executive health risk. J Occupa Med 19:354-357, May 1977.

Clark HH: Effect of chronic exercise on cardiovascular function. Phys Fitness Res Digest 2, July 1972.

Clark HH: Update—physical activity and coronary heart disease. Phys Fitness Res Digest 9, April 1979.

Cohen T: Why diets don't work, in Readings in Health 80/81. Guilford, CT, Dushkin Publishing Group, Inc, 1980.

Coleman RE: Manipulation of self-esteem as a determinant of mood of elevated and depressed women. J Abnorm Psychol 84:693-700, December 1975.

Collinwood TR: The effects of physical training upon behavior and self attitudes. J Clin Psychol 28:583-585, April 1972.

Collinwood TR, Willet L: The effects of physical training upon self-concept and body attitude. J Clin Psychol 27:411-412, March 1971.

Combs BJ, Hales DR, Williams BW: An Invitation to Health—Your Personal Responsibility. Menlo Park, CA, Benjamin Cummings Publishing Co, 190.

Cooper D. Coping with the new 'fitness.' JAMA 241:1319-1320, March 30, 1979.

Cooper DL, Flair J: Stretching exercises for flexibility. Physician Sportsmed 5:114-116, March 1977.

Cooper KH: The Aerobics Way. New York City, Bantam Book, 1978.

Coopersmith S: The Antecedents of Self Esteem. San Francisco, WN Freeman, 1967.

Corbin CB, Lindsey R: Fitness for Life. Glenview, IL, Scott, Foresman and Co, 1979.

Corbin CB, Noble L: Flexibility—a major component of physical fitness. J Phys Ed Rec 51:23-24, June 1980.

Creager JG: An overture: improving student motivation. Am Bio Teach 38:523, September 1976.

Definition of physical fitness. J Phys Ed Rec 50:28, October 1979.

DeMoss V: Sweet solution. Runner's World 15:56-59, July 1980.

DeMoss V: The good, the bad, and the edible. Runner's World 15:42-45, June 1980.

Deutsch RM: The Family Guide to Better Food and Better Health. Des Moines, Meredith Cooperation, 1971.

deVries HA: Health Science—A Positive Approach. Santa Monica, CA, Goodyear Publishing Co, Inc, 1979.

deVries HA: Physical education, adult fitness programs: does physical activity promote relaxation? J Phys Ed Rec 46:53-54, September 1975.

deVries HA: Physiology of Exercise for Physical Education and Athletics. Dubuque, IA, Wm C Brown Co Pub, 1974.

Dickie RS: Diet in Health and Disease. Springfield, IL, Charles C Thomas, 1974.

Dressendorfer RH: Endurance training of recreationally active men. Physician Sportsmed 6:120-131, November 1978.

Dressendorfer RH, Gahagen H: Serum lipid levels in male runners. Physician Sportmed 7:119-125, January 1979.

Dunnett W, Williams J: Strength through stress. Runner's World 15:54-57, February 1980.

Dweck CS, Gilliard D: Expectancy statements as determinants of reactions to failure: sex differences in persistence and expectancy change. J Personal Soc Psychol 32: 1077-1084, December 1975.

Eckholm E, Record F: The affluent diet—a worldwide health hazard, in Readings in Health 80/81. Guilford, CT, Dushkin Publishing Group, Inc, 1980.

Elliott J: An 'ideal' serum cholesterol level? JAMA 241:1979-1980, May 11, 1979.

Emmett A: Are you overdosing on vitamins? The ABC & D of vitamin lore, in Readings in Health 80/81. Guilford, CT, Dushkin Publishing Group, Inc, 1980.

Employee fitness: coroporate philosophy for the 1980s. Athletic Purchasing and Facilities 4:12-14, July 1980.

Enger SC, Herbjφrnsen K, Erikssen J, et al: High density lipoproteins (HDL) and physical activity: the influence of physical exercise, age, and smoking on HDL-cholesterol and the HDL-/total cholesterol ratio. Scand J Clin Lab Invest 37:251-255, May 1977.

Erickson DJ: Exercise for the older adult. Physician Sportsmed 6:98-107, October 1978.

Exercise and the cardiovascular system (A Round Table). Physician and Sportsmed 7:56-71, September 1979.

Fabry P, Tapperman J: Meal frequency—a possible factor in human pathology. Amer J Clin Nutr 23:1059-1068, August 1970.

Falls HB, Baylor AM, Dishman RK: Essentials of Fitness. Philadelphia, Saunders College, 1980.

Farinaro E, Stamler J, Upton M, et al: Plasma glucose levels: long-term effects of diet in the Chicago coronary prevention evaluation program. Ann Intern Med 86:147-154, February 1977.

Felker DW, Stanwyck DJ, Kay RS: The effects of a teacher program in self concept enhancement on pupil's self-concept, anxiety, and intellectual achievement responsibility. J Educ Res 66:443-445, October 1973.

Folkins CH, Lynch S, Gardner MM: Psychological fitness as a function of physical fitness. Arch Phys Med Rehabil 53:503-508, November 1972.

Fried H: "Plain Talk" about stress. Plain Talk Series, National Institute of Mental Health.

Friedman M, Rosenman RH: Type A Behavior and Your Heart. New York City, Alfred A Knopf, 1974.

Fry, PS: Success, failure, and self-assessment ratings. J Consult Clin Psychol 44:413-419,   June   1976.

Gadzella BM, Fournet GP: Differences between high and low achievers on self-perceptions. J Exper Educ 44:44-48, Spring 1976.

Garrison L, Read A: Fitness for Everybody. Palo Alto, CA, Mayfield Publishing Co, 1980.

Gatti C: Sometimes less is more. Runner's World 14:13, July 1979.

Germain RB: Self-concept and self-esteem reexamined. Psychol Sch 15:386-390, March 1978.

Getchell B: Physical Fitness—A Way of Life. New York City, John Wiley and Sons, 1979.

Getchell B, Cleary P: The caloric costs of rope skipping and running. Physician Sportsmed 8:56-60, February 1980.

Gillian TB, Katch VL, Thorland W, et al: Prevalence of coronary heart disease risk factors in active children, 7 to 12 years of age. Med Sci Sports 9:21-25, Spring 1977.

Ginter E: Decline in coronary mortality in the United States and vitamin C. Amer J Clin Nutr 32:511-512, March 1977.

Glasser W: Positive Addition. New York City, Harper & Row, 1976.

Glick Z, Kaufmann NA: Weight and skinfold thickness changes during a physical training course. Med Sci Sports 8:109-112, Summer 1976.

Glover E: Aspirin—is it the next wonder drug for everyone? Runner's World 15:67-70, April 1980.

Goldman J: Effect of a faculty development workshop upon self-actualization. Education 98:254-258, March-April 1978.

Greist JH, Klein MH, Eischens RR, et al: Running out of depression. Physician Sportsmed 6:49-56, December 1978.

Guggenheim FG: Basic considerations in the treatment of obesity. Med Clin N Am 61:781-796, April 1977.

Gustafson J: Teaching for self-esteem. Phys Educ 35:67-69, May 1978.

Gwinup G: Effect of exercise alone on the weight of obese women. Arch Intern Med 135:676-680, May 1975.

Gwinup G, Chelvan R, Steinberg T: Thickness of subcutaneous fat and activity of underlying muscles. Ann Intern Med 74:408-411, March 1974.

Hammen CL, Krantz S: Effect of success and failure on depressive cognitions. J Abnorm Psychol 85:577-586, December 1976.

Hanner R: Beginning running. Runner's World 14:68-71, July 1979.

Hartung GH, Foreyt JP, Mitchell RE, et al: Relation of diet to high-density-lipoprotein cholesterol in middleaged marathon runners, joggers, and inactive men. N Engl J Med 302:357-361, February 14, 1980.

Hartung GH, Squires WG: Exercise and HDL cholesterol in middle-age men. Physician Sportsmed 8:74-79, January 1980.

Havey AL: Goal-setting as a compensation for fear-of-success. Adolescence 10:137-142, Spring 1975.

Harris L and Associates, Inc: Health Maintenance Survey. Newport Beach, CA, Pacific Mutual Life Insurance Co, 1978.

Heart Attack study promotes exercise. Wilmington Star News, Wilmington, NC, March 30, 1980.

Hickler RB: Mild hypertension—implications and management. Primary Cardiol 6:41-43, February 1980.

Higden H: Can running cure mental illness? Runner's World 13:36-43, February 1978.

Higden H: Can running put mental patients on their feet? Runner's World 13:36-43, January 1978.

Higden H: Fitness After Forty. Mounain View, CA, World Publications, 1977.

Hirsch J, Van Itallie, T: Diet books be damned, in Readings in Health 80/81. Guilford, CT, Dushkin Publishing Group, Inc, 1980.

Hoffberger KS: Activities for over sixty. J Phys Ed Rec 51:26-27, January 1980.

Horn JC: The element of success—competitiveness isn't that important. Psychol Today 11:19-20, April 1978.

Hulley SB, Cohen R, Widdowson G. Plasma high-density lipoprotein cholesterol level. JAMA 238:2269-2271, November 21, 1977.

Huse DM, Nelson RA: Basic balanced diet meets requirements of athletes. Physician Sportsmed 5:52-56, January 1977.

Ilfield FW: Current social stressors and symptoms of depression. Am J Psychiatry 134:161-166, February 1977.

Insel PM, Roth WT: Core Concepts in Health. Palo Alto, CA, Mayfield Publishing Co, 1979.

Iso-Ahola S, Roberts GC: Causal attributions following success and failure at an achievement motor task. Res Q 48:541-549, October 1977.

Jacks ML: The importance of motivation in the typewriting classroom. Bus Educ Forum 30:20-22, August 1976.

Jacobsen M: The deadly white powder, in Readings in Health 80/81. Guilford, CT, Dushkin Publishing Group, Inc, 1980.

Jenkins CD: Psychologic and social precursors of coronary disease (Part I). N Engl J Med 284:244-255, February 4, 1971.

Jenkins CD: Psychologic and social precursors of coronary disease (Part II). N Engl J Med 284:307-317, February 11, 1971.

Jenkins CD, Rosenman RH, Zyzanski SJ: Prediction of clinical coronary heart disease by a test for the coronary-prone behavior pattern. N Engl J Med 290:1271-1275, June 6, 1974.

Johnson PB, Updike WF, Schaefer M, et al: Sport, Exercise and You. New York City, Holt, Rinehart and Winston, 1975.

Kasch FW: Choosing an activity. Physician Sportsmed 5:105-106, May 1977.

Kasch FW: Rope skipping offers a good aerobic alternative. Physician Sportsmed 4:122, April 1976.

Kasch FW: The effects of exercise on the aging process. Physician Sportsmed 4:64-68, June 1976.

Kasch FW, Wallace JP: Physiological variables during 10 years of endurance exercise. Med Sci Sports 8:5-8, Spring 1976.

Katch FL, McArdle WD: Nutrition, Weight Control, and Exercise. Boston, Houghton Mifflin Co, 1977.

Kaufman WL: The Natural High Fiber Diet. New York City, Jove Publication, Inc, 1977.

Kerrigan M: Dinner with Nathan Pritikin. Runner's World 14:38-46, August 1979.

Kerrigan M: The whole vitamin C story. Runner's World 14:53-57, November 1979.

Kogan BA: Health. New York City, Bruce Jovanovich, Inc, 1980

Kostrubala T: The Joy of Running. New York City, Pocket Books, 1977.

Kuntzleman CT: Rating the Exercises. New York City, William Morrow and Co, Inc, 1978.

Lampman RM, Santinga JT, Hodge MF, et al: Comparative effects of physical training and diet in normalizing serum lipids in men with type IV hyperlipoproteinemia. Circulation 55:652-659, April 1977.

Lay NE; The effect of learning to swim on the self-concept of college men and women. Completed Res Health Phys Ed Rec 13:98, 1971 (Doctoral dissertation, Florida State University, 1970).

LeBow MD: Can lighter become thinner? Addict Behav 2:87-93, April-July 1977.

Lee RE III, Schroder HM: Effects of outward bound training on urban youth. J Sp Educ 3:187-205, Summer 1969.

Leklem J: Can the food you eat cause cancer? Runner's World 15:54-57, May 1980.

Leklem J: The role of the B vitamins in daily life. Runner's World 14:59-61, September 1979.

Leon GR: A behavioral approach to obesity. Am J Clin Nutr 30:785-789, May 1977.

Leonardson GR: Self-esteem—an important correlate of physical fitness. J Phys Ed 75:16, September-October 1977.

Less is more. Runner's World 14:13, November 1979.

Lewinsohn PM: Engagement in pleasant activities and depression level. J Abnorm Psychol 84:729-731, December 1975.

Lydiard A: With Lydiard. Runner's World 15:25, August 1980.

Maltz M: Creative Living for Today. New York City, Pocket Books, 1970.

Maltz M: Psycho-Cybernetics. New York City, Pocket Books, 1969.

Manis E: The Houstonian Preventive Medicine Center's Nutritional Advice. Houston, TX.

Martin J: In activity therapy, patients literally move toward mental health. Physician Sportsmed 5:84-89, July 1977.

Mayer J: The bitter truth about sugar, in Readings in Health 80/81. Guilford, CT, Dushkin Publishing Group, Inc, 1980.

McIntosh HD: Jogging. Thou shalt not kill (thyself). JAMA 241:2547-2548, June 8, 1979.

Metzner HL, Lamphier DE, Wheeler NC, et al: The relationship between frequency of eating and adiposity in adult men and women in the Tecumseh Community Health Study. Am J Clin Nutr 30:712-715, May 1977.

Michael ED: Stress adaptation through exercise. Res Q 28:50-54, March 1957.

Miller DK: Flexibility for tennis and racquetball. Physician Sportsmed 5:21-22, September 1977.

Miller DK, Allen E: Fitness: A Lifetime Commitment. Minneapolis, Burgess Publishing Co, 1979.

Miller GJ, Miller NE: Plasma-high-density-lipoprotein concentration and development of ischaemic heart disease. Lancet 1:16-19, January-March 1975.

Miller NE, Forde OH, Thelle DS, et al: High-density lipoprotein and coronary heart disease—a prospective case control study. Lancet 1:965-968, April-June 1977.

Moody DL, Kollias J, Buskirk ER: The effect of a moderate exercise program on body weight and skinfold thickness in overweight college women. Med Sci Sports 1:75-80, June 1969.

Morgan WP: A pilot investigation of physical working capacity in depressed and nondepressed psychiatric males. Res Q 40:859-860, December 1969.

Morgan WP: Negative addiction in runners. Physician Sportsmed 7:56-70, February 1979.

Morgan WP: Running into addiction. Runner 1:72-76, June 1979.

Morgan WP, Horstman DH, Cymerman A, et al: Use of exercise as a relaxation technique. J Sc Med Assoc 75:596-601, November 1979.

Morgan WP, Roberts J, Brand FR, et al: Psychological effect of chronic physical activity. Med Sci Sports 2:213-217, Winter 1970.

Morris JM, Chave SPW, Adam C, et al: Vigorous exercise in leisure-time and the incidence of coronary heart-disease. Lancet 1:333-339, January-March 1973.

Muscle fuel for competition (Round Table). Physician Sportsmed 7:49-58, January 1979.

Nelson RA: What should athletes eat? Unmixing folly and facts. Physician Sportsmed 3:66-72, November 1975.

Nelson, RE; Craighead WE: Selected recall of positive and negative feedback, self-control behaviors and depression. J Abnrom Psychol 86:379-388, August 1977.

Okin D: Stress—our friend, our foe, in Miller E (Ed): Stress. Chicago, Blue Cross Association, 1974.

Oldridge NB: Compliance in exercise rehabilitation. Physician Sportsmed 7:94-103, May 1979.

Ostwall R, Gebre-Medhin M: Westernization of diet and serum lipids in Ethiopians. Am J Clin Nutr 31:1028-1034, June 1978.

Overcoming overprotection of the elderly. Physician Sportsmed 4:107, June 1976.

Paffenbarger RS Jr, Laughlin ME, Gima AS, et al: Work activity of longshoreman as related to death from coronary heart disease and stroke. N Engl J Med 282: 1109-1114, May 14, 1970.

Paffenbarger RS Jr, Wing AL, Hyde RT: Contemporary physical activity and incidence of heart attack in college men, abstracted. Circulation (Suppl III) 56:15, September 1977.

Pollock ML: How much exercise is enough? Physician Sportsmed 6:50-64, June 1978.

Pollock ML, Miller HS, Ribisl PM: Effect of fitness on aging. Physician Sportsmed 6:45-48, August 1978.

Rabkin SW, Mathewson FA, Hsu PH: Relation of body weight to development of ischemic heart disease in a cohort of young North American men after 26 year observation period: The Manitoba Study. Am J Cardiol 39:452-458, March 1977.

Ravelli GP, Stein ZA, Sasser MW: Obesity in young men after famine exposure in utero and early infancy. N Engl J Med 295:349-353, August 12, 1976.

Redford SR: How to handle job stress. Family Weekly, February 17, 1980.

Rhoads JM: Overwork. JAMA 237:2615-2618, June 13, 1977.

Roitman JL, Pavlisko JJ, Schultz GW, et al: Exercise prescription by heart rate and met methods. Physician Sportsmed 6:98-102, April 1978.

Rosen GM, Ross AO: Relationship of body image to self-concept. J Consult Clin Psychol 32:100, February 1968.

Rosswork SG: goal setting: the effects on an academic task with varying magnitudes of incentive. J Educ Psychol 69:710-715, December 1977.

Rubin D: Everything You Always Wanted to Know about Nutrition. New York City, Simon and Schuster, 1978.

Runner's World update. Runner's World 15:12, January 1980.

Ryan AJ: Don't overdo it. Physicians Sportsmed 6:3, December 1978.

Sander N: Light at the end of the run. Runner's World 14:96-103, May 1979.

Schafer RB: The self-concept as a factor in diet selection and quality. J Nutr Ed 11:37-39, January-March 1979.

Schemmel R, Mickelsen O, Gill JL: Dietary obesity in rats: body weight and fat accretion in seven strains of rats. J Nutr 100:1041-1048, September 1970.

Schultz P: Flexibility: day of the stretch. Physician Sportsmed 7:109-117, November 1979.

Schuster K: Aerobic dance: a step to fitness. Physician Sportsmed 7:98-103, August 1979.

Selye H: Stress and the reduction of distress. J SC Med Assoc 75:562-566, November 1979.

Selye H: The Stress of Life. New York City, McGraw-Hill Book Co, 1956.

Sevene B: Beginning Running. Runner's World 14:48-51, June 1979.

Shephard RJ, Kavanagh T: The effects of training on the aging process. Physician Sportsmed 6:32-40, January 1978.

Shrauger JS, Sorman PB: Self-evaluations, initial success and failure, and improvement as determinants of persistence. J Consult Clin Psychol 45:784-795, October 1977.

Sidney KH, Shephard RJ: Attitudes towards health and physical activity in the elderly. Effects of a physical training program. Med Sci Sports 8:246-252, Winter 1976.

Sidney KH, Shephard RJ: Frequency and intensity of exercise for elderly subjects. Med Sci Sports 10:125-131, Summer 1978.

Simonelli C, Eaton RP: Cardiovascular and metabolic effects of exercise: the strong case for conditioning. Postgrad Med 63:71-77, February 1978.

Snodgrass J: Self concept. J Phys Ed Rec 48:22-23, November-December 1977.

Solow C, Silberfarb PM, Swift K: Psychosocial effects of intestinal bypass surgery for severe obesity. N Engl J Med 290:300-304, February 7, 1974.

Spillane R: You and Smoking. New York City, Ramapo House, 1970.

Stanhope JM, Sampson VM: High-density lipoprotein cholesterol and other serum lipids in New Zealand biracial adolescent sample. Lancet 1:968-970, April-June 1977.

Stare FJ, Whelan EM: Health—facts and fallacies. Family Weekly, April 6, 1980.

Subotnick S: 9 mistakes runners make. Runner' World 15:72-73, April 1980.

Suinn RM: Easing athletes' anxiety at the winter olympics. Physician Sportsmed 5:88-93, March 1977.

Swartz D, Wayne R: How to mentally prepare for better performances. Runner's world 14:90-95, November 1979.

Teasdale JD: Effects of real and recalled success on learned helplessness and depression. J Abnrom Psychol 87:155-164, February 1978.

Terborg JR: The motivational components of goal setting. J Appl Psych 61:613-621, October 1976.

Thomas D: The positive view of self. NASSP Bulletin 60:24-29, November 1976.

Toufexis A: That aching back. Time 116:30-38, July 14, 1980.

Tutko T: Stress of the positive kind. Runner's World 15:57, February 1980.

Twenter CJ: Self-concept: the missing link in perceptual motor development. Phys Educ 34:8-11, March 1977.

Upton AC: Status of the diet, nutrition and cancer program. Statement before the Subcommittee on Nutrition, Senate Committee on Agriculture, Nutrition, and Forestry, October 2, 1979.

Utermohlen CR: What are you? player or prospect? NASSP Bulletin 60:58-61, November 1976.

Vaisrub S: Editorial: Psychoneurosis and obesity—the hen and egg dilemma. JAMA 230:591, October 28, 1974.

Van Aaken E: The Van Aaken Method (Special Book Excerpt). Runner's World 15:111-120, August 1980.

Viscott DS: How to Make Winning Your Lifestyle. New York City, Dell Publishing Co, 1972.

Vuori I, Mäkäräinen M, Jääskeläinen A: Sudden death and physical activity. Cardiology 63:287-304, July-August 1978.

Waitley D: The Psychology of Winning. Chicago, Nightingale-Conant Cooperation, The Human Resources Co, 1979.

Watsen AWS: A three-year study of the effects of exercise on active young men. Eur J Appl Physiol 40:107-115, February 1979.

Weight hikes risk of breast cancer. Wilmington Morning Star, Wilmington, NC, May 12, 1980.

Weinstein CJ: Self-image in business and life. Train and Devel 30:42-47, September 1976.

Wherry RJ, South JC: A worker motivational scale. Personnel Psychol 30:613-636, Winter 1977.

William CR: In the beginning ... goals. TIP 15:86-89, April 1976.

Williams P, Robinson D, Bailey A: High-density lipoprotein and coronary risk factors in normal men. Lancet 1:72-75, January-March 1979.

Williams RJ: Nutritional individuality, in Readings in Health 80/81. Guilford, CT, Dushkin Publishing Group, Inc, 1980.

Wilmore J: Exercise's role in promotion of health among adults. President's Council on Phys Fitness & Sports Newsletter, March 1980.

Wood PD: Running away from heart disease. Runner's World 14:78-81, June 1979.

Wood PD: Smoking and running. Runner's World 14:80-83, September 1979.

Young CM: Planning the low calorie diet. Am J Clin Nutr 8:896-900, December 1960.
Young RJ, Ismail AH: Comparison of selected physiological and personality variables in regular and nonregular adult male exercisers. Res Q 48:617-672, October 1977.
Zuti WB, Golding LA: Comparing diet and exercise as weight reduction tools. Physician Sportsmed 4:49-53, January 1976.
Zyzanski SJ, Jenkins CD, Ryan TJ, et al: Psychological correlates of coronary angiographic findings. Arch Inter Med 136:1234-1237, November 1976.

About the Author

David K. Miller is a professor of physical education at the University of North Carolina at Wilmington. He received his Ph.D. in Physical Education from Florida State University. He is co-author of a college textbook, *Fitness: A Lifetime Commitment,* and his articles on health and physical education have appeared in a number of professional journals. As an instructor of health & fitness and a non-competitive running enthusiast, Dr. Miller believes that everyone can develop a well being—good health program that meets their individual needs.